Leadership for World-Class Universities

Leadership for World-Class Universities reveals how "world-class" thinking and policy can help university leaders employ modern solutions to the challenges facing higher education today. Readers will benefit from best practice advice offered by distinguished international contributors who have excelled by thinking globally without losing sight of their respective national and local environments. Their essays are grounded in empirical research and written to engage the reader, stimulate reflection and enhance performance. This book focuses especially on developing and middle-income countries, which face special problems where higher education is expanding most rapidly.
Key themes include:

- strategic planning
- governance of academic institutions
- the role of the academic profession
- fundraising
- student access and equity
- the impact of globalization.

Leadership for World-Class Universities is a valuable resource for senior university administrators. At the heart of this volume is a focus on how academic leaders can work towards resolving the complex issues facing universities today.

Philip G. Altbach is J. Donald Monan, S.J. University Professor and director of the Center for International Higher Education in the Lynch School of Education at Boston College.

Leadership for World-Class Universities

Challenges for Developing Countries

Edited by Philip G. Altbach

Routledge
Taylor & Francis Group

NEW YORK AND LONDON

First published 2011
by Routledge
270 Madison Avenue, New York, NY 10016

Simultaneously published in the UK
by Routledge
2 Park Square, Milton Park, Abingdon, Oxon OX14 4RN

Routledge is an imprint of the Taylor & Francis Group, an informa business

© 2011 Taylor & Francis

The right of the editor to be identified as the author of the editorial material,
and of the authors for their individual chapters, has been
asserted in accordance
with sections 77 and 78 of the Copyright, Designs and Patents Act 1988

Typeset in Minion by
Swales & Willis Ltd, Exeter, Devon
Printed and bound in the United States of America on acid-free paper by Sheridan Books, Inc

Library of Congress Cataloging in Publication Data
Leadership for world-class universities : challenges for developing countries / Philip
G. Altbach, editor.
p. cm.
Includes bibliographical references and index.
1. Universities and colleges—Administration. 2. Educational leadership—United States.
3. Education, Higher. I. Altbach, Philip G.
LB2336.L43 2010
378.1'01091724—dc22
2010014980
British Library Cataloguing in Publication Data
A catalogue record for this book is available from the British Library

ISBN13: 978–0–415–80028–0 (hbk)
ISBN13: 978–0–415–80029–7 (pbk)
ISBN13: 978–0–203–84217–1 (ebk)

Contents

Acknowledgments

Leadership for World-Class Universities: Challenges for Developing Countries stems from a longstanding commitment by the Boston College Center for International Higher Education to understanding the challenges of development in higher education. We recognize that developing countries face special challenges and that their senior academic leaders must understand not only global higher education issues but also the context of development. This volume is dedicated to those leaders—the rectors, presidents, vice chancellors, and other senior managers in the parts of the world where expansion today is most rapid and the impact of globalization and other factors most intense.

Several of the chapters in this book are based on publications issued by the Center for International Higher Education. "Higher Education's Landscape of Internationalization," by Philip G. Altbach and Jane Knight, appeared in *Tradition and Transition: The International Imperative in Higher Education* (Boston College Center for International Higher Education, 2007), as did "The Academic Profession: The Realities of Developing Countries" by Philip G. Altbach. "The Challenge of Establishing World-Class Universities in Developing Countries," by Jamil Salmi is based on a conference presentation.

We are indebted to our authors as well as to Edith Hoshino, the Center's publications editor, for their contributions. This volume is a project of the Boston College Center for International Higher Education.

Philip G. Altbach
Chestnut Hill, Massachusetts
March 2010

Contributors

Philip G. Altbach is J. Donald Monan SJ University Professor and director of the Center for International Higher Education at Boston College. He served as Distinguished Scholar Leader of the Fulbright New Century Scholars program. He is coauthor of *Trends in Global Higher Education: Tracking an Academic Revolution* (UNESCO, 2009), author of *Tradition and Transition: The International Imperative in Higher Education,* and other books.

Andrés Bernasconi is dean of graduate studies and research, Andrés Bello University, Santiago, Chile.

David E. Bloom is Clarence James Gamble Professor at the Harvard School of Public Health and was codirector of the Task Force on Higher Education and Development.

Kai-ming Cheng is chair professor in the Faculty of Education and former pro vice chancellor at the University of Hong Kong. He has had responsibility for the university's fund-raising efforts.

Ying Cheng is a lecturer at the Graduate School of Education, Shanghai Jiao Tong University. He has been a postdoctoral fellow at the Ecole des hautes études en sciences sociales. He has worked in the Office of Planning and Institute of Higher Education of Shanghai Jiao Tong University since 2000. He is responsible for the annual update and new development of the Academic Ranking of World Universities.

Fred M. Hayward taught at the University of Wisconsin–Madison and was on the staff of the American Council of Education. He is currently a higher education consultant and has worked throughout Africa as well as in Afghanistan, Pakistan, and elsewhere.

D. Bruce Johnstone is Distinguished Professor of Higher and Comparative Education Emeritus at the University at Buffalo, State University of New York, where he continues to direct the International Comparative Higher Educational Finance and Accessibility Project. He served from 1979 to 1988 as president of the State University College at Buffalo and from 1988 to 1994 as chancellor of the multicampus, 400,000-student, State University of New York System.

Jane Knight is an adjunct professor at Ontario Institute for Studies in Education of the University of Toronto. Her research focuses on the international dimension of higher education at the institutional, system, national, and international levels. Her work in over 60 countries helps to bring a comparative development and international perspective to her research, teaching, policy work, and numerous publications. She was a Fulbright New Century Scholar 2007–2008.

Nian Cai Liu is dean of the Graduate School of Education at Shanghai Jiao Tong University and director of the Academic Ranking of World Universities project. He has been responsible for planning at his university.

Goolam Mohamedbhai is secretary-general of the Association of African Universities, based in Ghana, and former vice chancellor of the University of Mauritius. He has been president of the International Association of Universities.

Daniel J. Ncayiyana is currently a higher education consultant in South Africa. He served as the vice chancellor of the Durban University of Technology, the deputy vice chancellor of the University of Cape Town, and the dean of medicine at the University of Transkei, all in South Africa.

Liz Reisberg is a research associate at the Boston College Center for International Higher Education, where she supports the development of the center's Web site, coordinates grants, conducts research, and contributes to center publications. She also teaches in the graduate program in higher education administration. She is the founder and former executive director of The MBA Tour, a company that organizes professional recruitment tours throughout the world to help business schools meet talented candidates for their MBA programs.

Álvaro Rojas is currently Chile's ambassador to Germany. For 15 years, he served as the rector of the University of Talca in Chile and was responsible for the university's transformation into a respected public institution.

Henry Rosovsky is Geyser Professor of economics emeritus and former dean of the Faculty of Arts and Sciences at Harvard University. He codirected the Task Force on Higher Education and Development.

Pedro Rosso is professor of medicine and rector of the Pontifical Catholic University of Chile, Santiago.

Jamil Salmi is the World Bank's tertiary education coordinator. He is the principal author of the Bank's Tertiary Education Strategy entitled "Constructing Knowledge Societies: New Challenges for Tertiary Education." In the past 17 years, he has provided policy and technical advice on tertiary education reform to the governments of more than 60 countries in Europe, Asia, Africa, and South America. His latest book, published in February 2009, addresses the *Challenge of Establishing World-Class Universities.*

David Watson is a historian and principal of Green Templeton College, Oxford. He has been professor of Higher Education Management at the Institute of Education, University of London. He also served as vice chancellor of the University of Brighton between 1990 and 2005. His most recent books are *Managing Civic and Community Engagement* (2007), *The Dearing Report: Ten years on* (2007), and *The Question of Morale* (2009). He has contributed widely to developments in UK higher education. He was knighted in 1998 for services to higher education.

Preface

GOOLAM MOHAMEDBHAI

This book on leadership in universities could not have come at a more appropriate time. Universities have played and continue to play a crucial role in the development of their countries, especially in the developing world. At one time views were expressed about the lower rate of return on investment in universities in developing countries as compared to investment in basic education, especially at times of economic crisis. These concerns have now been cleared, and all stakeholders acknowledge the long-term social benefits of university education. Indeed, the importance of universities in improving the lower levels of education through teacher training and educational research, and thus in attaining the Millennium Development Goals and the Education For All targets, vital for achieving global sustainable development, is now widely recognized. For universities to fully play their role in promoting development, however, they need good leadership, and that is what this book is all about.

The scene is set in the introductory chapter by Philip G. Altbach. He clarifies that the book is essentially about public-funded universities and the focus is on developing and middle-income countries. He emphasizes that universities are complex organizations, a point made in several chapters of the book. Universities have increasingly become similar to large corporations, and yet they remain academic communities. Álvaro Rojas and Andrés Bernasconi (chapter 2) mention that universities are not just organizations but legal entities, communities, and institutions simultaneously, and they operate more like cooperatives, the employees being stakeholders and decision making requiring the agreement of members of the organization. Universities have even been described as "organized anarchies" with multiple, ambiguous, and conflicting goals. Yet another characteristic of universities is that they are conservative institutions, reluctant to change. This institutional complexity of universities must therefore be recognized by those who lead them, as well as by those who have a say in appointing those leaders.

This brings us to the question: how do we define university leaders and what should their attributes be? It is clear that university leadership is not confined to the institution's chief executive officer, whether a president, rector, or vice chancellor. It includes, according to D. Bruce Johnstone (chapter 10), all those who have the capacity to effect change and who form part of the executive team. Universities nowadays require leaders who are not just professors having come up the rank of academia through scholarship but can also operate as professional managers. In addition to having academic credibility, they should be strategic thinkers, have a reputation for integrity, be good communicators, and be able to manage crises effectively. They should be fair and consultative in their approach but equally bold and firm in their final decisions. As eloquently outlined by David E. Bloom and Henry Rosovsky (chapter 4), good governance of universities requires that their leaders defend academic freedom, encourage shared governance, promote accountability, ensure meritocracy in selection, and strive for excellence.

A key attribute of university leaders, therefore, is the ability to understand their institution, to have a future vision for it, and then to help bring about change in a consultative manner. The best way to effect this is through strategic planning, which has now become a common tool in all higher education institutions and often a requirement by those who fund the institution. Fred M. Hayward and Daniel J. Ncayiyana (chapter 1) take us through the process, outlining the pitfalls, emphasizing the need for the institution to take into account the internal and external environment, and highlighting how the best results can be achieved. The process of preparing the strategic plan is in itself an exciting and valuable exercise as it helps to create institutional understanding and cohesion and a shared vision for the institution. However, its effectiveness in the long term is limited if it is not accompanied by a realistic plan to fund the strategies over the plan period. This is where most universities in developing countries encounter difficulties. In many cases, public universities are still funded on an annual-grant allocation basis, which invariably is based not on the institutional needs according to its plan but rather on the availability of public funds in a particular year. The strategic plan then needs to be regularly modified to take this factor into account. Nevertheless, the plan is a vital tool for the institution to make its case for funding to government and, indeed, to mobilize resources from other sources. It is, therefore, important for public institutions to involve and seek the views of the relevant government ministries (education, finance, and planning) in the process of preparing the plan.

As mentioned by Altbach (introduction), there has been a concern that since most university leaders arrive in their executive positions as a result of their academic achievements, their management, administrative, and planning capabilities need to be strengthened. It is with this objective in mind that the Association of African Universities has developed a series of Leadership Development and Management Development workshops, catering for university leaders and managers, respectively. These two-week workshops provide a unique opportunity to university leaders and managers to be exposed to a range of institutional governance issues and challenges, facilitated by experienced resource persons, and to share their own experiences with colleagues from different institutions in Africa.

Johnstone (chapter 10) identifies several specific challenges that university leaders in the developing world have to deal with. An important issue involves increasing access. University education has been shown to enable upward social mobility and to improve the well-being of the population. Thus, universities have a responsibility to provide access to as large a number of students as possible, especially in countries where the tertiary enrollment ratio is low. In some countries, such as the ones in Francophone Africa, access to higher education is prescribed by national policy, and all secondary school leavers having obtained a baccalaureate are entitled to admission to a university. This poses enormous challenges to universities, which are obliged to accommodate numbers of students far in excess of their institutional capacity. Even in countries where university admissions are regulated, as in most Anglophone universities, the social and political pressures to admit large numbers of students are inescapable. Should quality of teaching and learning be sacrificed at the expense of increasing access? How should systems cope with uneven levels of entry qualifications of students, which often result in high rates of dropouts or students having to repeat several years? How should the limited human resources and physical infrastructural facilities be managed, including students' accommodation? These are some of the major issues related to access that university leaders inevitably have to grapple with.

An issue closely related to access is equity, which is comprehensively dealt with by Liz Reisberg and David Watson (chapter 11). All societies have inequities whose origins can be social, racial, religious, gender based, or ethnic, to quote a few. Such inequities are often reflected in the distribution of student participation in higher education. While inclusive and equitable participation in higher education is unquestionably accepted as essential from a social justice point of view, it is equally recognized that the means to achieve that objective can be complex, sensitive, and difficult. The measures commonly used to redress inequity in higher education include affirmative action in the selection of students, reservation of a quota for a particular disadvantaged group, or provision of financial assistance to those unable to finance their education. India is a well-known example where quotas have been reserved for the disadvantaged and underrepresented "lower" castes. Malaysia is another often-quoted example of where overrepresentation of the minority affluent Chinese community in universities has been reversed by establishing a limiting quota for the Chinese. In sub-Saharan Africa a major concern is gender inequity in higher education. Kenya and Uganda, for example, have used affirmative action to increase the admission of female students, especially in science and technology fields. Clearly, in the majority of cases in developing countries the matter of redressing inequity in higher education is decided at the national policy level, with universities simply implementing the measure. Obviously, inequity at the higher education level has its roots in the other lower levels of education. So while university leaders may have limited influence on admissions criteria of students in order to redress inequity, they ought to encourage open and dispassionate discussion on the issues and to undertake research so as to inform policymakers on the benefits and negative consequences of the various measures. Moreover, they need to recognize that facilitating the access of disadvantaged students is but a first step in the process; ensuring their success is their responsibility, and this may require special attention given to the students through, for example, additional tutoring.

One issue of inequity in higher education that is rarely addressed and has been discussed only to a limited extent in this book is gender inequity in university leadership. However, Reisberg and Watson do discuss gender in their chapter on access and equity. This is particularly important for developing countries. While considerable improvement has been made in attaining gender equity among university students in the developing world, not much progress has taken place in achieving equity among faculty and, especially, among university leaders. For example, women are conspicuously absent in university leadership positions in Africa; at present, there are no more than a handful of women as rectors or vice chancellors in the whole of sub-Saharan Africa. There is clear evidence that women perform as well as and often excel over men at various levels of education. Why, then, do they experience difficulty in climbing the academic ladder to reach the top? If a glass ceiling exists, in the name of equity and justice it is the responsibility of university leaders to ensure that it is broken down.

Another major challenge facing university leaders in developing countries is the funding of their institution. A key issue raised by Johnstone (chapter 3) is: how can universities increase their income when their costs are escalating, the numbers of students are increasing, and government funding is either stagnant or even decreasing? Whether in developing or developed countries, the solution seems to be increasingly through charging of tuition and user fees from students and their parents. But university leaders must recognize that cost recovery (a term first coined by Johnstone in 1986) is a socially and politically charged issue and needs to be implemented with caution and after full consultation with their respective government. The argument of equity inevitably comes into play. The often-proposed palliative solutions of providing scholarship and loan schemes for needy students are fraught with challenges in their successful implementation. Universities in some developing countries, such as Uganda and Kenya, have found an ingenious way of overcoming the resistance to the introduction of fees and at the same time increasing access, through a dual-track policy of admitting and charging full-economic fees to students who fail to be among the prescribed quota of government-sponsored, non-fee-paying students. While such a policy may resolve the funding crisis in the short term, it could have negative consequences for the institution in the long run. One source of funding to higher education that has remained largely untapped in developing countries is philanthropy through private donations, a point forcefully made by Kai-ming

Cheng (chapter 9). This, however, requires appropriate government encouragement and dynamic institutional leadership.

Reduction in expenditures is another means of coping with shortage of funds. In most universities in developing countries, personnel costs constitute the largest proportion of the budget, sometimes being as excessive as 75 percent. This is, therefore, the area where some economy can be achieved through freezing of faculty or staff replacements or laying off or redeployment of underutilized faculty and unproductive staff. Yet here again the political and social implications of such measures and their impact on the institution need to be considered. Also, not all university leaders, especially those in developing countries, have the freedom to "hire and fire" personnel and, as pointed out by Johnstone (chapter 10), the legal and contractual obligations of the institution toward its staff should never be ignored.

Yet another challenge for university leaders in developing countries is the acute shortage of qualified faculty. It is becoming increasingly difficult in countries such as those in sub-Saharan Africa to recruit or retain good faculty, especially in some key areas. "Aging faculty" is now a well-known phenomenon. This has a direct impact on the quality of teaching and even more on research output. Brain drain is the main but not the only cause and, as explained by Altbach (chapter 12), it has become an extremely complex phenomenon. Neither stemming brain drain nor encouraging the diaspora to return to their country of origin is feasible. A better option is to get universities to involve the diaspora in their various activities. This is already happening in individual cases, but a more organized mechanism for such involvement of academic diaspora has yet to evolve.

With the advent of globalization, university leaders need to understand that their institutions now operate in a global-knowledge society and that their graduates must not only cope with national development priorities but be equally equipped to deal with global challenges. Indeed, internationalization of higher education has gained prominence in every continent of the world. Also, as pointed out by Altbach and Jane Knight (chapter 6), internationalization is expected to cause a dramatic increase in student mobility: from the current 2 million to 15 million by 2025. This trend raises a number of issues that will need to be addressed by the heads of higher education institutions—namely, visa requirements and national security; the tension between accommodating domestic students and attracting foreign ones; the pressure for homogenization of programs and use of English as the main language and the effect of these on the cultural environment of some nations; the growing cross-border delivery of higher education in developing countries and the need to ensure its quality; and other matters.

An important instrument for globalization and internationalization is information technology, which has witnessed unprecedented developments over the past decades. However, as rightly pointed out by Altbach (chapter 12), a digital divide exists between developed and developing countries. Internet connectivity in African universities, for example, is sporadic and prohibitively expensive. It is clear that while institutional efforts in improving connectivity must continue, collective action at national or even regional levels can produce more tangible results. This is what led the Association of African Universities to play a catalytic role in sensitizing African university leaders to the essence of creating National Research and Education Networks, which can then play an effective advocacy and lobbying role vis-à-vis policymakers and private Internet service providers in relation to increased access and cheaper connectivity on behalf of African knowledge institutions, especially universities.

Globalization has also ushered an era of unprecedented competitiveness in higher education, as exemplified by global university rankings and the notion of world-class universities. Governments, including those in developing countries, have become obsessed with having some of their universities positioned in the global university rankings or being considered as world class. Jamil Salmi (chapter 13) identifies the following characteristics of a world-class university: a concentration of talent recruited from across the world; abundant resources, especially for research; and a governance structure that makes it relatively independent of the state. Clearly, using these criteria, few public-funded universities in the developing world would be classified as world class. But an institution that does not satisfy these criteria of a world-class university should in no way be denigrated as one of poor quality. Indeed, using the well-established notion of fitness of purpose commonly utilized in quality assurance of universities and that verifies the responsiveness of an institution to national socioeconomic needs, one can well arrive at the conclusion that an African university, for example, claiming to be world class may not be of quality. The main pursuit of leaders of universities in developing countries should be achieving quality of their institutions, not world-class status. As Bloom and Rosovsky (chapter 4) rightly point out, university leaders in developing countries should establish realistic and operational standards that meet the needs of their country and institution. Merely copying practices of universities in the developed world, simply because of the attraction of being classified as world class, can be ineffective and detrimental.

With regards to global rankings, it is unfortunate that so much media publicity is given to the institutions that are ranked, but hardly any mention is made of the specific criteria used for such rankings. Such standards would reveal their inappropriateness to most universities in developing countries. As explained by Nian Cai Liu and Ying Cheng (chapter 8), global rankings are more appropriate for institutions that aim for global competence and competitiveness and are not relevant to universities in developing countries that focus on addressing local needs. The authors go further and warn that a blind pursuit of global ranking by such universities could be harmful to them and their countries. It is, therefore, imperative for university leaders in developing countries to first fully understand the methodology and criteria used in the various university rankings and then explain these to their stakeholders, especially the policymakers. They could also assist in establishing specific criteria of direct relevance to their institutions at national and regional levels, set appropriate standards, and then accept being rated against these. This is the current approach being adopted by the African Union Commission for rating (not ranking) universities in Africa.

Politics invariably has some degree of influence on public universities in developing countries, and several chapters (Altbach; Bloom and Rosovsky; Rojas and Bernasconi) address this issue from different perspectives. The nature of political interference would depend on a number of factors, such as the type of government in the country, the governance structure of the institution, the way university leaders are appointed, and others. In Korea all university staff are considered public officials and would, therefore, owe allegiance to the government of the day. In Vietnam, research areas at universities are determined by government, and government even selects the researchers. In several countries in Africa, as well as in some universities in China and India, university leaders are appointed by government and can therefore be subjected to political directives. There are well-documented instances when university leaders resisted political interference. In the majority of cases those leaders either resigned or were removed. In Ethiopia, for example, university leaders resigned in protest when government interfered in the evaluation of faculty; government appointed new leaders. University leaders also often have to deal with faculty and students being actively involved in politics on campus. In such complex situations there can be no simple recipe for how university leaders should counteract political interference. Ultimately, they need to be guided by the governance provisions of their institution, act in the best interest of their institution, follow their conscience, and manage with integrity.

To sum up, the common thread that runs through this book concerns the imperative function for university leaders to know the complex nature of their institutions, to be fully aware of the social and political environment in which their institutions operate, and to be conscious of the major global trends in higher education that will inevitably have an impact on their institutions. This comprehensive book should appear on every university leader's bookshelf as it helps to sensitize them to the wide range of issues and challenges they have to face and on some of the approaches being adopted in addressing them. The authors of the various chapters are eminent scholars who have wide experience on leadership of universities, not only in their national institutions but also in other parts of the world, and who are renowned for their expertise in the areas they deal with here. However, this book should be valuable not only to university leaders but equally to those who invariably have to interact with them— government, faculty, students, the business world, and the civil society.

Introduction

PHILIP G. ALTBACH

Universities everywhere require leadership and expertise capable of participating in an increasingly complex and globalized world. Universities can demonstrate "world-class" thinking and policy development in the sense that they employ state-of-the-art solutions to pressing challenges of the twenty-first century. Regardless of the national or cultural context in which they operate, world-class universities are committed to providing the best-possible academic services to students, academic staff, and the community. These institutions "think" globally without losing sight of their national and local environments. They achieve this goal by taking lessons from academic trendsetters around the world and then adapting relevant ideas and practices to meet local needs and goals. This kind of strategic thinking requires an understanding of how the broad themes of the day—such as, competition in the global academic marketplace, privatization, and new mechanisms for financing universities—affect the daily operation of a university and the policy decisions required of academic leaders.

Senior academic administrators often assume their jobs without adequate knowledge about the complex institutions they are called upon to lead and are usually uninformed about how universities relate to national and international systems of higher education. In the past, this lack of expertise was not considered a serious liability; most presidents, rectors, and vice chancellors were elected for limited terms from among senior professors and routinely returned to their academic positions. Universities were relatively isolated institutions with a great deal of autonomy. Governments or other authorities, such as the Catholic Church, that provided funding and legitimacy generally left universities alone. Major decisions remained in the hands of the senior professors. Autonomy constituted the rule, and accountability had not yet entered the vocabulary of higher education.

Universities constitute complex institutions and are becoming more so in the era of massification and globalization. Any university, however small, features all of the organizational complexity of a company or government department. Moreover, larger universities' budgets have proven comparable to those of major enterprises. People who are called upon to lead universities in the twenty-first century face a difficult task for which they are, in general, unprepared. This book has a simple yet daunting purpose—to provide some perspectives for

1

academic leaders concerning many of the key policy issues they must address in managing universities. We place a special focus on universities in developing and middle-income countries, where the challenges are especially problematic and the need for enlightened and effective leadership perhaps forms the greatest issue.

This book is not a "how to" publication; it provides a broad analysis of key issues—access and equity, fund-raising, governance, and others. These themes are relevant for all academic leaders to understand. While the chapters do not offer solutions, they provide analysis broadly relevant to academic leaders everywhere but with a special focus on developing and middle-income countries. The full extent of topics is not covered—that would require an encyclopedia.

We are concerned in this volume with universities and not specifically with other postsecondary institutions such as community colleges, vocational institutes, and the like. While many of the factors prove relevant to anyone involved with postsecondary education, our specific concern is with the university sector. This book focuses on nonprofit public and, to some extent, private universities. The new and rapidly growing for-profit private sector is not considered here. In some ways, the differences between public and private are less distinct as public universities are privatized and some private universities are taking on many of the characteristics of public institutions.

All universities cannot become world class in the sense of competing for the top positions in the global rankings and league tables. But they can be world class in serving in the best way possible their particular mission, region, or country. In this book, we define world class as doing the best-possible job in the context of mission or location. In this sense, all universities can be world class if they are provided with wise leadership and the resources to their mission.

The Complexity of the Twenty-First-Century University

Universities have become large and complex institutions as a result of massification and the expansion of student numbers and in part because of the growth of science and the many new functions that universities have taken on. A typical university has, among others, the following roles:

- Undergraduate teaching
- Graduate (postgraduate) teaching
- Professional teaching in many fields, often including law, medicine, management, and others
- Basic and applied research
- University-industry collaboration
- Public service such as cultural programs for the community
- International relationships of many kinds

- Generating income from a growing number of sources, including student tuition, sale of intellectual property, philanthropic gifts, and others

University budgets in many cases run into hundreds of millions of dollars annually, with income coming from many places, including allocations from governments, student tuition, income from the sale of services and products, intellectual property, and others.

Universities as Corporations—and Much More

One of the complexities of modern university management is the fact that universities have in some ways become similar to large corporations given their size, budgets, and complexity. At the same time, they are also academic communities, with strongly held traditions of academic governance and participation. Indeed, that contradiction is one of the central dilemmas of university leadership and management.

University management requires many specializations, including financial accounting, real estate management, dining services, psychological consulting, enrollment management, student services, extracurricular activities, legal expertise, police services, and many others. These specializations extend beyond the expertise and the management of skills of academics. Thus, management skills of all kinds are required for the modern university.

At the same time, the core function of the university remains academic—teaching, learning, and research. Traditionally, academic work has been managed by academics through shared governance—with strong participation from the academic staff. To maintain the integrity and the creativity of the academic work of the university, the academic community must be involved in the governance of the key academic work of the university.

Many observers have argued that the faculty must maintain essential control over who is admitted to the university to study, the curriculum and key decisions concerning the approval of academic degrees, and who is recruited, appointed, and promoted to the academic staff itself. These issues are the core functions of academic governance.

Contemporary universities require a combination of professional management and administration as well as the traditional participation of the academics in the essential academic functions of the institution. In much of the world, there is little awareness of the significance of professional administration and few methods of providing training for administrative staff. At the same time, the traditional academic governance policies may not meet today's challenges. As a result, conflicts between academic governance and university management can occur, and appropriate expertise in management is often unavailable.

Thus, universities are complex organizations and require professional management and administration—in many ways similar to any large organization.

4 · Philip G. Altbach

Yet, the spirit of a university is antibureaucratic in the sense that academic decision making involves the entire academic staff at the same time that size and complexity of the institution necessitate an element of bureaucracy. The challenge is to ensure an appropriate balance between these two realities. In most countries, the balance of power has shifted to the managers and away from the academics.

The New Responsibilities of Academic Leaders

Persons occupying the highest levels of leadership in universities—presidents, rectors, vice chancellors, and those with institution-wide responsibilities in positions just below chief executives in rank—face unprecedented challenges. Top academic jobs have become more complex and variegated.

As noted earlier, presidents now typically serve as chief executive officers (CEO) as well as academic leaders. A CEO typically oversees the administrative and financial affairs of an institution or company—as well as the academic sector of the university. In most cases, administrative leadership has acquired an increasing amount of time and energy as universities have expanded.

A university's financial team includes a president, financial vice president, and often other senior leaders. Income sources are often diverse and include tuition, allocations from governmental or other public sources, research-based income, university-industry collaboration funds of various kinds, income raised from intellectual property, and philanthropic and other donations. University expenditures, as well, have become more varied and diverse. Most university budgets are devoted to teaching and learning—with academic salaries and funds for laboratories, libraries, and other facilities devoted directly to the educational mission of the university.

University funds are also increasingly devoted to information technology, student services including athletic and extracurricular facilities, outreach programs for local and national communities, and many other policies. Research has become a central part of the budget of a small number of research-focused universities. Historically, universities were relatively small and did not spend large amounts of money. Now, a medium-sized university in North America or western Europe may have an annual budget of close to US$1 billion. Budgets elsewhere, while not as large, are nonetheless quite substantial.

University presidents are increasingly involved in fund-raising—from alumni and other donors, philanthropic foundations, and other sources. In the United States and increasingly elsewhere, presidents and other top academic officials spend quite substantial amounts of time on fund-raising and development. For every top administrator, the intricacies of this responsibility are entirely new and often involve the acquisition of new skills and ways of thinking about leadership responsibilities.

External relations have also become increasingly urgent duties of university presidents. In part because universities have such large and complex organizations, they must deal with many more groups in society. Senior university leadership used to be focused mainly on the institution itself; now it is equally externally oriented. The mass media has taken an increased interest in higher education as universities have become significant social institutions, and presidents must often deal with newspapers, television, and Internet media as well. Universities are often involved in community affairs—from assisting in neighborhood development to traditional "town-gown" conflicts—and in the social and cultural affairs of the region or even the nation. In a few cases, such as the National Autonomous University of Mexico, which serves as the national library of the nation and operates several major national scientific institutions (and sponsors a well-known football team as well), universities maintain a major public presence.

In an era of university-industry collaboration, universities engage as never before with the economy. This means that presidents must interact with businesses of all kinds, especially in the emerging high-technology sector such as biotech companies and other types. Joint research projects may engage universities in complex intellectual property or other arrangements with for-profit companies. University policies relating to profit sharing and intellectual property as well as specific contractual arrangements may be in the hands of top leadership.

University presidents are much more enmeshed with local and sometimes national political authorities of many kinds. Although the portion of public university budgets coming from the state has decreased in most places, accountability has tended to grow. Government officials often ask questions about the role and function of universities, which must be answered. Funding agencies, public and sometimes private, are also involved in university affairs.

In some countries, politics intrudes onto the campus, and university presidents may be directly affected. In some cases, presidents of universities are directly appointed or must be approved by political authorities. This is the case in some Chinese and Indian universities, among others. Political parties or factions sometimes achieve a presence on campus, and academic decisions are occasionally subject to political interference. Student unrest proves to be endemic in some countries and occasional in others. These kinds of political interference in the affairs of universities weaken university autonomy and cause a negative impact on academic quality and morale. Thus, it is important that presidents deal as constructively as possible with often quite difficult circumstances.

Finally, university presidents at times become international decision makers and ambassadors of their institutions. Globalization has brought many universities into international relationships, often for the first time. Global university networks, specific academic collaborations with foreign institutions, international students, branch campuses, and many other international relationships have become common features, and the president is very often the representative and policymaker of the institution.

The job of top university leadership has clearly changed significantly in the past half century and is now much more diverse and complex than ever before. Presidents continue to serve as the academic leaders of their institution, but they have many more responsibilities, both within the university and when interacting with society.

Education of the University President and Top Management

Worldwide, top university leaders are not specifically trained for their jobs. Indeed, in most countries, almost none of the professionals in university administration are specifically educated for the positions they occupy. University presidents almost universally emerge from the professoriate and are selected in several ways. Probably the largest number of leaders are chosen from the ranks of the academic staff at their own university and either elected, usually by the faculty but sometimes with student and occasionally staff participation, or are appointed internally through various mechanisms, for a limited term. After serving one or two terms, they return to the faculty of their university. In some countries, the common practice is to search outside the university for a president or top administrative job within the country or in some places internationally. In such cases, the person chosen will tend to possess some previous administrative and leadership experience.

Almost without exception, university presidents hold a doctoral degree in an academic discipline and have spent much or all of their careers teaching in their field. While they have an interest in university leadership, they have no training for the job and most have little if any experience in administration. It has been urged that research universities should be led by top scholars because experts need to be led by people who are also experts and understand the nature of academic life. The best leaders are considered as those who have a deep understanding of the organization they are leading. The most competent presidents seem to learn "on the job."

University presidents almost always emerge from the ranks of the professoriate, with the majority returning to teaching after their term of office. Thus, most do not develop either leadership skills or a deep knowledge of the nature of the higher education enterprise. Moreover, most presidents do not serve in office long enough to develop the needed expertise. Further, those leaders who know that they will be returning to their institution's professorial ranks do not have much incentive to "rock the boat" or provide innovative leadership.

A small number of universities seek to provide their top management relevant training concerning university management and leadership as well as some of the skills needed to be effective in their jobs—usually through seminars and short courses. In a few countries, most notably the United States, middle management frequently has specialized training in the field of higher education and often a master's or doctoral degree in the field of higher education or a related specialty. Without question, university leadership requires specialized skills and an understanding of the academic enterprise that goes beyond being a professor and experiencing academic life.

The Future of Academic Leadership

A central challenge for university presidents is the dual problem of management and leadership. Top university leaders are expected to serve both positions in providing leadership to an increasingly bifurcated academic community, representing the university externally, and managing a large and complex organization. These dual responsibilities must be performed in an increasingly politicized and economically difficult environment. Twenty-first-century university leadership may become an impossible task. At the very least, this work needs knowledge concerning the university, higher education generally, and about the growing number of tasks required of academic leaders.

Academic leadership also requires a strong personality and a significant capacity for hard work. Academic leaders must highlight a commitment to higher education as a central enterprise in society and to their university. And these leaders must provide a strong commitment to the best values of the university—meritocracy in all aspects of academic work and the centrality of the university's mission of teaching, learning, and research. In many ways, the future of the university depends on the quality, commitment, and stability of its leadership.

1

Strategic Planning for Higher Education

FRED M. HAYWARD AND DANIEL J. NCAYIYANA

[T]he strategic plan . . . was in the true sense of the expression, an act
of liberation, not just a plan or framework for action.
—Njabulo Ndebele[1]

A fundamental purpose of strategic planning in higher education is to provide an ongoing process of examination and evaluation of an institution's
strengths, weaknesses, resource requirements, goals, and future prospects and
to set out a coherent plan to build a stronger, better, and more effective institution. That plan needs to be one that can be altered and shaped as goals are
achieved, the environment changes, or new goals are identified. Strategic planning is intended to strengthen and enhance the performance and quality of an
institution. It should not occur in a vacuum but should take place within and be
shaped by the higher education environment, national higher education policy,
and available resources, as well as the needs and goals of the faculty, students,
community, and the nation.

The Whys and Wherefores

Leaders in higher education know that the path to success will be long and
difficult—calling for new ideas, hard work, and the ability to mobilize the best
minds in the institution and the nation. The pressure for immediate action by a
leader, especially a new leader, can be overwhelming. And yet, one of the most
important attributes of successful leadership consists of hearing the calls for
change, yet listening to the voices of people who know the institution well, to
critics as well as supporters, and in particular to those who have demonstrated
creativity and talent essential to effective change. One of the best ways to begin
the process of listening is through strategic and financial planning,

> a conscious process by which an institution assesses its current state and
> the likely future condition of its environment, identifies possible future
> states for itself, and then develops organized strategies, policies and proce-
> dures for getting to one or more of them.
>
> (Peterson 1980, 113)

Strategic planning seeks to answer the questions: What is this university about? What would we like it to be? What would that entail? How can we get there? (Hayward and Ncayiyana 2003, 7)

The strategic-planning process helps to provide an overview of the institution in an open and transparent way that is often not possible in individual interviews or meetings. It allows leaders to explore current values, missions, and goals and to examine them in the context of the current state of the institution, the community, the national economic and political setting, and the international environment. Understanding the current context, existing goals, and institutional aspirations marks an important starting point for thinking about the future. This process provides a sounding board for ideas and a context in which the leaders of an institution can make their own critical contributions to a creative vision for the future. This is a moment when planners should dream—what would we like the institution to look like in 5 to 10 years? What might we do to realize those dreams? The task then is to put those dreams into a strategic plan and if necessary temper them to meet the context in which the institution operates.

Strategic and financial planning allow higher education leaders to take the pulse of the institution, review and assess its current direction, and create a new vision for the future that will mobilize the university community in new, creative ways. The process will also allow new leaders time to become a more integral part of the institution, to listen to colleagues, staff, students, supporters, and critics throughout the community and to develop strategies and goals for change in the context of where the institution is at the moment and where leaders hope to take it.

If done well, the results can be revolutionary, as they were in the example cited in the quote at the beginning of this chapter from Prof. Njabulo Ndebele shortly after the end of apartheid and the establishment of a democratic government in South Africa. That process brought together people who had been on opposite sides of the struggle, had different values, and, in some cases, contempt for those who had opposed them. Yet, during the strategic-planning process they became united in their effort to create a new, high-quality university in the North—an institution in which the future was defined not by an elite backed by force, as in the past, but by the university community as a whole. Although the 60 participants (administrators, faculty, staff, and students) on the strategic-planning committee differed on many aspects of the plan, the most important institutional condition they achieved as a result of their deliberations was to meet a "shared understanding" of their needs and goals. As Vice Chancellor Ndebele recalled some years later:

This becomes the basis on which the roles of various institutional partners are discovered and embraced rather than assigned. Intervention for

change then has a greater chance of being self-motivated and self-directed, either at the level of individuals or at the level of organizational units.
(N. Ndebele, personal communication, March 4, 2007)

The results of this effort included changes that were truly revolutionary in the context of apartheid South Africa.

To what extent is this experience relevant to other circumstances? One's environment may seem more benign, but in the experience of the authors, the conditions on most campuses echo many of the conflicts, differences, and tensions mentioned here. Where such tensions exist, they need to be resolved before a shared understanding can be achieved. The strategic-planning process can help create that understanding and develop consensus, set the stage for a new vision for the future, and spell out the process for successful change in the long run.

In this process, the undertaking is based on where we are to what we want to be, taking into account the external environment and the internal environment. Part of the planning process includes consensus building and a shared understanding of the current situation. Do we have a *consensus* for the desired change? If not, what can we do to create the consensus needed? What are the major institutional values? Do they accord with our stated mission? Do we have the human and monetary *resources* needed to meet our goals? Do we have the *capacity* to effect change? If not, what can we do to foster it? What mechanisms should we set in place to monitor implementation and adjust to unforeseen challenges? How can we institutionalize the process? These questions set the stage for a discussion of the components of strategic and financial planning, which will be elaborated in the sections that follow.

Why Strategic Planning becomes Tangential and Unimportant in Many Institutions

Universities are Intrinsically Resistant to Change

Universities are, by their very nature and tradition, conservative organizations and thus resistant to change. Universities of today "stem from the same historical roots" of the medieval European university, particularly the faculty-dominated University of Paris (Altbach 2007, 24). The university remains one of the most resilient and enduring of human institutions, thanks in large part to its dogged dedication to the preservation of its traditions and ways of doing things. Clark Kerr (2001, 115) observes that of the human institutions established in the Western world since 1520, only 85 have persisted to the present day, including the Catholic Church and some 70 universities. Of these institutions, the universities have seen the least transformation:

Higher education institutions, steeped in historical origins and precedence, are more likely than most organizations to have a culture that
naturally resists change. With their long history of practices and tradition
based on an accumulation of consistently acted out values . . . higher education institutions are often too entrenched to change easily and prefer the
comfort of the status quo.

(Freed, Klugman, and Fife 1997, 120)

Consequently, few universities have succeeded in "transform[ing] themselves dramatically." Others have been able to make important changes
in parts of their operations. . . . But many institutions have stumbled,
dissolved into controversy, or lost their nerve.

(Rowley, Lujan, and Dolence 1997, 54)

The professoriate, largely strong-willed and sometimes fiercely independent
members with a track record of individual achievement and success in freely
chosen fields of endeavor and endowed with a strong sense of certainty regarding their goal, will generally be more competitive than cooperative and value
independent enterprize more than "joining the herd" in a quest for common
objectives. Senior faculty members are likely to be quite resistant to planning
perceived as setting boundaries and dictating direction. Some senior managers,
used to being in control and calling the shots at their whim, may be another
source of resistance to change.

Constraints Embedded in the Governance System

Authority and power—the intangible elements that ultimately determine what
can or cannot be accomplished at a university—and the manner in which these
are distributed will have a significant bearing on the success or failure of strategic planning at a higher education institution. For this reason, it is useful to
begin by reviewing the stereotypical governance models of universities internationally in order to better understand the interface between governance and
the capacity to plan.

Burton Clark has described three models of authority distribution in international higher education systems (Clark 1983). The first is the continental
(European) model, which tends to be strongly state controlled and state steered
and in which real planning authority is vested in the government (the ministry of education), with the university operating essentially as a government
department. In this model, the university management structure is thin on the
ground with little or no planning capacity or authority. Funding is tightly controlled at the center, and the government determines what academic programs
are offered. Although the most extreme versions of this model were to be found
in the Warsaw Pact countries before the collapse of the Berlin Wall, varying

shades of it characterized many western European education systems such as in Finland, Portugal, the Netherlands, and particularly in France in the *écoles superiors*. While European higher education policies have gradually if unevenly shifted toward greater institutional autonomy in recent years, many universities in Africa, South Asia, and other developing countries continue to adhere to this model and to be severely constrained by lack of management autonomy and control over their finances.

Clark's second model is the British tradition of weak state control and constitutionally entrenched institutional autonomy, coupled with a powerful professoriate. This so-called "collegial model" vests much authority and power in academic governance structures dominated by the professoriate such as faculty boards and senates. The executive head of the university is the vice chancellor who belongs to the professoriate, to which he or she is accountable, and is vested with moderate authority as a primus inter pares—first among equals—to facilitate and coordinate the running of the university largely in the interests of the "community of scholars." In this model, laissez-faire is the rule, university development is somewhat haphazard with minimal planning, and there is little accountability to society at large. This model was particularly extant in the epoch of elite higher education systems.

As this model has changed in recent years from a collegial to a managerial form, driven by "the central realities of higher education in the twenty-first century—massification, accountability, privatization, and marketization" (Altbach 2007, 138), the university administration has also grown in numbers and power. The vice chancellor now fulfills the role of a chief executive officer with enhanced powers, supported by a large number of nonacademic management professionals in fields ranging from student affairs to human resources. This in turn has tended to undermine the position of the professoriate, introduce greater tensions between the faculty and the administrators, and complicate the setting for strategic planning.

Institutional autonomy affords the university the leeway to recruit and employ staff at its own discretion, determine its own academic programs, frame its own criteria for student admissions, raise funds from nongovernment sources, engage in revenue-generating entrepreneurial activities, and manage its own finances and budget, albeit within the framework of national legislation and policy. While this autonomy should serve to facilitate strategic planning, the academic freedom enjoyed by the often conservative and sometimes unhappy professoriate has served as a counterweight. Recounting his experiences of stiff resistance by the faculty to his efforts to set a new strategic direction for the University of Zimbabwe, former vice chancellor Walter Kamba recalls:

> The heads of [academic] departments behaved as if they owned the departments, following the traditional behavior associated with the post

[of professor] in Britain. They ran the department as if it was personal property, consulting with only those whom they wished to consult.

(Kamba 2000, 41)

Clark's third model is the generic American university, in which the university is vested with substantial autonomy, faculty authority is weaker than in the other two models, and the university or college president is more powerful than a vice chancellor or a (European) rector. As will be discussed in the later sections of this chapter, although the power of the professoriate is being eroded, the faculty still exercises enough power and influence in decisions regarding strategic planning with the capacity to significantly hinder or facilitate the process.

Institutional Culture

There is no single definition or characteristic of the concept of institutional culture, but the term is widely used to describe the personality of institutions and encompasses: attitudes, values, practices, governance, and intercampus constituency relationships that underpin the functioning of the institution.

Robert A. Sevier notes that "on campus, times of change are usually seen as times of angst" (2003, 1) and lists the following fears and concerns, among others, that act as deterrents to the embrace of planning within the university community: loss of power and prestige, reallocation or loss of resources, loss of autonomy, intrusion into personal and professional domains, changing definitions of success, altered reward systems, fear of technology, and fear of having to relearn.

In a sense, the tendency for faculties to resist change draws from a basic human trait. Sevier further elaborates:

> People, and the organizations they create and inhabit, seldom welcome change. For the most part, they are resistant and reluctant, believing that there is great comfort in the familiar and greater security in the status quo. As a result, they tend to resist new ideas and new ways to think about old ideas. They suffer, as one wag reminded me, from hardening of the categories.

(Sevier 2003, 1)

In many developing nations, planning is bedeviled by the absence of a shared vision and a common understanding of the societal role and purpose of the university, with the faculty seeing the university as a place for the creation and transfer of knowledge, the students seeing it as a place to extract the entitlements of free education and free boarding and lodging, and the often excessively numerous administrative and support staff (and, not unusually, the politicians) seeing it as just another state-owned enterprize with the primary purpose of providing jobs. Indeed in some African and Asian towns and cities, the university is the largest if not the sole employer. These conflicting expectations lead to a polarized campus culture often dominated by student militancy and radical labor union activism. In these circumstances, agreeing on a common vision and mission with academic excellence as a priority becomes a tall order.

Autonomy and Academic Freedom

Institutional autonomy and academic freedom, the acknowledged and often conflated hallmarks of a good academic cultural environment, are quite distinct. *Institutional autonomy* is concerned with governance and refers to the right of institutional self-government, free of external interference, in accordance with universal academic values. Accordingly, the university is free to conduct its academic and administrative business and determine its own policies without external vetting. Autonomy is not absolute, however. There will always be a tension between this freedom and the obligation to comply with high-level policy and statutory regulation in the interests of the common good.

An institution that is tightly controlled by government will be profoundly hard put to plan. Testifying before the Task Force on Higher Education and Society convened by the World Bank and UNESCO (United Nations Educational, Scientific, and Cultural Organization), a senior observer of the African scene, related how

> with the government in many countries having assumed the power to appoint and dismiss the vice chancellor, governance in the universities has thus become a purely state-controlled system . . . . There are countries where even deans and heads of departments are also appointed by government and where heads of institutions change with a change in government.
>
> (Task Force on Higher Education and Society 2000, 62)

The university leadership in these circumstances may therefore see little sense in engaging in time-consuming planning activities if the plan is destined to be set aside by the minister of education with the power to determine what the university may or may not do and with absolute control over the size and shape of the budget. In many African and Asian countries, the custom is for universities to submit their budgets to the ministry for funding in competition with other ministerial funding obligations. In these circumstances, the funding allocation is totally unpredictable and may be up one year and down the next. What is invariably predictable in these resource-constrained nations is the inevitability of a budget cut. The university rarely, if ever, gets what it has requested. Worse still, remittances to the university often occur in tranches of unpredictable quantum at unpredictable times. Given the centrality of the budget process to planning and the need for assurance that the activities in the plan will be funded, it is difficult to conceive of a more planning-averse scenario.

Invariably, in such settings, academic freedom is also constrained, with the academics too intimidated to complain publicly or to express themselves freely on such topics as corruption, government waste, or wrongheaded education policies. They are also prevented from conducting research that may be perceived as unflattering to the powers that be.

It is our experience, however, that even in severely conflicted settings planning can be an important and useful intervention to build bridges among contending parties. Planning provides the neutral space for mutual dialogue, institutional introspection, and the quest for a modus vivendi. Only through such a participatory process can the contending campus constituencies arrive at common values and objectives. In these circumstances, external consultants can be usefully brought in as honest brokers and advisers.

The story of the Durban University of Technology in South Africa presents an instructive case study. This university was the result of a merger between two neighboring higher education institutions, ML Sultan Technikon and Technikon Natal. Though only separated by a crooked white fence, the two institutions could not have been more different in terms of their histories and institutional cultures. ML Sultan Technikon was founded on a postage-stamp-sized lot with limited state-financial support, by indentured laborers imported from India to work in sugarcane plantations in South Africa in the mid-1980s. Despite severe apartheid restrictions, ML Sultan Technikon developed into a well-managed and academically successful academic institution with cash reserves in the bank, thanks largely to proverbial Asian frugality and community solidarity and, in the 1980s, to sensible strategic planning following training sessions by one of the authors (Hayward). Technikon Natal, on the other hand, was established as an institution for the white community on expansive land with liberal state support and relatively opulent facilities. Understandably, the relationship between these proximate institutions was marked by longstanding resentments and animosities. Despite its privileged position, Technikon Natal was poorly managed in a top-down fashion with severe budget deficits.

In 2002, in compliance with mandatory postapartheid higher education restructuring, ML Sultan Technikon and Technikon Natal were merged into one institution, under the leadership of one of the authors (Ncayiyana) to form the Durban University of Technology. Predictably, the merger resulted in seismic institutional cultural clashes that rendered Durban University of Technology a crisis-ridden institution of the sort described in the foregoing paragraphs, and planning with the support of external consultants became a significant and fruitful intervention in the endeavor to identify and evolve a common vision, mission, values, and objectives. Today, the Durban University of Technology is a relatively stable and successful institution.

The planning process is as important as the product, and ownership of the plan by all the stakeholders is paramount. The Durban University of Technology case demonstrates that under limited capacity or a lack of mutual trust and of internal cohesion, the use of external experts for facilitation and expertise can be a useful intervention. However, the plan must be a product of internal dialogue.

Universities as a species are intrinsically conservative, inclined to resist any move that seeks to change their long-held traditions and practices. Even in universities with the freedom to run their own affairs, issues of institutional culture (internal conflict, lack of trust, entrenched sectional interests, fear of change, weak or incompetent leadership, and so forth) may act as deterrents to planning.

On the other hand, strategic planning can transform a campus, bring it together in new ways, create an active creative community, and foster a new sense of identity on campus. It can be an "act of liberation" if those involved create the conditions for such change. It can also be an important process for change and renewal or an equally important process to reassure the university community that the institution is heading in the right direction and should remain steady on the course.

The Critical Role of Leadership

Defining Leadership

Leadership is critical to successful planning by universities. But leadership defies precise definition. Many authors have endeavored to describe it in numerous different ways. Robert Birnbaum's definition is probably one of the better known, namely that "Leadership involves moving others towards a shared perception of reality, towards a common understanding of where the organization is and where it should be going, and toward an increased commitment to those ends" (1992, 16).

Attributes of a Good Leader

Broadly, leadership refers to the skills to set the institutional tone, direction, and cohesion by influencing people, whereas management refers to the skills to implement institutional policies and decisions and to run the institutional administration. The two attributes are not mutually exclusive, however, and the ideal leader of a higher education institution should in this context be in possession of both. He or she must be a visionary, able to see the bigger picture and to identify the broad priorities but also an implementer able to see institutional decisions through to realization. To be able to give direction and influence people, a person must have a keen understanding of the institution and its culture, values, and political paradigm. Above all,

at its most basic, leadership is all about managing change. It is about antic-
ipating it; framing it in ways the organization understands; finding a path
through it. In many ways, the hallmark of a great leader is how well he or
she manages change.

(Sevier 2003)

University leadership can only be as good as the institutional context in which
it is exercised. Therefore, we shall now explore constraints that may threaten
leadership effectiveness and planning success in the context of current realities
in institutional governance.

Distributed Leadership

Although this section focuses on the university president, chancellor, or vice
chancellor as the institutional leader, successful planning and implementation cannot rely on the leadership of one person. Strategic planning requires
capable and appropriately empowered leadership at all operational levels and
in all sections or departments of the institution. Unless all the leaders in all the
organizational units and other influential formations on campus are successful
in creating a commitment to the initiative, a plan that is impressive on paper
may fail to achieve its goals. Defining leadership roles and responsibilities at
these levels is essential to a plan's effectiveness. Each member of this leadership
cadre must have deep organizational knowledge and a thorough understanding
of when and how to make decisions in line with the discretionary authority and
boundaries of their mandate.

Governing boards and councils have a critical leadership role in planning.
Although strategic planning is led by the president, chancellor, or vice chancellor within the university, the governing board's role is "to consider the issues of
mission and overall goals, to state clearly what it expects the planning process
to address, and to participate willingly in the process" (Ncayiyana and Hayward
1999, 21). Above all, it is important that the governing body lends appropriate
support to the chief executive officer throughout the formulation and execution of the plan.

Students are an important constituency of the university community and
must be represented on all committees and working groups concerned with the
formulation, implementation, monitoring, and evaluation of the plan.

Leadership and Governance

The traditional university is under pressure from a number of fronts ranging
from demands for greater relevance from business and government to calls for
greater access and massification around the world. Costs are rising faster than
public funding, causing severe financial stresses for the university. There has

been a shift in the public perception of higher education being a "public good" that should be funded by the state to it being a "private good" that should in large part be borne by the beneficiary (the student). There are also political pressures from governments and others who see the university as a hotbed of political activity that should be tamed.

Financial pressures are exerting unprecedented changes in academe. The autonomy of the professoriate is being eroded by demands for greater accountability and a re-examination of faculty employment conditions. On its web site the American Association of University Professors points with disapprobation to faculty "Facing hiring freezes, layoffs, furloughs, increased class sizes, and a diminished voice in institutional decision-making" (AAUP 2009). Financial pressures in the developing world are also resulting in increasing class sizes and expanding workloads from Ethiopia (Tessema 2009) to Afghanistan.

In some parts of the world a number of universities have sought to establish closer ties with business and corporations through endowments and even naming rights that many academics regard as exerting harmful influence and even unseemly control on the academy (Soley 1995). The American Association of University Professors asserts that "university corporatization [has led to] the domination of institutional governing boards by successful business leaders who favor the application of free-market business practices to higher education and who appoint like-minded presidents and academic administrators" (AAUP 2006).

University Leadership Challenges in Africa and Asia

As in many other parts of the world, South African universities are confronted with the conundrum of declining state financial support, burgeoning student numbers and increasing operating costs, as a result of which managerialism—managing a university like a business with the focus on the "bottom line" to the detriment of academic management norms and traditions—has begun to make inroads into institutional management and governance. It has become common practice by universities to pursue "third stream income" (the other two being state support and student tuition fees) in the form of grants, endowments, and the setting up of wholly owned for-profit enterprizes.

The challenges of leadership for the South African vice chancellor have been summarized as follows:

> In a very short period [since democracy], institutional leadership has had to deal with becoming both more skilled in a business management sense, and at the same time, more democratic; and with having to deal with new power relations between constituencies within the institution and between the institution and the rest of society.
>
> (Cloete, Bunting, and Kulati 2000, 2)

Academic leadership in many Asian nations is similarly constrained by political and/or religious restrictions. In China, academic freedom is severely restricted and is not accepted as an academic norm.

In Singapore, Malaysia and Taiwan, certain topics are considered highly sensitive for research and analysis by academics. In Malaysia and Singapore potentially volatile religious and ethnic questions must be treated with extreme care by the academic community. In Malaysia, there is an expectation that academics should belong to the ruling political party, Golkar.

(Altbach 2006, 74)

In Afghanistan, though the Ministry of Higher Education supports academic freedom (Ministry of Higher Education 2009, 19), religious conservatism makes many subjects difficult to deal with even in an academic setting, and they are thus generally left alone.

The Strategic-Planning Process

This section gives a brief overview of the strategic- and financial-planning process starting from preplanning activities through to plan implementation and monitoring. Because the strategic-planning committee and the budget committee each may do its work independently—or no budget committee is even involved—many plans fail. It has been said that "in the absence of a plan, the budget is the plan; and if a plan exists but is not linked to the budget, the budget is still the plan!" Also underscored is the importance of consensus building within the institution and, to the extent necessary, with other stakeholders.

Planning Initiation

A successful strategic-planning process usually develops from a good deal of thoughtful strategic thinking prior to starting the formal process. It might include an environmental scan laying out an overview of the current situation by a small team of major current challenges for the institution. It should also include careful consideration of potential members of the planning committee—individuals who are widely respected, noted for their constructive approach to issues, and represent a broad range of campus opinions. A successful strategic-planning committee must include some of the most distinguished faculty members, administrators, members of staff, and student representatives. Critical, too, is the choice of the committee chair who should be both a leader and a listener and someone able to bridge differences and foster consensus.

The impetus for starting the planning process might be the appointment of a new president or chancellor, fundamental changes in the economic condition of the institution, a desire to respond to imperatives growing out of globalization, the end of a cycle associated with the previous strategic plan and a need to start a new cycle, or a variety of other factors. Whatever the stimulus, some broad parameters for the committee should be set out in advance (suggestive but not restrictive), including a time frame, tentative schedule, and benchmarks.

Essentially, the quality, creativity, and commitment of the faculty create the university. The administrators, staff, and students also play a key role in setting the institution's reputation, and they too must have a major part in this process. There may be opposition to student and staff participation, yet if they are not an integral part of the planning process the campus community will miss out on critical inputs about teaching, the infrastructure and other issues that may not have reached the ears of either administrators or faculty members. Failure to include students in strategic planning efforts in Madagascar early in the process nearly derailed the effort because students believed the plan was an effort to privatize public higher education. In South Africa students played a major role in making a student-loan plan work—including convincing reluctant students of the need to repay their loans in a timely manner. Similarly, exclusion of staff members in one case brought about strikes that crippled one institution for weeks. In the experience of these authors, many of the most useful insights and suggestions have come from staff and students. Without them, major inputs will be missed and implementation will be more difficult.

The Strategic-Planning Committee

To serve as a member of a university strategic-planning committee will involve a major time commitment, which should be made clear at the outset. And in most cases, the staff best equipped to contribute to such a committee will have the least time to serve. They will be deeply involved in their teaching, research, and service obligations, and they may be involved in a substantial amount of consulting to supplement their incomes—especially where salaries are comparatively low. In a number of countries, the salary structure is such that most faculty members cannot meet their bills without a second job to supplement their income. Thus, service on a strategic-planning committee may be quite costly in personal financial terms, to their teaching, research, and family obligations. In some countries in which salaries are adequate, such as the United States, the honor of such service on a university-wide committee may be a sufficient reward. In others, such service may pose serious hardships for participants. For student members, committee service may eliminate the opportunity to work part time to cover the cost of their studies. Thus, part of the preplanning stage should include consideration of incentives for committee members who would have special needs if they were to participate. It might be that a one-course reduction of teaching load, payment of costs of travel, or a fixed stipend of several hundred dollars a month, as necessary in several developing countries, would facilitate desired participation. Working out these arrangements in advance will enhance the acceptance rate for potential committee members, avoid embarrassment for some of them, and facilitate a successful strategic-planning process.

The beginning of the strategic-planning process should be announced publicly, along with its charge, the names of members, and an invitation to the campus community to make their ideas for the future known to the planning committee. Openness and transparency will enhance both the process and encourage successful implementation. Suspicions and concerns about the process should be dealt with from the outset. The longer the problems fester, the more difficult they are to resolve.

The dangers involved if conflicts and major issues are not resolved at the outset became strikingly apparent to the authors on the first day of a facilitation of the strategic planning process in Malawi. Our efforts were nearly derailed when representatives of two of the units that made up the university's strategic-planning committee announced that both units were going to secede from the university. Some members of the strategic-planning committee felt this was "good riddance" and wanted to continue without them. Others thought that action would cripple the process—that a breakup of the university would be fatal for all of its parts in the long run. Still others thought we should reschedule the meetings to a later date once these issues were resolved. We decided that if a strategic plan existed for the institution it should be implemented immediately, but we also believed that the institutions would do better remaining as a cohesive unit than as several independent institutions. Thus, our suggestion was to facilitate discussions with each of the two institutions separately during the following day, ensure that the institutions as a whole were prepared for the consequences of the breakup, and, with or without them, continue the planning process with whoever remained, the day after.

The next day was one of marathon discussion sessions with each of the units—in both cases starting with a fairly hostile crowd. We laid out the options and consequences, followed by an open discussion—often heated. People weighed the advantages and disadvantages of succession, the costs of breakup, and the chances of success. It was an exhausting day for everyone, but we called for a decision by the end of the day and promised to resume strategic planning with whatever was left of the university the next morning. In the end, the two secessionist units realized that they were much better off working together as part of the university than each setting up its own institutions, its own strategic plan, and seeking funding in competition with the other institutions. The planning process resumed the next day with new vigor. In the end, an excellent plan was developed over the next few months.

In this case, the success of the strategic-planning process depended on early resolution of the conflicts that threatened to derail it. Here, external facilitators proved vital to a resolution. The outcome illustrates the importance of confronting conflicts and divisions at the outset so that the process thereafter can move forward appropriately.

Identifying Institutional Values and Mission

Most institutions have a mission statement and often a statement of key values, which should be revisited at the beginning of the planning process. The objective is to clarify that the institutions are committed to some enduring values—such as, open and free discussion, gender equity, rural development, excellence in teaching and research, amelioration of poverty, or protecting the environment. The mission and values that emerge from that review should guide the work of the strategic-planning committee over the next few years and move the institution in the direction of what it wishes to be.

Environmental Assessment

An environmental assessment, sometimes called a SWOT analysis (for strengths, weaknesses, opportunities, and threats) is essential to successful planning. It will help the committee assess the current condition of the institution including both its strengths and weaknesses. An environmental assessment might present new opportunities or help us consider an unknown future and explore areas that might otherwize be neglected. In strategic-planning facilitations in which we have been involved, the environmental assessment has been critical in helping the strategic-planning committee focus on key issues related to building the kind of university it envisions.

The vice chancellor of the University of Development Studies in Ghana, thinking back on the strategic-planning process in 2002/2003, emphasized the importance of the environmental assessment (SWOT analysis) to the success of the university's process. First, it helped "sensitize" stakeholders to the issues and to future expectations of the university. He went on to say that

> Secondly, the identification of the strengths, weaknesses, opportunities and threats through the SWOT analysis helped Management to take advantage of the strengths and opportunities and to work towards reducing the weaknesses and threats. The University, for example, continued to encourage its "young, dynamic and enthusiastic staff members" and "motivated students" while ensuring that the "poor infrastructure base" and "poor communication networks" were substantially improved. Without a Strategic Plan, it might not have been easy to be that focused and much less would have been achieved in terms of concrete results.
>
> (J. Kaburise, personal communication, February 17, 2007)

An environmental scan encourages the strategic-planning committee to make a careful, systematic assessment of the institution in ways that might not otherwize occur. As such, it sets the stage for a careful review of the current situation in ways that highlight the most critical goals and priorities.

Setting Goals for the Institution

Once the committee has assessed the university environment, the goals for the institution are much more obvious, and agenda setting can begin. Some institutions ask individual units to forward their goals to the committee which then sifts through them to identify priorities. However, that action tends to produce long *wish lists* with little coherence or likelihood that many of the goals will be realized. This approach tends to raise expectations with most hopes then dashed at a later stage. Taking a university-wide approach helps the planning committee identify key issues, many of which will have implications for the whole institution. For example, upgrading science and technology laboratories benefits only those programs. A commitment to improved teaching or "writing across the curriculum" affects all programs but does not preclude priorities that focus on a single unit.

Overall, the most effective approach to setting goals, in our experience, involves assessing the need of the university as a whole, rather than unit by unit. Are university graduates being employed? What areas are most successful? Which ones have large numbers unemployed after six months? Are employers happy with graduates? Do students feel they have been well prepared for the world of work? Is the publication of the faculty the record that the institution would like? How are faculty members faring in terms of citation indexes? How do the various fields rank nationally? What kinds of recognition do faculty members receive nationally and internationally? Is the faculty involved in knowledge production in significant ways? What is the evidence? Are there a number of distinguished teachers on campus? How do they fare in student evaluations? Have they received institutional or national awards? How does the institution's current condition reflect the institution's vision and mission? What areas need support to achieve the mission and vision of the institution?

The answers to these questions will help shape the goals of the strategic plan. Job placement results might suggest that the university should train fewer journalists, although that is the most popular major among students. In one Midwestern university half the students, in the college of letters and science, wanted to be journalism majors. How many journalists does a country need? These decisions must be grappled with by the strategic-planning committee. In Afghanistan, teacher education was flooded with applicants but only because all other areas were full. Teaching was discovered to be the last choice of these students. What could the university do to raise the attraction of teaching—to become something other than the last choice for applicants? What changes would assist the urgent national need for teachers and produce teacher education graduates who feel good about their choice of field, excited about the teaching profession, and eager to meet those challenges? Are there ways to inculcate values among students that will encourage them to become teachers? Are there other incentives that can be used to support teaching? The answers to these questions are "yes," but that process requires a different approach to teacher training along with improved working conditions and pay for teachers.

Planning can help shift students to desired fields. South Africa encountered a desperate need for more graduates in science and technology. Most of the graduates in early 2000 were in arts and letters. How could higher education meet the requirement for science and technology? Those areas required a math and science background, starting in primary and secondary school—that is, not merely being provided late in a student's training. Nonetheless, strategic plans at most tertiary institutions focused on increasing the number of science and technology graduates. Teachers and students in secondary schools responded to the new requirements, and these efforts succeeded remarkably in a relatively short period of time. In another institution, the University of Wisconsin–Madison, starting in the early 1980s there was growing concern about the quality of teaching and the inability of students to write well. The university made teaching and learning its top priority, emphasizing writing in every course—writing across the curriculum—providing grants for innovative courses and creative approaches. Student writing improved measurably as did student evaluations of teaching. Although the University of Wisconsin–Madison has always been a large institution of over 30,000 students, it gained a reputation for high-quality teaching and produced students who knew how to write well.

Strategic-plan goals should focus beyond new programs or enhancing existing programs. The strategic-planning committee should consider eliminating programs that are underenrolled or no longer fit into the mission or vision of the institution. In a number of cases examined by the authors, institutional goals involved the elimination or consolidation of programs. In South Africa, the University of Durban-Westville reduced the number of faculties and eliminated several programs. Indeed, one of these programs had more faculty members than students.

Prioritizing the Goals

Achieving an agreement on goals for the future is not nearly as difficult a task as prioritizing them. As a result, some excellent and worthy goals often fall outside the scope of the plan. It should be accepted that some good projects will need to be put off to a later date. Such issues are the hard choices of strategic planning. Nonetheless, it is important to maintain the priorities set. Thus, external funding or new initiatives outside the framework of the mission and goals should not be added to the process if they divert funds or attention from the priorities set by consensus. No matter how hard the committee tries, it may be impossible to gain total consensus about planning priorities.

However, in observing more than a dozen strategic-planning efforts in a number of different countries, we have seen several practices that help foster agreement. One option is the ability of the chairperson to foster open discussion and exchange. A second practice occurs when the members build a common sense of identity with the institution rather than the separate units. Some committees develop an effective culture of compromize—a willingness to put decision making in the context of the institution as a whole. Another factor that often contributes to agreement is *time*. We have seen incredible rancor, walkouts, boycotts, even threats during a strategic-planning discussion. But if the leadership is able to keep people talking usually at some point, almost everyone realizes that there has been enough talk, enough debate, that it is time to make tough decisions. And then consensus occurs—usually very quickly.

Some simple rules of thumb can provide assistance as well (Hayward 2008). In most cases some goals can reflect the needs of the institution as a whole. It might be the need for a digital library in Afghanistan, more bandwidth in Madagascar, or an equitable health system for faculty and staff in South Africa. An additional rule of thumb is that priority should be given to faculty and academic programs. What can be done to improve academic programs, support teaching and research, attract, and keep the best minds in the country? In the long run, the success, reputation, and future of a university depends on the ability of academics to develop new knowledge, pass on the findings of the past, and teach students how to be creative members of society. If the strategic-planning committee comes to recognize that the teaching and research staff are the most important resource of the university, decisions about goals and their priorities will be much easier to implement. Cost will be another determining factor. What goals fit within the budget constraints of the strategic plan? How does that affect priorities? Usually, the answer is clear.

Financial Planning

Strategic planning without financial planning is of limited value given that the cost is a critical factor in preparing a realistic plan and insuring that it is implementable. Careful calculation of the cost of each goal will lead to setting priorities and will eliminate goals that are unlikely to be funded. Linking the strategic plan to the budget will help set targets for fund-raising and establish contingency plans if such goals are not met. In the end, successful implementation will depend on the care and thoroughness of the financial planning that goes into costing the strategic plan year by year.

Budget software that includes income and expenditures by major category for all items in both the recurring and development budget is a useful tool for this process. Year one is the last completed budget year with the next five-year totals reflecting each year of the strategic-planning budget. It should include all elements of the institutional budget. Planners then enter costs associated with the strategic plan each year over the next five years. All income and expenditures related to the strategic plan should be included in the year in which the projects will be implemented, including any savings that are expected to result from elimination of programs or from expenses that no longer meet the mission or needs of the institution. Thus, for example, the additional cost of new faculty members would show up in the year they are expected to be employed; income from additional student fees would be reflected in the years of enrollment, growth and construction costs as they are expected to be paid over the life of construction projects. In addition, the annual budget should include calculations for annual inflation. This cost is often neglected with dire consequences. If inflation is 10 percent per year, for example, the budget must reflect that cost. Without it, there will be an annual equivalent shortfall of the amount of inflation that will have an ongoing cumulative effect on the budget.

Funding the Plan

Ideally, funding for the strategic plan is available when the plan is written, but this is not always the actual case. The completed strategic plan itself is often a key to obtaining funding from government, funders, or the public. Indeed, many funders require a strategic and financial plan as a condition of considering funding.

A good strategic plan does not always involve budget increases. Indeed, a thoughtful strategic plan should cut programs that no longer fit the needs of the institution or have ceased to be effective. This is especially the case in tight financial circumstances where new initiatives may have to be funded by cutting some current budget expenditures.

Critical to obtaining funding is making an effective case for higher education. Too often we fail to justify goals, adequately explain the mission, clarify values, and show how the contributions of the university foster national development and the individual well-being of the graduates. Too often we assume that the case for funding is self-evident. Great care and thoughtful planning should go into making the case for the funding needed.

Facilitation of the Process

The institution may wish to seek the assistance of a specialist on strategic and financial planning. Some consultants offer to help write the strategic plan. However, such a bid should be avoided since such plans almost never result in effective planning or implementation. Successful strategic plans, in our experience, are always the product of the institution itself and broad participation by faculty, administration, staff, and students. Nonetheless, having an experienced external facilitator can be helpful both in dealing with ongoing institutional conflicts and bringing to the strategic-planning process the experience of other institutions and countries. In the end, however, the plan must reflect the values, goals, and priorities of the institution as a whole. Only that will help mobilize faculty, student, community, and national support.

Mobilizing the Community to Support the Strategic Plan

Most strategic plans involve major changes in some aspects of the institutional operation—sometimes involving layoffs, curtailment of some programs, as well as expansion of others. Part of the process of strategic planning should involve regular consultations with the constituents, keeping them abreast of the process, changes proposed, goals, and new priorities. Laying the groundwork for change becomes a critical aspect. Part of that aspect involves recognizing the fears and concerns of members of the community who may be affected by the new strategic plan and helping them prepare for the changes that are underway.

Leading change is a critical part of mobilizing people to implement the strategic plan.

> Successful execution of strategy and building of organizational capacity require committed and active leadership. In parallel with organizational planning and budgeting, leaders should develop an action plan for navigating change, leveraging expeditionary initiatives, developing and mobilizing leadership, developing organizational capacity, and communicating/engaging participants across the enterprize.
>
> (Norris and Poulton 2008, 38)

Part of leading change is developing trust (Eckel et al. 1999, 14). Broad campus participation and communication are essential in developing that trust. In the end, a plan succeeds because the vision and goals are shared by the majority of the campus community and people recognize what has to be done to achieve them.

Faculty, staff, students, and alumni can also be valuable partners in fundraising for the strategic plan. They can be especially effective in making the case before legislative bodies, local government, and funders. Alumni groups have also been effective in raising funds among graduates, making major contributions in a number of places including remarkable support at the University of Ghana, Legon. Making alumni and friends of the university part of the ongoing process early gives them the information to become effective ambassadors for the institution and its funding needs.

Implementation and Monitoring the Plan

Far too many strategic plans do not include an implementation strategy. As Norris and Poulton make clear, the plan is only a start: "planners must deal with the execution of strategy and the development of the organizational capacity necessary to compete effectively and in new ways" (2008, 34). How is the plan to be implemented? What aspects of the plan should be implemented first? Are there short-term goals that can be realized quickly? Will some goals need to await fund-raising successes? How can we best respond to the opponents of change? Who will be responsible for the implementation of each goal? What are the timelines for each? These and other questions should be answered and strategies established before the implementation process begins. Responsibilities for each set of goals must be assigned and reporting mechanisms developed. An overall timetable for the strategic plan should also be set out with realistic deadlines reflecting preparation time, reviews, construction time, approval time, setup, and training where needed.

Monitoring the plan is also a critical part of the process. Where unexpected obstacles occur, the plan may need to be modified. In some cases major changes will be needed to achieve desired ends. The strategic-planning committee should meet regularly to review progress on the plan, consider modifications, and keep the university community aware of successes and achievements as they occur. The budget should be monitored on an ongoing basis and where costs change, the appropriate adjustments made.

Strategic and budget planning should be an ongoing process. Use the planning process to institutionalize strategic planning. The planning committee might be institutionalized as a permanent university committee. It should have a permanent staff with the technical capacities and financial training to assist the strategic-planning committee and serve as both support for and an archive of the planning process.

Measuring Success and Lessons Learned

Monitoring and Evaluation

Monitoring and evaluation is critical to tracking progress and success in the implementation of a strategic plan to ensure that the organization is adhering to the institutional objectives agreed on during the strategic-planning process and that lessons are learned from implementation failures. In the absence of such tracking, the strategic plan is destined to collect dust on the institution's bookshelves. Brian Figaji, former vice chancellor of the Peninsula Technikon (as it then was) in Cape Town recalls how:

> In the 1980s the senior management would compile an annual strategic plan. We would perform SWOT analyses, hold discussions and try to produce a successful strategy. During the year this strategy tended to fall by the wayside, and thereafter business was conducted with little change. The next year, we would review our strategy, but the process was neither taken seriously nor performed rigorously.
>
> (Figaji 2000, 88)

Like so many other institutions, Peninsula Technikon had gone through the motions (however imperfectly) of strategic planning but had neglected to incorporate plans for the follow-through. At the heart of all strategic-planning models that have been proposed is a triad of inseparable elements: researching and planning, resourcing and implementing, and monitoring and evaluating the plan.

Institutions have tended to measure success in terms of inputs (funds raised, faculty hired, and student numbers) rather than outputs. At an institution headed by one of the authors, success indicators for student uptake included numbers of students enrolled, dropout rates, and throughput rates; and research output was assessed regarding numbers of research-oriented graduate students and postdoctoral fellows enrolled, master's and doctoral degrees conferred, and the quantity of published peer-reviewed articles and books. Indicators that are more difficult to measure may also include quality, a new curriculum, transformed approaches to teaching and learning, community involvement, job placement, satisfaction of graduates looking back on their education, and realization of other qualitative objectives or goals set.

Responsibility and Time Frames

The process of implementation, monitoring, and evaluation should be clearly spelt out in the plan. First, it is critical that the strategic-plan document specifies who is responsible for the implementation of the plan, and for achieving each goal and objective. Ordinarily, this responsibility rests in the first instance, with the leadership of the respective academic and administrative units. Second, the document should specify who is responsible for monitoring the implementation of the plan and evaluating whether the stated goals are being achieved.

At the institutional level, monitoring is exercised through the leadership cascade beginning with the department chair or administrative unit director, whose function is to ensure that sections deliver on the strategic-plan undertakings according to the agreed time frames, and that any obstacles are dealt with by the relevant people or bodies within the institution.

Formal monitoring and evaluation at agreed intervals is the responsibility of the authority or structure identified in the plan, such as the university planning committee. Formal reports are submitted at agreed intervals to the chief executive officer (president, chancellor, or vice chancellor), who in turn reports to the governing board, council, or to the ministry. The reports are also deliberated on and evaluated at university forums such as school or faculty boards and senate. Third, and as already suggested, the plan must lay out clear schedules, time frames, and performance indicators for implementation and evaluation.

Outcomes of Monitoring and Evaluation

Monitoring aims to determine whether the goals and objectives of the plan are being achieved according to the timelines specified in the plan and if not, why not; whether deadlines should be adjusted; plans altered; whether some planned projects or activities should be cancelled; and whether personnel have adequate resources (money, equipment, facilities, training, etc.) to achieve the goals. Moreover, monitoring should answer the question: what can be learned from our monitoring and evaluation to improve future planning activities and also to improve future monitoring and evaluation efforts?

Because a strategic plan is a high level, longer-term document in a fast changing world, it is important that it be regarded as a road map rather than a dogmatic catechism and to accept that the university may be obliged to change or modify direction as it proceeds through the coming years due to changes in the organization's external and/or internal environment. Significantly, the reasons for change are critically interrogated and understood. Some reasons may be quite obvious, such as the emergence of new regulatory legislation or drastic changes in institutional funding. Others may be more subtle, such as the attrition of key researchers or the inability to populate specific courses with suitably qualified students.

On the other hand, "quick wins" must be explicitly celebrated. Celebration is as important as accomplishing objectives. Without a sense of progress, acknowledgment, and fulfillment from a job well done, the next planning cycle becomes a grind. Sevier observes that "While significant change is typically a long-term undertaking, people need to know immediately that their efforts are having some impact" (Sevier 2003).

To sustain the momentum of success, good performance should be rewarded:

> For strategic planning to succeed, faculty should be rewarded for a broader range of things [beyond teaching and research]. People participate in activities that get rewarded, so universities have to be willing to shift resources and allocate funds for strategic priorities. In essence, strategic planning goals and objectives should be linked to the reward system.
>
> (Lerner 1999, 11)

Lessons Learned

Implementation of a strategic plan will invariably produce lessons linked to successes as well as failures. Better and more efficient ways of doing things, as well as how not to do things, will be learned. Problems will emerge, requiring a reconsideration of the specific strategy, and some projects will prove to be unhelpful or unaffordable and will have to be discarded. New ways of monitoring and evaluation will be discovered, and some predetermined performance indicators will be found not to work out as planned. Conversely, some actions and interventions will be found to work well or even better than predicted. These and other lessons learned must be documented, deliberated at the appropriate level, acted upon, and retrievably archived.

It is not possible to implement a strategic plan without regularly taking stock at predetermined intervals using predetermined performance indicators and time frames. The plan should be sufficiently flexible to accommodate alterations occasioned by changes in the internal or external environment.

There are indicators of success that may have long-lasting impacts, including creating a "culture of negotiation" or a "culture of planning," making the case successful for the strategic-plan funding needed, fostering integration and a sense of identity with the institution, creating legitimacy for new processes or structures, mobilizing support where there was none, building greater participation, institution building, and institutionalization of the process.

Strategic planning can transform a campus, bring it together in new ways, create an active creative community, and foster a new sense of identity on campus. It can be an "act of liberation" if the people involved create the conditions for such change. It can also be an important process for change and renewal or an equally important process that reassures the university community that the institution is heading in the right direction and should remain steady on course.

Notes

1. Vice Chancellor Njabulo Ndebele, personal communication, March 2003.

References

AAUP (American Association of University Professors) (2006) How we can resist corporatization. Available: www.aaup.org/AAUP/pubgres/academe/2006/MJ/. . ./andr.htm (accessed September 20, 2009).
—— (2009) Faculty facing troubling trends. Available: www.aaup.org/AAUP/newsroom/Highlights/Pricevid.htm (accessed September 20, 2009).
Altbach, P.G. (2006) International Higher Education—Reflections on Policy and Practice, Chestnut Hill, MA: Boston College Center for International Higher Education.
—— (2007) Tradition and Transition: The International Imperative in Higher Education, Rotterdam: Sense.
Birnbaum, R. (1992) How Academic Leadership Works. San Francisco: Jossey-Bass.
Clark, B. (1983) The Higher Education System—Academic Organization in Cross-National Perspective, Berkeley: Univ. of California Press.
Cloete, N., I. Bunting, and T. Kulati (2000) "Higher education leadership challenges, 1999," in N. Cloete, T. Kulati, and M. Phala (eds) Leadership and Institutional Change in Higher Education, Pretoria, South Africa: Centre for Higher Education Transformation.
Eckel, P., M. Green, B. Hill, and W. Mallon (1999) On Change III: Taking Charge of Change, a Program for Colleges and Universities, Washington, DC: American Council on Education.
Figaji, B. (2000) "Grappling with change: case studies—Peninsula Technikon," in N. Cloete, T. Kulati, and M. Phala (eds) Leadership and Institutional Change in Higher Education, Pretoria, South Africa: Centre for Higher Education Transformation.

Freed J.E., M.R. Klugman, and J.D. Fife (1997) "A culture of academic excellence: Implementing the quality principles in higher education," *ASHE-ERIC Higher Education Report*, 25 (1).

Hayward, F. (2008) "Critical issues in institutional accreditation: Observations from a multi-country perspective," in *Proceedings: 2nd International Conference on Assessing Quality in Higher Education*, Lahore, Pakistan: Punjab Univ. Press.

Hayward, F. and D. Ncayiyana (2003) *Strategic Planning: A Guide for Higher Education Institutions*, Cape Town, South Africa: Centre for Higher Education Transformation.

Kamba, W. (2000) "Leadership strategies for institutional change: The case of the University of Zimbabwe," in N. Cloete, T. Kulati, and M. Phala (eds.) *Leadership and Institutional Change in Higher Education*, Pretoria, South Africa: Centre for Higher Education Transformation.

Kerr, C. (2001) *The Uses of the University*, Cambridge, MA: Harvard Univ. Press.

Lerner, A. (1999) A strategic planning primer for higher education. Available: www.sonoma.edu/aa/planning/strategic_planning_primer.pdf (accessed September 23, 2009).

Ministry of Higher Education (2009) *National Strategic Plan for Higher Education: 2010–2014*, Kabul: Ministry of Higher Education, Afghanistan.

Ncayiyana, D. and F. Hayward (1999) *Effective Governance: A Guide for Council Members of Universities and Technikons*, Pretoria, South Africa: Centre for Higher Education Transformation.

Norris, D. and N. Poulton (2008) *A Guide to Planning for Change*, Ann Arbor, Michigan: Society for College and University Planning.

Peterson, M. (1980) "Analyzing alternative approaches to planning," in P. Jedamus and M. W. Peterson (eds.) *Improving Academic Management*, San Francisco: Jossey-Bass.

Rowley, D., H. Lujan, and M. Dolence (1997) *Strategic Change in Colleges and Universities*, San Francisco: Jossey-Bass.

Sevier, R.A. (2003) "Overcoming internal resistance to change," *University Business*. Available: http://findarticles.com/p/articles/mi_mOLSH/is_7_6/ai_105556098/ (accessed August 31, 2009).

Soley, L. (1995) *Leasing the Ivory Tower: The Corporate Takeover of Academia*, Boston, MA: South End Press.

Tessema, K. (2009) "The unfolding trends and consequences of expanding higher education in Ethiopia: Massive university, massive challenges," *Higher Education Quarterly*, 63 (1): 29–45.

The Task Force on Higher Education and Society (2000) *Higher Education in Developing Countries: Peril and Promise*, Washington, DC: World Bank.

2

Governing Universities in Times of Uncertainty and Change

ÁLVARO ROJAS AND ANDRÉS BERNASCONI

In the context of globalization and the new economy, the problem of governance in higher education has gained prominence, as governments, universities, and other societal actors face new challenges. This chapter examines the challenges facing university leaders and administrators in the context of the massification of higher education and its diversification, the rise of accountability, revenue streams, and the professionalization of management. Dealing mainly with the internal management of universities—not with the governance of higher education systems—involves relationships with government authorities and stakeholders, the governance roles of faculty and students, the nature of executive power and the attributes of an effective leadership team, the connection between strategic planning and organizational structure, the management of faculty, and the modern concept of audit and control.

The knowledge economy's emphasis on advanced training for human capital and technology-driven innovation has put universities—society's designated institutions for advanced education and research—under a new light. No longer peripheral to the cast of actors engaged in the engineering of development and progress, universities find themselves center stage and largely scrutinized for efficacy, now that so much depends on their performance and efficiency, given the new expectations of accountability.

Inevitably, the extension of higher education to new demographic groups, more diverse constituencies, and new sets of preoccupations has initiated new conceptions of the relationship between the state and higher education. "Hands off" is no longer a viable policy recipe, as governments increasingly view higher education as strategic to any long-term vision of the country's role in a global economy and society. As a result, a series of reforms were introduced to the governance of higher education systems, starting in the 1980s, in countries across western Europe, North America, Latin America, and Asia. The collapse of communism also contributed to this wave of reforms in the areas previously under Soviet influence. These reforms seek to increase higher education systems' productivity and efficiency, align them to national priorities, increase access, bring in private sources of funding, associate science more closely with the technology needs of the business sector, and reinforce accountability, among other goals (Kogan et al. 2000; Amaral, Jones, and Karseth 2002).

Most of these measures pertain to the funding of the system, the redefinition of the jurisdiction of diverse government agencies, the revision of the scope of degree-granting authority in institutions of higher education, the creation of new coordinating councils, or the establishment of accreditation agencies—and therefore not directly affecting the structure and practices of governance within universities and other institutions of higher education. But some reforms do target organizational governance directly—such as introducing a board of directors at a public university for the first time—and even other reforms none-theless end up influencing the way in which universities set priorities, manage their resources, and generally conduct themselves.

Strategic Policymaking

Mission and Role Differentiation

As higher education expands its reach and functions, governments and mul-tilateral lenders supporting reform programs in developing countries propose diversification as the strategy for matching the institutional platform to the new clienteles and tasks to be performed by the system. Whether the creation of new institutions or the revamping of existing ones will occur is often unclear in a government's diversification policy. While governments dread mission sprawl and unsustainable overreaching in existing institutions, they do hope the same institutions tackle the new challenges by becoming more entrepreneurial and determined in their quest for the new frontiers of the knowledge economy.

From the perspective of a university leader, the question then becomes: spe-cialization or diversification? Should the institution focus on developing high performance in a few areas of knowledge or selected types of programs forg-ing unique and thoroughly colonized niches? In contrast, should the strategy spread out over more functions and clienteles, to hedge the risk associated with the ever-accelerating pace of change in the competitive environment?

Making the right strategic choice relates to the history of the institution, the strengths and weaknesses of its human resources, its image and reputation, its connections with the relevant external community, and its geographical location.

Accountability versus Autonomy

As a condition for the public trust invested in them, institutions are required to account for the integrity, efficacy, and efficiency of both their procedures and results in all spheres of action. Accreditation has formed accountability's favorite vehicle but does not constitute the sole device for scrutiny. Consumer protection agencies, research funding councils, regulations on health and welfare (human and animal), credit-rating bureaus, and scores of other sectors take an active interest in universities' mission and function.

Higher education has become a regulated industry. University managers must understand that responding to demands is a condition of "doing business." Hopefully, they will also recognize the benefits to this level of inspection: not only is transparency enhanced and difficult questions posed and answered, but senior leaders may discover that essentially reports to external agencies actually produce hard data on what their institutions are actually undertaking.

Accountability, therefore, does not only serve an external function and should not be approached just as red tape (which, however, it often is) to be executed quickly and painlessly as possible. Perhaps its most enduring benefits are internal, as responsibility, transparency, and integrity become part of the institutional culture—in much the same vein as peer review has been internalized by researchers worldwide as a natural form of academic examination.

Thus approached, no contradiction exists between accountability and autonomy. The latter refers to academic freedom and the capacity of the institution to steer its resources toward its self-defined ends. But in democratic societies those prerogatives are to be exercised within the boundaries of legitimate action defined by the body politic.

Managerialism: Discourse and Techniques

Traditionally, in universities, middle and even upper management has been entrusted to elected academics with little training or experience in administration and often without a vision of higher education beyond their fields of study. Full professors and chair holders could make decisions without challenge from the institution, which holds no capacity to sustain such a confrontation. This statement does not imply that professorial decisions were wrong: in the absence of a clear definition of mission and institutional goals, professors filled in the void through their choices, thus defining, by accretion, the university.

This bottom-up generation of the administrative cadres provides advantages: professors enjoy the legitimacy of their election to the post and remain accountable to their peer electors. But the benefits usually come at the expense of technical ability and willingness to make hard choices.

Should top administrators be elected or appointed? Should a rector be elected and serve for a fixed term or be appointed by a board and report to it? Should academic committees be charged with legislative, executive, or advisory roles? Clearly, the growing complexity of university endeavors, the source and volume of resources involved, and greater accountability, among other pressures, have called for the professionalization of administration and administrators. Moreover, responsibilities previously allotted to faculty committees have been reassigned to individual officeholders, both in central administration and in the schools or faculties. While academic affairs remain the province of the professoriate, areas such as planning, infrastructure development, procurement, marketing, finances, admissions, alumni relations, library development, human resources, information technology, and many others fall nowadays under the purview of appointed specialists. Academics promoted to posts like dean or rector are now expected to hold managerial experience to enable them to negotiate the world of administration—its language, tools, and principles.

Cost Recovery

Closely related to the managerial era is the effort deployed by administrators to discover the precise cost of everything the institution does, press for more productivity on the basis of this information, and seek new sources of funding. Finding unit costs in teaching, research, or service is often viewed with skepticism by academics who do not believe that everything can be priced. Still more resisted is the consequence that follows costing, essential to managing outlays: comparing expenditures to productivity—at the institutional, school, department, program, or individual level—and confronting academic and administrative units with this information to elicit greater output from them.

Along with managing the costs' side, revenues need to be increased. In the case of private institutions, their long-term ambition is to tap public funding, for tuition payments can go only so far in financing quality higher education. Conversely, in the current political economy of higher education, public universities are required to look into the private sector for funding opportunities.

Universities as Complex Organizations

While universities are organizations, they are jointly legal entities, communities, and institutions. As legal entities, they are empowered to appoint their authorities, hire staff and faculty, enter into contracts, and acquire property, as well as other activities. They usually have a board of directors or overseers, officers accountable to the board, employees, and clients. As a college (collegium), universities are communities of professors, experts in their fields, who autonomously direct the study and transmission of knowledge to new generations. As institutions, universities are webs of cultural patterns and relationships established over centuries, universal in scope, and slow to change.

Clark Kerr (2001) has designated four "estates" in the university: the administration, vertically organized; faculty, deployed horizontally—save for times of crisis, when they act as political assemblies; students, acting either individually as consumers, grouped as a constituency in student unions, or serving as interest or pressure groups; and the external overseers, acting by the power of budget or administrative command.

The early communitarian structure of the university, where the academic project was entirely determined inside of the institution, has over the past three centuries been ceding ground to the demands of society. Academic self-determination through collegial deliberation and decision making is still a distinct feature of universities, especially those with a critical mass of scholars primarily devoted to the pursuit of knowledge. Nonetheless, society—projecting itself politically through government or as customers in market exchanges—does exert influence over these autonomous structures, so much so that the idea of the university as a cloister or ivory tower separated from the pulse of the quotidian life of the city is no longer valid and needs to be replaced by an open-systems perspective.

Therefore, public or private, national or local, teaching or research oriented, old or new, the university is a complex organization. This complexity is a result of (a) multiple organizational levels; (b) various channels of interaction among and within these levels and with the external environment; (c) the relative weakness of hierarchical power as compared to other types of organizations; (d) its dense and diverse value system; and (e) its dynamic relationship with the political, social, economic, and cultural milieu. As a result, authority is diffused, structures are highly fragmented, purposes are varied, complex and not always complementary, goals are difficult to measure, and autonomy coexists with resource dependence (Birnbaum 1988).

These unique organizational features reveal how authority appears disseminated across intermediate and lower structural levels, which by virtue of their substantive competence benefit from a sort of delegated decision-making power. The top leadership requires an attitude of dialogue and mechanisms of negotiation to accommodate bottom-up decisions with general corporate objectives. This horizontal model of governance, characteristic of academic affairs, coexists with the much more vertical style of management of the administrative and financial operations.

Faculty tend to construct their worldview—and hence, their vision of the university—through the looking glass of their discipline or profession, bringing with them the depth and narrowness of their highly specialized understanding of the world when asked to serve in management and leadership roles. Private companies' management teams have been trained in the same body of knowledge. The leaders of the public-sector bureaucracies do not necessarily share the same educational background but are nonetheless intellectually synchronized by their interest and service in any one field—like defense, health, or public works. Unlike these two sectors, in universities the same difficulties that bog down academic cross-disciplinary communication do, however, affect the coordination ability of heterogeneous management teams with various professional backgrounds and worldviews.

Given these issues, higher education literature has stressed the chaotic aspects of universities as organizations: they appear from the outside as "organized anarchies," in the famous Cohen and March (1974) description, with multiple, ambiguous, and conflicting goals that are permanently contested and changing. On these permanently shifting bases, rational administration seems implausible. The source of this permanent wrangling is not only internal. It also results from interactions with external power groups, especially in public universities, which are expected to respond to multiple legitimate interests.

Clever organizational design can help navigate the always shifting configuration of interests and demands, internal and external, but it is not the ultimate solution. Permanent dialogue and discussion are essential to forge alliances and induce agreements, while keeping a vision of the whole of the university in the minds and hearts of its members and constituencies.

External Governance

Universities sustain numerous relationships with their external environment—as previously stated, one of the sources of their organizational complexity. Of course, along with significant international links, domestically, universities have to deal with the government through various ministries, chiefly the education or science ministries responsible for higher education policy. In federal countries, communication often presents a more intense practice with state authorities than with federal agencies.

Private universities must contend with their owners, who are typically also their administrators, but not always: proprietors, churches, foundations, and transnational holdings tend to delegate daily management and retain instead control of the governing boards of the institutions.

Relations with other universities in rectors' councils or conferences are also relevant. Accreditation agencies and other scientific and professional regulatory bodies also require commitments, as do business associations and organizations of the civil society.

Therefore, governance not only pertains to internal issues. The quality of the relationships enounced earlier strongly affects an institution's opportunities. A university leader must play the role of articulating her university with the larger environment. A rector is, in the most complete sense of the word, also a politician. He is supposed to represent, persuade, cajole, mediate, and broker agreements in favor of his university. Unfortunately, this dimension of a rectorship is not always fulfilled, because facing the enormous stress of running the university, many presidents and top administrators tend to focus their energy on the internal problems of their campuses. This option includes political benefits: making leadership visible among the electoral body should be a concern for elected university officials, but neglecting external affairs will, in the long run, damage the standing of the institution.

Relations with Government Ministries

The fruitfulness of the relationship with national or state agencies in charge of higher education policy depends in large measure on their formality. In several countries the ministers or secretaries responsible for higher education host regular meetings with rectors, individually or in conferences of rectors. Structured, regular encounters of this kind are an asset, for they give rectors the chance to define issues as problems of policy, participate in the deliberation over solutions, and generally influence policy design. Of course, all of this can be done also through informal lobbying, but regular channels of exchange are preferable for their transparency and the permanent and equal opportunity they provide to all institutions to participate in policy discussions.

Therefore, university leaders are well advised not to relinquish the occasional campus visit, phone call, or urgent meeting with the minister, but to complement those instances with more regular meetings in which not the urgent, but the important issues can be aired.

Relations with Regional and Local Authorities

As indicated before, the activity of a university produced direct consequences amidst its social, economic, cultural, and political settings. Many demands of the community are directed toward the university, either officially through its representative or unofficially through the press and other vehicles of expression. Not all public opinion can be effectively satisfied by the university. Some issues will fall beyond the university's mission and others will lack funding. In addition, for certain issues, the university will lack the structure necessary for taking care of that particular problem.

Even when the university cannot accommodate a request of this sort, its leaders must maintain a relationship of openness, trust, and empathy with local and regional authorities. A large part of the student body will be local, the university's employees will live in the community, and most of the business sector will usually operate locally as well. Therefore, good relations with the immediate environment are advantageous to both parties.

Further, universities concentrate on highly qualified human resources. Outside large metropolitan areas, they are usually the largest employer of such talent. They can help local civil servants develop better services, or small businesses prosper. This technical capacity becomes influential political capital in the hands of university leaders negotiating with local authorities. Well managed, it can generate much synergy of direct consequence for the general welfare.

The Place of Politics

Again, governing a university, especially when it is a public institution, serves as a function with a political dimension. This description does not imply that rectors or other university leaders ought to be registered party members. However, it needs to be stressed that the political system makes decisions of consequence for universities and that it is unwise for universities not to try to influence those decisions. Politicians are sometimes gatekeepers to the realization of the strategic goals of universities, and for this reason they should be permanently informed of the situation of the university, its strategic plans, its strengths, and its weaknesses.

Yet, militant political activity on the part of faculty and staff ought to be avoided inside the campus. Students should view their professors as independent of political factions, notwithstanding the clear stance they may have on issues of political belief or policy. Likewise, elected officials should not run on the bases of national political platforms. Professors' politics are irrelevant to the functions they will be elected to assume and should be kept out of their electoral profile.

Internal Bodies

As noted before, universities are subject to oversight by agencies and concerns external to the organization. Within the universities, their executives are under the scrutiny of collective bodies representing the interests of the owners and society at large, as represented in boards of governors or trustees and the internal "estates" of the institutions, mostly faculty, but also students and administrative staff. It is to these groups that we now turn. The management of the relationship with these internal bodies of control forms part of the duties of the chief executive and her team.

Managing Governing Boards

Boards of directors or trustees are meant to represent the position of the owners and other external stakeholders of the university. In public universities, the owner is the state—national or provincial; in private universities, it is the individuals or groups who provide the capital for the foundation of the university and continue to be responsible for its support. Often, both in public and private boards, individuals prominent in the professions, science, government, or the private sector are invited to join as trustees to lend their expert judgment and experience to the deliberations of the board.

Governing boards do not provide solely oversight and control. Indeed, this activity perhaps forms their least relevant function. For the exercise of this role they depend upon the information the rector furnishes. However, they can exert little control over a rector who does not want to be controlled. More importantly, boards of directors offer a valuable forum for discussion of the major issues, give advice, muster support for the university, and generally serve to project the work of the university into the community and bring the resources of the community closer to the university. They are, in brief, the permanent bridge between the institution and its external environment.

Therefore, openness and transparency is called for in the relationship between the rector and his board. Written reports and oral presentations should be carefully prepared, to provide real information and bases for a fruitful debate. The financial commitments associated with every plan ought to be clearly spelled out, and the board should be kept permanently informed of every major development, planned or not, that affects the institution. It is a good practice for the rector to bring along the staff member in charge of the matter under discussion, so that, if required, he can illustrate to trustees the details of the issue at hand.

Faculty Senates and Other Internal Legislative Bodies

In many countries tradition dictates the existence of a university-wide deliberative body composed solely or mostly of senior faculty, whose role it is to debate and approve policy in academic matters. While it is often the case that these councils or senates slow down decision making and tend to favor negotiated middle-of-the-road alternatives that a majority of their members can tolerate, they can introduce visions not always represented in the executive team and a healthy dose of moderation to the governance of the institution.

Given that the executive team, if it is appointed by the rector rather than independently elected, tends to consist of like-minded people, it is generally helpful that a forum exists for divergent—even outlandish—thought to be expressed. This enriches deliberation and, properly managed, can improve decision making. Moreover, these senates also carry on the history of the institution, an important asset when the rector is a newcomer or younger than the average faculty member. It is not unusual that new measures proposed today had already been tried in the past, failed, and were largely forgotten.

However, it is significant that the functions assigned to these bodies remain of a legislative or judicial nature. Dangerous situations of paralysis or factional division at times ensue when assemblies overstep the executive function. Drawing the line is sometimes a difficult task—for example, the executive prerogative in matters of budget, or real estate investments or divestments, or opening of new programs and centers. When agile policymaking is essential, which seems to be the rule in the current environment for higher education, it is perhaps advisable to err on the side of enlarging executive authority and limiting senate authority to the strategic, long-term policies in the academic area.

Participation of Students, Alumni, and Staff in Governance

Also a matter of tradition, the extent and scope of the institutionalized involvement in governance of students, alumni, and administrative staff vary considerably from country to country. To some extent the rationale for their inclusion parallels what was outlined earlier with respect to faculty senates, but three key differences exist.

First, universities are not democracies, where all are equal and one person represents one vote. Even among faculty, hierarchies exist where senior professors command a weightier say over academic matters than junior colleagues. Second, students are transient members of the organization, and therefore the range of their vision is often limited by their immediate interests, while the concerns of alumni are rather opportunistic and have their ebbs and flows. Finally, politicization is a larger risk for students and administrators, who do not have the anchoring of the academic ethos as a counterbalance.

Thus, the benefits of adding the voices of the nonfaculty members of the university—such as a broader scope of deliberation and more acceptance over the policies they participated in shaping—need to be carefully weighed against the vulnerabilities of a governance system based on constituency representation. Many universities give student leaders and administrators a minority participation in university councils, significant enough not to be mere tokens, but never so large that it may compromise faculty control of these bodies. This approach seems a sensible policy.

Executive Power

The mounting complexity of university management, described earlier, forms one of the forces separating the roles of faculty from those of senior leadership, including deanships. Yet, progress and recognition in the academic career are strongly associated with a track record of externally funded research and abundant publication, while obtaining research grants and managing them has become a time-consuming operation. New teaching methods also involve permanent dedication by instructors. Management cannot be carried out in the spare time left by teaching and research, any more than science and instruction can be successfully taken care of during the lulls of running an administrative office.

In most countries, greater institutional autonomy in public universities has made it necessary to migrate from a bureaucratic, public-administration culture, in which everyone is concerned solely with their piece of the whole, toward an organizational culture uniquely attuned to the singular characteristics of universities. This culture gives every member of the institution a stake in its future and the necessary emotional attachment and compromise to support the efforts to keep up with permanent change and increased competition. Private institutions have less of a legacy of bureaucratic practices to contend with but face similar demands of agility to respond to their environment.

The Role and Functions of the Rector or President

The chief executive of a university can be nominated in different ways: he can be appointed by a board of trustees or by a government authority; or elected by faculty with or without participation of students. Whatever her origin may be, the rector is usually expected to carry out functions that go beyond her statutory role. She is ultimately responsible for institutional decisions, even if those resolutions are previously discussed and approved in collegial bodies. This is due in part to the transformation of internal government of universities from the "parliamentary" model predominant from the late 1960s onwards, to the "presidential" mores prevalent today. In the current scenario, more policy continuity and responsibility for actions are required than government by assemblies can provide.

A vision of the future of higher education in the relevant environment—local, national, or international—is possibly the single most useful attribute concerning the chief executive of a university. Little was at stake for management when universities were largely undifferentiated, faced excess demand, met little or no competition, and received guaranteed funding. Academic charisma and intuitive management sufficed. The university of today requires of its chief executive (a) leadership in the strategic steering of the organization; (b) dedication to fostering a healthy organizational climate through internal communications, motivation, and sense of belonging; (c) cultivation of relationships with the political, business, cultural, and social environments; (d) a horizontal management structure based on delegation and responsibility centers; (e) a capacity to lead innovation in structure, culture, and above all in the management of strategy and communications; and (f) the ability to harmoniously bring together different perspectives through dialogue and persuasion in collective governing bodies.

An accessible style of leadership, a permanent commitment with both the big and the small dramas of the university and its people, and a degree of visibility and influence in the scientific and academic world and in the local and national community also help a rector fulfill this demanding role

Building an Effective Executive Team

The leadership of the chief executive and the attributes the office entails are decisive for a successful stewardship of the university. In due measure, these qualities ought to be present also among his key collaborators. We refer here to the executive authorities who are appointed by the rector, as opposed to deans and department heads usually elected by their peers.

The executive team must not only hold the larger definitions of mission, vision, and strategic objectives but, ideally, would have participated in the development of the mission. If the team members did not share in the development of those ideas, they should nonetheless immerse themselves in the overall principles and premises guiding the development of the institution.

Coherence among chief administrators is, therefore, paramount, for the times are not forgiving of improvisation, intuitive leadership, or individualism.

In each area, managers are required to match the larger strategic goals of the organization with those specifically related to their office. This formula is not incompatible with impressing a personal mark on each job, based on temperament, style, or particular interests. Certainly, the reading and interpretation of the scenarios of the day continuously provide room for adjustments and special emphasis.

Thus, members of the executive team are to be made aware of two key directives. First, the standard option bringing new, personal elements to the task defined for each position means the actions must coincide with the broad policies defined by the governing board, the faculty councils, and the rector himself. Second, the true capacity of a senior administrator is tested by these opportunities for innovation, when she can anticipate alternatives, foresee difficulties and, most importantly, create new possibilities in undetected or uncharted terrains.

Not only do managers need to be faithful to the vision ahead, they must also align their action with the tradition and rituals every institution has developed over its history and that constitute its organizational culture. Some of these actions are university-wide; others pertain to specific areas. This approach is easier when effective communication exists with the academic units—such as colleges, schools, or departments—based on trust, respect, and a sense of commonality of purpose, beyond the disagreements that may emerge over the means.

The physical distance between top management and the academic units, the facility to coordinate meetings solely among the members of the executive team, the better working relationship that exists within this group, and other all too human factors at times cause the top leadership to ensconce itself and loose contact with "the real" university. When this happens, the leadership begins to be seen by academia as a remote bureaucracy operating with no checks and balances, self-serving, and removed from the true university—even where, paradoxically, the rector has been elected by academia. There is only one antidote to this situation: to venture away from the office and into campus. long and often.

Administrative and Academic Structure

Revisiting the organizational structure is usually not a high priority in the "to-do" list of administrators—in part, because the organizational form is taken for granted, as a natural arrangement of sorts and because it is difficult and time-consuming to make changes. It is easier to hire someone and expect things will run better with the new person in charge or to create additional offices to accommodate fresh demands. As a result, in most universities administrative structures are "sticky": units established long ago tend to remain while new structures are installed alongside, usually responding to functional urgencies or opportunities rather than attempting to match structure with strategy. While this approach may well release short-run pressures, in its preservation of obsolete structure it limits the ability of the organization to act swiftly and proactively.

The university structure conditions the application of a development strategy even when that strategy does not call for a change in structure. In effect, the results of the planned actions will depend on the degree of bureaucratization in the organization, the existing flows of information, and the technology available for management support. Therefore, there is no option for escaping the influence of the organizational chart.

How Should the Managerial Function be Organized?

There is no dearth of literature on the proper way of designing the structure of an organization. However, most of this work focuses on business firms, and as we have argued, universities are quite different species. In many ways, they are closer to a cooperative: its employees are stakeholders and elect the managers, much decision making requires the agreement of the members of the organization, and surpluses are rare.

The structure works best if it is flexible, that is, if it can be readily changed when new forms are required. A structure that requires an act of congress to change is not flexible. Units in rigid structures interact with their environment, internal or external, from the perspective of the unit's position, routines, and procedures, not from the clients' situation. Typically, units "solve" a problem by passing it along to the next office. Plasticity, which entails the possibility that a unit will be wiped out if underperforming, makes the members more attuned to the point of view and needs of whoever is requiring their service. Functionality is favored over formality, efficient procedures over bureaucratically correct ones, and visible outcomes over opaque paper trails. Flexible structures are also nimble—in the sense that they have more horizontal links than vertical ones, as well as when their costs are small.

How Should Academic Units be Organized?

The university structures its academic operation in large units encompassing entire sciences or professions, usually under the name of colleges, faculties, or schools, and these in turn are subdivided in smaller units to gather the members of a discipline. The organizational conservatism noted earlier is also reflected in the academic structure: rather than scrapping schools, faculties, colleges, or departments, new ones are created next to the old ones, or centers and institutes are founded with the explicit mandate of tearing down disciplinary walls, which is always a challenge beyond the organizational issue.

Academic structure is a sensitive matter because it not only corresponds to managerial convenience, but, rather, it reflects epistemic beliefs deeply held by academics. The academics' identity as scholars is at stake when there is an attempt to redraw the boundaries of a department or school. Whereas for the case of the administrative structure, we argued for boldness on the part of the would-be organizational designer; here caution is in order. The safest strategy appears as bypassing the heated arguments about what constitutes this or that field of knowledge through the creation of seemingly unthreatening units—such as, interdisciplinary centers and programs, technology transfer institutes, and the like.

At any rate, when contemplating both the academic and the administrative structure of the university, it is important to bear in mind Thomas Hammond's (2004) admonition that the organizational chart affects decision making at the top of the hierarchy in certain ways: (a) what information will be conducted (or not) to the upper echelons, determining which events are defined as problems and how they are defined; (b) and who will be heard when the time comes to decide what to do about the defined problem.

The Management of Faculty

Typically, universities seek to increase their prestige. A reputation of excellence is the closest the world of universities reaches a universal criterion of success. Although the notion of prestige allows various meanings, possibly the dominant idea is that prestige is equal to research achievement and selectivity in admissions. Insofar as these attributes depend on the performance of the faculty, the management of faculty work should become a central concern for administrators intent on maximizing the reputation of their universities.

This concern would extend to the whole institutional life cycle of the professor: search and selection of prospective faculty members, forms of appointment, rules on tenure and promotion, workload definition and control, performance evaluation, compensation, and participation in governance. Nowadays autonomy is generally not judged as diminished by accountability, although it is increasingly understood that the management of faculty work is not necessarily antithetical to academic freedom.

Yet even if it preserves academic freedom, the management of faculty work affects the governance role of faculty, for it underlines the position of professors as employees at the expense of their prerogatives as partners. Therefore, a trade-off exists here concerning which senior leadership ought to be mindful: a tighter control on how faculty spend their time may weaken professors' sense of ownership, limiting their relationship with the university to the quid pro quo of providing professional services for a fee.

The relevance of faculty for the vitality and development of the university, however, has not been a priority object of managerial attention. Much effort and deliberation go into finding and selecting new professors, but once hired, they have been traditionally left alone. There are good reasons for this lax attitude on the part of administrators. Academic freedom, an essential value of the university as an institution, protects the autonomy of the professor. Moreover, quality control over the work of a professor legitimately belongs to his colleagues inside and outside the university, acting as peer reviewers and referees, rather than to administrative authorities. Further, often these authorities are also academics, elected by their colleagues, and relations of collegiality trump those of authority or control.

But this laissez-faire attitude on the part of the administration seems to be coming to an end. Just as the relationship between the university and its environment is undergoing a redefinition, with society demanding greater output at the least possible expense, faculty finds itself under great pressure to produce more (Schuster and Finkelstein 2006). Thus, in spite of the enhanced social position universities have come to occupy with the emergence of the knowledge economy, observers of the academic profession worldwide agree that the status and work conditions of the professoriate are declining in the developed world (Altbach 2000; Kogan and Teichler 2007).

The massification of higher education over the past decades has been identified as a chief cause of deterioration in the work environments of professors, creating pressure to increase teaching efficiency—more students per professor. Furthermore, it tends to separate research from teaching and drives the recruitment of scores of adjunct, part-time instructors and fixed-term academics to serve to the ever-expanding ranks of new students.

Cost-recovery policies in public universities and the growth of the private sector of higher education have had an impact in the economic conditions of the professoriate. Although faculty salaries have not decreased, the complaint is that they have not kept up with the income gains of other professionals with comparable levels of training and that more hours of work are needed to complete a decent remuneration. In developed and emerging economies, professors boost their consulting and technical assistance activities, while in developing countries they hold other jobs or teach at the new private universities.

Accountability goes hand in hand with increased power among administrative cadres at the expense of the faculty, and buttressing policies and mechanisms of supervision of academic productivity is often seen by professors as a dent in their intellectual autonomy. Job security has ceased to represent the essence of the academic profession, as temporary jobs multiply and performance evaluation becomes the norm, even for tenured faculty. Furthermore, besides satisfying intellectual curiosity, research is expected to serve a useful purpose, such as leading to economically relevant results. Faculty are not only asked to teach more but also to assure learning outcomes, which requires participation in teaching-methodology training programs and in curriculum development.

Some of the measures adopted by university administrators directly bear upon the traditional aspects of the academic profession. For instance, the search and selection of new faculty members have traditionally been entrusted to the academic unit into which the professor will be hired. While this continues to be the prevailing method for recruitment, it is not unusual for the central administration to reserve for itself the final approval of the new appointment—especially in the higher professorial ranks—to ensure that new faculty members conform to the university's development plan or to that of the respective school.

The formalization of an academic career with its tracks and ranks helps to provide some sort of hierarchical structure to the professoriate. The formulas for this are quite varied: in most universities the academic career is only available for regular (full-time) faculty, but a parallel track can be designed for adjuncts. Even though in the regular track the promotion to the higher ranks of associate and full professor depends on research performance, a separate track for faculty who only teach may help confirm progress and excellence in teaching. Yet, in any case, it is helpful, as a stimulus for people to improve, to establish an "up or out" rule, signifying the maximum time a professor can remain in the assistant rank without progressing to the next stage. To make certain that promotion decisions are consistent across all colleges, schools, or departments, promotion committees often operate at the university-wide level—and not only in each academic unit.

The stability of employment, or tenure, is a treasured conquest of professors for the protection of academic freedom. Particularly in developing and transitional nations with weak conditions of rule of law, threats to academic freedom are not a thing of the past, and tenure can play an important function. However, also in developing countries situations are found where academic ethos is weak, salaries are low, and university jobs are assigned as perks to friends, family, and political cronies. These series of factors, specifically lethal to serious scholarship, are sometimes compounded by tenure, which induces free riding among those who take the protection it affords as a permission not to work and forms an adverse selection whereby only individuals who fail to find employment elsewhere end up as professors. These problems have no easy resolution. In balance, it seems advisable to combine tenure with some manner of performance evaluation. For instance, tenure could be granted after a probationary, fixed-term period, in which the professor needs to demonstrate his worth to his peers. Additionally, the performance of tenured faculty can be evaluated at regular intervals on academic grounds, with the option of termination of employment if a professor repeatedly fails to satisfy the required criteria.

Professors have traditionally become quite autonomous in allocating their time to the diverse tasks under their job definitions. Increasingly, though, regulations are appearing that mandate certain functions, such as teaching undergraduate courses. The composition of faculty jobs is classified, quantified, and periodically recorded, and these records serve as the basis for post hoc evaluations. Although these exercises can become a mere ritual if the dean or department chair is lenient, in the hands of administrators willing to use them as management tools the detailed planning of a professor's output and its evaluation in due time can be quite powerful.

Salary policy is also a relevant management instrument. While some aspects of ideology may cause the academic profession to demand equal pay for equal function, nowadays faculty salaries tend to reflect the hard facts of the academic labor market: wages vary considerably by field and discipline, and professors in the same rank do not obtain similar compensation across schools and departments. Moreover, often variable sources of income are added to base salaries, consisting of consulting and speaking fees, research honorariums, and other forms of compensation that reflect the variable capacity of professors to raise funds for the university and for themselves.

Through instruments such as these, universities seek to align the work of the professors with the goals the organization has defined for itself.

Audit and Control

For decades, audit and control were regarded almost exclusively as financial and accounting matters. The idea was that the analysis of the execution of a budget would provide insight into the performance of academic and administrative units as cost centers. Typically, also, in this view budgets were mostly carried over from the previous year, with a few increments or cuts depending on the fiscal situation of the university or some particular emphasis defined by the central administration.

These strategies are not very effective from the point of view of strategic management, but they are often necessary due to regulatory norms in public universities, and in older private ones that often adopted the practices of their public peers for want of other models.

Beyond the necessities of budgetary control and financial audit, modern management requires integrating audit and control into a larger system of accountability, to satisfy the information, monitoring, and evaluation needs derived from the strategic development plan.

Every strategic plan contains performance indicators, benchmarks for comparison, monitoring systems, and assessment methods to ascertain whether the university is moving toward the desired goals. Progress need not only to be mapped through milestones, and then measured, but those measurements should be susceptible to auditing by internal and external opinion.

In practice, what this means is that the executive team and the technical unit responsible for follow-up and evaluation will achieve useful, valid and on-time information regarding the execution of the budget as well as the achievement of targets and the progress of the development plan.

The most effective mechanism to create this system of accountability is to call for the academic units to define their own goals and priorities within the framework of the general strategy of the university and to amalgamate the perspectives and plans of the academic groups, programs, and units within their jurisdiction. The idea is for the lower units to identify how their planned actions will support the goals of the larger structures in which they are positioned and contribute to the university's strategic design. This sort of pyramidal structure of commitments can be combined by formal agreements between each organizational layer and the next, going all the way up from the individual professor to the rector.

The overall system of accountability makes sense and becomes transparent in the context of a culture of assessment. While in some academic systems this culture may be firmly established, that is not the common case in developing countries. For this reason, the role of the chief executive is key: leadership is required for this process of accountability to be perceived not as compulsory control but rather as a system for continuous quality improvement. This policy is a deep cultural change and will take time, but results can be obtained with persistence and if people at all levels of the organizational structure are held accountable, through sanctions or incentives, to their stated commitments.

Conclusion

Governance has become a critical issue as institutions and enrollments multiply worldwide, competition in the marketplace and accountability norms gets tougher, public funding responds to new, performance-oriented models, and running a university becomes a job for professionals. In this environment, it is patent that governing a university without a well-defined goal, a clear vision of the road ahead, or a deep understanding of the organization is tantamount to courting failure.

In defining a distinctive goal or mission for the university, the old platitudes about knowledge creation and dissemination are no longer good enough. The mission needs to be more specific so as to guide decision making and rally the community toward a well-understood and shared description of the future. The problem of differentiation and mission distinctiveness is compounded in our time by the global emergence of the research university as the sole or dominant standard of excellence in higher education. Research universities in the world are few and far between, even in large academic systems such as that of the United States. Developing a research- and postgraduate-intensive university may be a reasonable path for a few institutions in emerging academic systems. However, for the vast majority of institutions, the Harvards, Berkeleys, and Oxbridges of the world are not the relevant model. Those institutions will have to come up with strategies to differentiate themselves by stressing dimensions of excellence that are not research based—such as educational results, internationalization, language training, employment outcomes, service to a cultural orientation, and the like.

Turning to teaching is the easy part, for education forms the essence of the university. Here, the question is: What kind of education will distinguish this university from others? And the next question is: What else, if anything, should the university generate, in addition to educated citizens and trained professionals? For most universities, the question is moot, because they do not see a mission for themselves beyond teaching, and if they do, they lack the resources to carry it out. Some institutions may take on additional dimensions of service to the community. A university is not immersed only in science; it is also a part of the national and local community. Therefore, many universities would rather make their impact felt across their immediate environments, contributing to tangible social, economic, and political progress. Here, another form of strain for leadership emerges, as faculty with scientific vocations coexists with others who find their calling in deploying their knowledge to serve the needs of the community. The standards of excellence for either type of work are substantially different, and seldom are they harmoniously integrated. A compromise must be reached to accommodate both, equally important, uses of the university for progress and development.

However, no amount of collective deliberation through strategic planning or other instrument will leave all internal and external constituencies happy with the choice the institution makes, in this or in any other fundamental matter. Therefore, decisiveness in decision making, leadership in rallying the community toward the selected goals, and sustained persuasion about the advantages of the chosen path are indispensable attributes of effective governance.

References

Altbach, Philip G. (ed.) (2000) *The Changing Academic Workplace: Comparative Perspectives.* Chestnut Hill, MA: Boston College Center for International Higher Education.

Amaral, Alberto, Glen A. Jones, and Berit Karseth (2002) *Governing Higher Education: National Perspectives on Institutional Governance*, Dordrecht, Netherlands: Kluwer Academic.

Birnbaum, Robert (1988) *How Colleges Work. The Cybernetics of Academic Organization and Leadership*, San Francisco: Jossey-Bass.

Cohen, Michael D. and James G. March (1974) *Leadership and Ambiguity: The American College President*, New York: McGraw-Hill.

Hammond, Thomas (2004) "Herding cats in university hierarchies: Formal structure and policy choice in American research universities," in Ronald G. Ehrenberg (ed.) *Governing Academia*, Ithaca, NY: Cornell Univ. Press.

Kerr, Clark (2001) *The Uses of the University*, 5th ed., Cambridge, MA: Harvard Univ. Press.

Kogan, Maurice, Marianne Bauer, Ivar Bleiklie, and Mary Henkel (2000) *Transforming Higher Education: A Comparative Study*, London: Jessica Kingsley.

Kogan, Maurice and Ulrich Teichler (eds.) (2007) *Key Challenges to the Academic Profession*, Kassel, Germany: University of Kassel.

Schuster, Jack H. and Martin J. Finkelstein (2006) *The American Faculty: The Restructuring of Academic Work and Careers*, Baltimore, MD: Johns Hopkins Univ. Press.

3

The Funding of Universities in the Twenty-First Century

D. BRUCE JOHNSTONE

The funding of higher education throughout the world and especially within the low-income, or developing countries has faced dramatic changes in the last decades of the twentieth century and the first decade of the twenty-first century, which will only accelerate in the decades ahead. The funding-pattern shifts are caused by rising needs for higher education based on economies and democratic societies, by growing demands for higher education access, and by the worldwide expansion of higher education costs—or revenue requirements—above the corresponding rates of increase of available revenues, especially those that are dependent on government. The consequence in most of the world has been a shortage of revenue to accommodate both the greater costs of instruction and research as well as (and exacerbated by) the increasing revenue needs of rising enrollments.

These diverging trajectories—of rapidly increasing resource needs amidst static or even faltering revenues from state budgets—must, in turn, be met by solutions on the cost side and/or the revenue side. In the absence of solutions to the underlying dilemma of university funding, the resulting and steadily worsening austerity will compromize the goals of higher education throughout the world, that is, improving the quality of both teaching and research, expanding and assuring more equitable participation, and bringing greater economic and social benefits to the expenditure of scarce public revenues. At the same time, such solutions are exceedingly difficult, both politically and managerially, which is why their implementation, on the parts of both governmental ministries and university leaders, has been so elusive. Thus, higher education leaders as well as policymakers must understand the nature of this underlying funding dilemma, the so-called *solutions* that may be available (on both the cost and the revenue sides), and the cultural and political as well as the strictly managerial dimensions of this worldwide higher education funding dilemma.

The Higher Education Funding Dilemma

The underlying higher education funding dilemma is mainly propelled by three trends. These situations are worldwide and are not dependent on economic development, the prevailing political ideology, the form of government, or the current structure of a country's higher (or more broadly, its entire tertiary) education system. These trends, in summary, are: (1) the tendency of unit, or per student, costs to increase in excess of a country's prevailing rate of rising prices (that is, in excess of the prevailing rate of inflation); (2) the worldwide pressure of increasing enrollments, whether powered by demographics and/or by increasing rates of participation, which accelerates the previously mentioned rise in per student costs and thus in total revenue needs; and (3) the inability of governmental revenues (in all but a few countries) to keep pace with these surging revenue requirements.

Increasing Per-Student Costs

The per student costs of instruction (that is, before considering the additional costs of increasing enrollments) conform closely in most economies to the rate of increase among faculty and staff wages and salaries, which in most countries tracks over time the rate of increase of wages and salaries in the general economy—or, if there is any real growth in the economy, at inflation plus. This is the so-called cost disease, or the phenomenon of the rising relative unit *costs* in the labor-intensive and productivity-immune (or at least productivity-resistant) sectors of the economy. This condition meets relatively little of the cost-cutting substitution of capital for labor that is the source of productivity increases in the goods-producing sectors of the larger economy. This phenomenon, first articulated by William J. Baumol and William G. Bowen (1966), applies as well to such labor-intensive, productivity-resistant enterprizes as symphony orchestras, most governmental and nongovernmental organizations, schools, and universities. This rate of increase of unit costs (or revenue needs) may be driven even faster in colleges and universities by two additional cost drivers peculiar to higher education: (1) *technology*, which in institutions of higher education tends not to be a productivity enhancer or unit-cost reducer, rather increases unit-costs, altering the very nature (and supposedly improving the value) of the product, but still requiring more, not less, revenue; and (2) *curricular change*, in which new programs tend to be input faster than old programs or faculty can be shed.

Increasing Enrollment

Accelerating this natural rate of increase of unit (or per student) instructional costs or revenue needs, are growing enrollments. This expansion in low- and middle-income countries is a function of two main forces. The first of these is demographic: specifically the change (generally the growth) over time in the number of youth within the conventional college or university age cohort (usually ages 18 through 24). Some highly industrialized countries—such as, in much of southern Europe, Russia, and Japan—are experiencing demographic declines, for which they are trying to compensate via recruitment and matriculation of students from other countries (e.g., Japan through students from China and Indonesia and Russia through students from China and central Asia). However, most low- and middle-income countries, with the notable exception of China, have been experiencing sharp increases in youth populations.

The second force affecting enrollments consists of the increasing participation rates of these (generally increasing) university age cohorts. Increasing participation rates, in turn, are a function of three factors: (1) an increasing proportion of youth completing secondary education; (2) changing employment opportunities and a perception of increasing competition for fewer *good* jobs, the attainment of which is likely to be enhanced by higher education; and (3) an increasing regard for social and economic mobility and justice, leading to policies designed to increase higher education participation particularly among those who are traditionally underrepresented on account of poverty or other reasons for historical low participation rates—including gender, ethnic, and linguistic minority status; poor secondary schools; or any number of conditions associated with marginalized populations. Countries with high birthrates also tend to encounter low participation rates (especially in sub-Saharan Africa, Latin America, and the Caribbean). Such countries are likely to experience both of these enrollment accelerators—steeply rising participation rates of surging numbers of university-age youth—resulting in extreme enrollment pressures upon what is most likely to be a highly constrained university capacity.

The increasing enrollments impact the financing of higher education by accelerating the natural rate of increase among per student costs. Thus, steeply and continuously, an extension of public resources will be required to maintain the quality of the higher education product. Without the coming forth of more public resources—which is the case in most countries, the totally industrialized and affluent but especially most of the low-income or developing world—inevitably higher education austerity will be enforced, bringing with it both diminished quality and equity.

Faltering Governmental Revenues

The final crisis involving funding of higher education in low- and middle-income countries is the inability of governmental revenue to keep up with these rapidly increasing higher education revenue needs. And again, the causes are obvious. Governments everywhere, especially in the less-developed world, are burdened with the similarly escalating costs and revenue needs of other public spending obligations. Furthermore, growing middle-class electorates in many countries are becoming more fiscally conservative, particularly given the distaste for continually rising taxes and the perception of wasteful government spending. The so-called transitional, or postcommunist, countries also continue to labor under the enormous costs of building an internationally competitive productive infrastructure from their outmoded industrial factories and weaning a labor force away from its deeply rooted dependence on state enterprizes and guaranteed employment.

In developing countries, enrollment pressures and revenue needs are steeply rising. Yet, since production and incomes (and thus taxable wealth) tend to be low, taxation is also a difficult issue, technically. Governments face the financial challenge of obtaining a share of purchasing power when relatively little wealth comes from large, stable enterprizes that can be taxed and also counted upon to withhold taxes from their employees. For example, an analysis of taxation, tax capacity, and needed tax reforms in sub-Saharan Africa from Norway's Michelsen Institute found the tax-to-gross domestic product ratio around 21 percent in sub-Saharan Africa (as low as 10 percent in Tanzania and Uganda)—compared with an Organization for Economic Cooperation and Development-based average of some 32 percent—and cited many examples of ineffective, costly, and coercive tax collection efforts, especially at the local levels. Researchers also warned that "attempts to squeeze additional revenues from poorly designed taxes may exacerbate the negative effects of the tax system on the economy and the society in general" and concluded "it is unlikely that a substantial widening of the tax base can be achieved without increasing the tax burden of the poorer segments of the society" (Fjelstad and Rakner 2003, ix). Former communist countries, once dependent on easy and extensive turnover taxes on state-owned enterprizes, now need to tax personal or corporate incomes, retail or commercial transactions, and/or property—all of which are difficult to calculate, expensive to collect, and relatively easy to evade. To worsen the difficulty of taxation, the globalization of the world's economy makes it easier for businesses and individuals in many countries to hide or shield incomes or to simply move themselves and their taxable assets to lower-tax countries.

Finally, governments everywhere, but especially in the low- and middle-income countries, are contending with fiercely competing needs for the scarce public revenues. Many of these issues may become more politically and socially compelling than a voracious and still elitist pubic higher education sector—especially one that most citizens' children in low-income countries will probably not see. In much of the developing world and in many transitional countries, for example, the competitors for scarce public revenue include the replacement of decrepit public infrastructure, unfunded pension obligations, the need for a workable social safety net, and the cost of reversing generations of environmental degradation. In sub-Saharan Africa, competition for the scarce public dollar is truly formidable and includes, in addition to the needs listed earlier, public health, (e.g., the old scourge of malaria and new pandemic of HIV-AIDS), elementary and secondary education, and assistance to faltering economies. Thus, although the government (or taxpayer) will continue world-wide as the main revenue source for public higher education, the limited additional revenue can be squeezed out of the public treasuries for public colleges and universities will be forced to accommodate some of the inevitably expanding higher education enrollments, leaving little or nothing to maintain faculty and staff salaries, improve faculty-student ratios, or meet the needs of deteriorating physical plants.

Increasing Austerity in Higher Education

These trends on the financing of higher education—again, varying by country, but considerably more severe in low- and middle-income countries—have been increasing the austerity in universities and other institutions of postsecondary education as well as in national systems of higher education. This nearly universal and growing higher education austerity in turn has affected universities and other institutions of higher education as evidenced by: overcrowding of lecture theaters; insufficient or outdated library holdings, computing, and Internet connectivity; a deterioration of physical plants; less time and support for faculty research; and a widely assumed loss in the quality of both teaching and learning as well as of research. At the national or system level, the austerity is manifested by capacity constraints, the inability to accommodate all graduates of academic secondary levels who are capable and desirous of further study, a loss of the most talented faculty to countries with fewer financial troubles, and an increasing inability to compete in the global knowledge economy. Finally, the financial austerity effects students, who face tuition fees where there used to be none or meet rising costs where fees have existed, in addition to the rising costs of student living. These crises are contributing to the need to work and earn while studying or face going into debt, or both—for individuals fortunate enough to find a place at all (with many having left the system long before secondary school completion, never experiencing even the possibility of tertiary education).

This austerity has been most crippling in sub-Saharan Africa but is serious throughout the developing world, as in many of the *transitional* countries, especially those emerging from the former Soviet Union. The solutions, simplistically, are clear. First, governments can be urged to contribute more. This is invariably the solution preferred by university leaders, faculty and other staff, and students. However, as we noted earlier, governmental taxation in many low- and middle-income countries is frequently near the point of diminishing returns, as additional taxes can lead to increasing costs of collection, increasing tax avoidance and corruption, or the departure of taxable individuals and productive enterprizes from the country altogether. Furthermore, while systems and institutions of higher education almost certainly have a valid claim on additional public revenues, should they be found, so do a myriad of competing public needs such as elementary and secondary education, public health, and public infrastructure. Thus, while higher education leadership must not abandon pressing their claims for additional public resources, the solutions to the cost-revenue squeeze—particularly for low- and middle-income countries—must increasingly come from university leaders via solutions on the cost side, which in turn means getting more teaching and learning from fewer faculty and staff and, on the revenue side, obtaining more nongovernmental revenue. First, cost-side solutions will be discussed, which in theory are a quest for greater efficiency, or the elimination of waste, but in practice may frequently simply involve the cutting of costs.

Cost-Side Solutions

Solutions to the diverging trajectories of costs and revenues attempt to lower per student instructional costs. The claims of the faculty and staff—first, to preserve their jobs and, second, to maintain or enhance their emoluments—often have the highest political and emotional leverage. Thus, other noninstructional and nonpersonnel cuts tend to be made first: for example, deferring maintenance of the grounds and the physical plants, suspending the replacement of equipment, and freezing or cutting such current expenditures as books and journal subscriptions, replacement of computers, travel, and other noninstructional expenditures. In the most economically stressed countries, bills for utilities and other needed supplies and services may simply not be paid. Some of the regional universities in Madagascar were reported in 2008 to have had no phones or electricity for many hours a day for want of paying the bills. Supplies were not available, and the library was reported not to have purchased a textbook in years (World Bank 2008, 6). A less extreme example, but still demonstrating the priority-distorting political power in many countries of civil service and faculty unions (and the political parties beholden to them), are the many examples of critical noncompensation expenditures for computing, Internet connectivity, instructional equipment, and library acquisitions (not to mention needed repairs to roofs and plumbing) being sacrificed merely to save the jobs of faculty and staff (and sometimes well-paid administrators) whose value addition to the college's or university's instructional mission may be minimal.

Beyond the sacrifice of most nonpersonnel expenses to the preservation of jobs, but continuing at the most drastic, simplistic, and least-strategic level, governments or universities may cut costs simply by not paying or seriously delaying salaries of faculty and staff. Only slightly less simplistic but still decidedly *nonstrategic* are such relatively easy expense-cutting actions as the freezing of salaries or student bursaries—especially when increases are expected and counted upon, as in a highly inflationary economy—or the termination of staff who are part time or not yet entitled to any form of permanency or tenure. More politically or legally acceptable than the nonpayment of salaries, but still damaging to the university's instructional mission, is the freezing of faculty replacements. As the more productive faculty in many (not all) fields are the most mobile, they are frequently the ones who leave. Colleges and universities experiencing prolonged freezes may wind up with few—and oftentimes inferior—faculty in the new high-demand fields, with excessive numbers of faculty in older fields and programs that have fewer students. Again to return to Madagascar for an extreme but illustrative example, the government as of 2008 had enforced a strict hiring freeze for more than 10 years, driving up the student faculty ratios and greatly increasing the teaching loads of the remaining faculty (many of whom teach extra hours to compensate for their extremely low salaries). With no new faculty having been hired, the average age of the remaining faculty had risen alarmingly, with 81 percent age 50 or above and 22 percent in 2008 older than 60. Furthermore, as the nonteaching staff appear to have fewer options and thus rarely leave, Madagascar's main university, with only 500 full-time faculty, carried in 2007/08 a nonteaching and administrative staff of nearly 2,200 (World Bank 2008).

More strategic expenditure reductions at the institutional level—whether to meet an aggregate budget reduction or to free revenue for reallocation and investment—must reduce costs of personnel and do so selectively to shed the faculty and staff who are the least productive and/or least central to the core mission(s) of the university. The least productive and/or least central faculty may well be some of the most senior and politically powerful members, whose scholarly productivity or teaching effectiveness may have seriously declined. Otherwise, they may be administrative staff whose days could be spent in hard work but in work that no longer adds commensurate value to the mission of the institution. Eliminating faculty and staff positions may be both politically and legally difficult and at times impossible to carry out. Strategic cost cutting cannot ignore contractual obligations or be oblivious to sensitivity and decency when it comes to the excruciatingly difficult task of terminating faculty and staff. At the same time, if the future needs of the university and the quality of the instructional programs are to take precedence, university leaders must be allowed to make such hard decisions: in short, to maintain mission and quality, if necessary, at the cost of sacrificing lower-priority programs (as well as losing popularity, political support, and smooth labor relations).

The management of government agencies and the norms of civil service employment, especially in most developing and transitional countries, which prize continuity of employment above all else, are generally incompatible with strategic cost-side solutions to financial problems. Typical problems with government agencies include laws, contracts, and political pressures that forbid terminating staff for any but the most egregious causes, hiring part-time or temporary staff in place of full-time workers, or contracting out services. Additional frequent impasses involve denying other good management practices such as carrying unspent funds forward from one fiscal year to the next or shifting available funds from one budget category to another. However, a clear shift in such management-constraining laws and regulations has occurred in the last decade or two, especially in the highly industrialized countries of the Organization for Economic Cooperation and Development. Such reforms, most of which would give greater managerial autonomy and flexibility to universities, have been proposed and/or are on the table in many middle- and low-income countries as well. Such reforms often entail transforming universities from governmental agencies to public corporations with authority, for example, to: (a) establish wage and salary policies; (b) reallocate expenditures based on institutionally determined priorities; (c) carry forward unspent funds from one fiscal period to the next, thus supporting savings and institutional investment and discouraging spending to avoid loss or an excessive budget; (d) enter into contracts with outside agencies and businesses expeditiously and competitively; and (e) receive and own assets or borrow and incur debt. All of these powers, and more, in many developing and transitional countries were formerly reserved to the ministry or parliament and to the government's financial, personnel, and civil service bureaucracies.

Thus, managerial authority is being strengthened and vested in chief executive officers (presidents, rectors, or vice chancellors) who are selected by governing boards rather than by heads of state or ministries. Further strategic cost-side remedies to financial shortfalls may lower the average per student costs of instruction by increasing teaching loads and/or average class size. However, such strategies, as well as curtailing research, diminish the time the academic staff can spend with individual students and limit the possible instructional modalities, favoring larger classes, fewer examinations, and fewer or shorter written assignments over small classes, discussion-centered pedagogies, and more written examinations. Yet, such relatively obvious cost-side strategies may have already run their course, particularly in middle- and low-income countries. Decades of budget cuts and of absorbing more students and instituting new academic programs with little or no added public funding have arguably taken most if not all of the low-hanging fruit of obvious waste and budget cuts in most countries. Further across-the-board increases in class sizes or teaching loads sufficient to lower the average per student cost of instruction may not be possible without further serious deterioration in the quality of teaching and learning and a further loss in the desirability and attractiveness of the professoriate as a profession.

In many countries, including affluent and highly industrialized as well as middle- and low-income countries, the view remains that much more fundamental and drastic cost-side solutions must still be sought to lower per student costs and provide some cost-side solutions to the otherwize steeply rising trajectory of higher education costs. Three newer, more fundamental cost-side solutions are more radical sector diversification, institutional mergers, and more reliance on technologically assisted instruction—such as distance earning and virtual universities. We conclude our review of solutions on the cost side by consideration of these newer possible strategies for increased higher education efficiency.

Sector Diversification

This strategy constitutes a shift from a preponderance of higher education institutions being (or at least aspiring to be) research universities toward alternative short-cycle, less-expensive, less-selective, more vocationally oriented, and more hierarchically managed institutions, whose faculty are oriented to teaching rather than to research. Thus, sector diversification is commonly viewed as a partial solution to higher education's increasing austerity. The presumably lower per student costs of these so-called nonuniversity alternatives to the classical research university lie in their higher teaching loads, which in turn are a consequence of the lessened expectations for research, a less-extensive involvement in university governance, and the presumption of a lower-reliance on expensive equipment, laboratories, libraries, and technology as well as the shorter duration of study of their students. The form and extent of these alternatives to the classical university vary throughout the world. Among the best known are the German technical universities, or *Fachhochschulen,* the Dutch higher technical schools, the French *institutes universitaires technologies,* the Japanese public and private junior colleges, and the American community colleges—most of which attempt to provide, in these countries, tertiary level education shorter in duration, more practical, less academically rigorous, and less costly. Sector diversification will continue to meet resistance from university students and faculty, who frequently see alternatives to the classical university as lower in status and designed mainly to track less-well-prepared students—more likely from poor or otherwize marginalized families—into forms of tertiary education that will limit their opportunities. Nevertheless, sector diversification will likely remain prominent on the agenda of international higher education reform both for its presumed increased relevance and usefulness to many students (and employers), as well as for the presumption of greater cost-effectiveness.

Mergers

At least in theory, mergers can lower unit costs by increasing the scale of operations and achieving savings on such overhead expenditures as physical plant, libraries, and top-level administration. However, actual savings from mergers still require cutting faculty and staff, including highly paid administrators as well as closing facilities, eliminating some academic programs, and giving up precious institutional identity—measures that are often bitterly resisted, both institutionally and politically. If the merger is only nominal—that is, retaining most facilities, programs, and faculty and merely eliminating a president or rector and a few other top-level administrators—the result may simply be more complicated and less-effective management, a demoralized faculty (of both institutions), and a failure to realize the potentially significant savings of either a genuine merger or the outright closure of one of the supposedly "merged" institutions. At the same time, institutional mergers may be both necessary and possible—and indeed have occurred—in countries where many universities and colleges developed on small and frequently narrow scales for historical reasons that are no longer relevant or have been discredited. Examples of such fruitful settings for cost-effective mergers include South Africa's apartheid division of higher education institutions by race as well as the old Soviet communist model of small and academically narrow universities owned by and oriented to the research and employment needs of a single industrial sector or production ministry.

Technologically Assisted Instruction

Finally, an explosion of interest in most countries, especially in middle- and low-income countries, designates technologically assisted instruction, distance learning, and virtual universities. The most successful applications have focused on the margins, or peripheries, of higher education rather than radical transformations of existing universities. However, undoubtedly great interest will continue among existing universities in instructional technologies of all sorts—largely to supplement traditional modes of instruction. The mission will include the ability to deliver true distance learning to older or returning students as well as to midcareer professionals needing efficient refresher learning (perhaps to maintain licensure, as might one day be required of physicians, teachers, and lawyers). In developing and low-income countries, the potential of technologically assisted distance learning may lie more in serving traditional-age students in remote locations, where the principal costs of higher education are the living expenses away from home (although a lack of personal computers and good Internet connectivity may continue to form major barriers).

Whether new developments in instructional technology can ease the financial austerity of institutions is unclear, although experience from more-affluent industrialized countries suggests that these procedures may enrich the teaching and learning but rarely lower—and frequently increase, at least in the short run—the per student costs of instruction. In theory, of course, one professor, with considerable technological investment and extensive staff support, can teach at many locations and possibly to far more students than he or she could teach "face-to-face" at a single site. And if the goal is to reach out to otherwize place-bound students, unable to travel to a common site but able to get to remote sites to receive a transmission, distance learning can extend access at considerable savings over the alternative of placing faculty and a full facility at each remote site. In countries with surging enrollments, financially unable to build and staff more institutions, virtual or distance-learning universities may be a key to relieving some of the enrollment pressures, especially in areas remote from the metropolitan centers. China, India, Indonesia, Turkey, and sub-Saharan Africa (African Virtual University) all claim large enrollments in distance, or virtual, universities (World Bank 2002; Herbst 2006). However, for a single institution or even a national system of colleges and universities seeking to cope with diverging trajectories of costs and revenues, most applications of distance learning can enrich the learning but are unlikely to provide measurable efficiencies for the existing institutions.

In the end, while cutting instructional expenses needs to be part of the solution to higher education's underlying financial dilemma, cost-side solutions alone will be insufficient for both substantive and political reasons. More importantly, the gap from the diverging trajectories of higher education costs and available revenues is simply too wide to be closed by further cuts in expenditures, even with some of the more radical cost-side "solutions." In short—and as segue to the next section—higher education in almost all countries must turn to nongovernmental revenues to supplement the increasingly insufficient revenue available from governments.

Revenue-Side Solutions

These solutions to the diverging trajectories between surging costs, or revenue needs, and limited public revenues look to increasing nongovernmental revenue. The most efficient and robust stream—that is, a revenue stream that is potentially sizeable, continuous, and least likely to divert the faculty from their mission of instruction—is from the parent and/or student via tuition and other fees. In fact, tuition fees along with financially self-sufficient provision of food and lodging, and the rise of tuition fee-dependent private institutions, are increasing phenomena in most countries of the world. The issue of higher education costs being shifted from a predominate reliance on governments, or taxpayers, to families and students is at times referred to as cost sharing. This perspective was as first articulated and extended internationally by the author in the 1986 study of tuition fees and student finance in the United States and Europe (Johnstone 1986), and developed and documented further through the International Comparative Higher Education Finance and Accessibility Project at the University at Buffalo (Johnstone and Marcucci 2010). Having entered into common parlance in the discourse of higher education policy, the term *cost sharing* has become both a statement of fact—sharing costs of higher education among governments (or taxpayers), parents, students, and philanthropists—as well as a reference to a near worldwide policy shift of some costs from a predominate reliance on governments to sharing among parents and/or students in addition to taxpayers.

Cost sharing is associated with tuition fees and "user charges," especially for governmentally or institutionally provided room and board. However, a policy shift toward greater cost sharing can take several forms. The most common version is the introduction of tuition in systems where higher education was formerly free or nearly so. This would be the case in China in 1997, the United Kingdom in 1998, or a number of countries in sub-Saharan Africa in the first decade of the twenty-first century. In formerly Marxist countries such as Russia, most of eastern and central Europe, and other countries that were once part of the former Soviet Union, as well as in East Africa with its legacy of African socialism, a common variation is the addition of a special tuition-paying track within the public universities while maintaining free or low fees for the regularly admitted, state-supported students. Such a dual track tuition fee, particularly as practiced in Uganda and Kenya, preserves the legal and political appearance of free higher education, which is particularly important (and may be enshrined in a constitution or a framework law). At the same time, such a policy imposes high tuition fees on many (sometimes, as in Uganda's Makerere University, a majority) of the otherwize qualified university students. Furthermore, such a system is considered by most policy analysts to be inequitable in that the highest subsidies go disproportionately to the students whose parents could and would afford a modest tuition fee but who are accorded the limited number of free places in part because of the quality of their (frequently private) secondary education and all of the other cultural advantages of a middle- and upper-middle-class education.

Many countries contemplating the imposition of some form of cost sharing turn first to "user charges" or fees, to recover at least some of the expenses of governmentally or institutionally provided (and heavily subsidized) residences and dining halls. This has been happening in most countries, including virtually all the formerly communist/socialist countries and most of the countries in sub-Saharan Africa, where subsidized living costs at one time absorbed the bulk of higher education budgets.

Still another form of cost sharing is the elimination or reduction of student grants or scholarships. This approach is sometimes accomplished simply by "freezing" grant or loan levels or holding them constant in the face of general inflation, which then erodes their real value. This trend began with the once very generous grants in Britain (which were later abandoned altogether), as well as with the value of the maintenance grants in most of the communist or socialist countries of the former Soviet Union, eastern and central Europe, and Asia, as well as many countries in Africa. A similar policy change in the direction of greater cost sharing would be an increase in the effective cost recovery on student loans. This goal can be accomplished through a diminution of the subsidies on student loans (similar to the diminution in the value of nonrepayable grants) and possibly through an increase in interest rates, as was on the policy table in Kenya during 2009. Or, the additional cost recovery might be accomplished through a tightening of collections or a reduction in the instances of default—as has been occurring in South Africa and Kenya.

A final policy of cost sharing, would constitute the purposeful limitation of capacity in the low-cost or tuition-free public sector together with the official encouragement (and frequently some public subsidization) of a tuition-dependent private higher education sector. A number of countries—notably Japan, Korea, the Philippines, Indonesia, Brazil, and other countries in Latin America and East Asia—have avoided much of what would otherwise have formed a significant governmental expenditure on higher education by keeping a limited public sector—usually elite and selective—and shifting much of the costs of expanded participation to parents and students through the encouragement of a substantial and growing private higher education sector.

Although cost sharing may take on these different forms, the imposition of and/or large increases in tuition fees provide the greatest financial impact. This is because tuition fees—aside from the need to rebate some of the aggregate income in the form of loans, grants, or discounts to preserve accessibility—can be both financially significant and ongoing and even designed to regularly increase, thus keeping pace with the inevitably rising per student costs of instruction. Also, unlike most forms of faculty entrepreneurship, tuition fees do not divert faculty from the core instructional mission and, according to many observers, actually have a beneficial effect of improving the quality of teaching and the relevance of the curriculum. Perhaps for these reasons, tuition fees are also the most politically charged and ideologically resisted form of cost sharing and thus have become a symbol of the conflict between people who believe that government must continue to provide higher education free of any charge and those who believe in the imperative of cost sharing and especially of tuition fees.

Rationales for Cost Sharing

Cost sharing has three principle rationales. The simplest is the *austerity,* or the *sheer need,* rationale, which is a function of the afore-mentioned divergence between the increasing costs and revenue needs of universities and the limited availability of taxpayer revenues. Such a rationale is the most politically and ideologically neutral and is probably in itself sufficient to account for most of the recently observed worldwide shift in costs from governments to parents and students.

Many economists and policy analysts also see an *equity* argument for cost sharing. They observe that so-called *free* higher education (sometimes extended in the past, although rarely into the twenty-first century, to free tuition, free room, free board, and pocket money) is virtually everywhere partaken of disproportionately by the sons and daughters of the elite, who will clearly benefit handsomely in greater occupational choices and prestige and usually in income but is in almost all cases paid for at least proportionately by the average citizen and worker.

Finally, *efficiency* arguments have been advanced in favor of cost sharing: based on the principles of market economics, among which is the assertion that having to pay at least a part of the costs of higher education should make both parents and students more discerning consumers—just as having to charge at least a partial price for the higher education (or the food or the lodging), particularly with some competition, should make the university and/or the government a more efficient and responsive provider.

The economic rationale behind the case for students bearing a portion of the costs of their higher education identifies substantial private benefits, both monetary and nonmonetary, that accrue to the student from higher levels of education. These benefits are said to justify a tuition—especially a modest one that can be deferred and repaid through some form of loan or a surtax upon income or current earnings. The case for parents bearing a portion of the costs of their children's higher education is driven both by the assumption of private benefits extending to parents and by a cultural notion of parental obligation. This rationale includes the presumption that governmental or philanthropic subsidies will fill in for parents who cannot afford to pay. The fact that tuition fees have provided revenues to higher education throughout the world and that public needs, including public higher education, are outrunning the available public revenues means that free higher education is rapidly disappearing almost everywhere.

In most countries few policy alternatives seem to exist to the adoption of some tuition fees. The alternative (again, in most countries) would seemingly deny universities the revenue that they need and cause the losing either of higher education quality or capacity (and thus access.) The effects of these circumstances especially harm the poorest students, who lack the options of expensive private higher education or attending a college or university abroad. In fact, at least in the abstract, most economists maintain that tuition fees—means-tested grants and/or sufficient available student loans—are actually more equitable than free higher education, since students everywhere are largely from the middle and upper classes and the taxing systems in most countries tend to be proportional or even regressive (Marcucci and Johnstone 2007).

Student Loans

Any element of cost sharing that presumes a contribution from students requires a student-loan program, which is simply a way for students to bear a portion of the costs of their higher education. The financial burden is deferred into the future when the students should be able to pay—presumably from employment made more remunerative by virtue of the higher education they have received. Student loans have become widespread throughout the world

(Shen and Ziderman 2009). Some student loan schemes are small: (a) severely rationed by limited loan capital; (b) sponsored only by a single institution or consortium of institutions (generally private); (c) focused only on low-risk borrowers such as advanced professional students or borrowers who can produce multiple, credit-worthy cosignatories. A few schemes, including several in Africa, are financially fragile and have little record as yet of repayment recovery (although the loan schemes in South Africa and Kenya are at least financially viable). However, excessive subsidization of interest rates, high rates of default, and high costs of servicing and collecting seriously detract from the rates of recovery on many student-loan programs (Shen and Ziderman 2009). For this reason, student-loan schemes may be resisted both by ministers of finance and other governmental leaders, who may justifiably fear their financial cost to the treasuries, as well as by students, who may fear the further encroachment of tuition fees. Student-loan schemes are also complex, widely misunderstood, sometimes misrepresented, and frequently contested. However, although the political and ideological opposition tends to be aimed less at the notion of student borrowing itself than it is at a presumption that a governmental loan scheme is a kind of camel's nose into the tent of further cost sharing. Furthermore, some of the misunderstanding, on the part of student borrowers and politicians alike, is a result of the terms used by politicians and loan agencies alike—such as "free to the student at the point of entry," or "no tuition fee but only a deferred obligation"—to play down what remains an imposition of tuition fees and student loans (Johnstone 2006, 2004).

Some Fundamental Questions and Issues of Cost Sharing

As most low- and middle-income countries move further into forms of cost sharing, some critical questions or issues must be addressed at the outset by higher education leaders and government authorities. Five such questions are particularly salient. The first issue is whether cost sharing is to be advanced through tuition fees, through higher (that is, more nearly break even) fees for governmentally provided food and lodging or through encouragement (and even some partial subsidization) of a growing private sector—or any combination of the aforementioned? A second question that must be addressed at the start of a consideration of tuition fees is whether it is parents who are expected to contribute to the costs of higher education instruction—that is, via an *up-front* tuition fee (as, for example, in the United States, the Netherlands, China, Canada, and Japan)—or whether the burden of a shared cost of instruction is to fall mainly on the student in the form of deferred fees or loans (as in Australia, England, and Ethiopia).

Once a decision has been made to impose a tuition fee and on whom to impose it (in low- and middle-income countries usually on families who are financially able to contribute), the third question is the approximate percentage of public college or university instructional costs that ought to be covered by the tuition fee. The range throughout the world in 2009 seems to be from strictly nominal, as in 5 to 10 percent, to the 20 to 25 percent sought in China, up to the relatively high percentages in some American states of 35 to 40 percent. In almost no countries, however, (save possibly in Mongolia) do tuition fees at public colleges and universities exceed 40 percent, which means that virtually all governments, even those having embraced the appropriateness of tuition fees, continue to believe in substantial public benefits from higher education and commensurately substantial public subsidies.

If there is to be a tuition fee, then, a fourth critical question is whether the fee should be the same for all institutions, faculties, and degree levels. Or, might the tuition fee be greater, for example, for the most selective faculties or for the institutions, faculties, and programs in greatest demand (and likely to lead to the most remunerative careers)?

The fifth and last, but absolutely critical for policymakers and university leaders to debate, question is how accessibility is to be maintained given the increasing costs shifted to parents and/or students. The principal answer in all cases rests with some mix of need-based or means-tested grants and loans. But grants and loans are expensive and can quickly undo the revenue benefits presumed to have stimulated cost sharing in the first place. In other words, subsidies—whether in the form of grants, bursaries, tuition fee discounts, subsidized food and lodging, or the subsidies embedded within most student loans—must be cost effective, that is, make a difference in the enrollment behavior of the student, rather than merely reduce what would otherwize be parental contributions or reasonable student borrowing or enhance the students standard of living with no effect on enrollment or persistence.

Other questions and issues need to be faced in the consideration of a policy of increasing the higher education cost shares borne by parents and/or parents. But these five are essential to be faced and answered as a part of any cost-sharing policy. The answers will be contested, but the stakes are high. In the end the revenue needs of higher education in virtually all countries are high and will continue to rise. The alternatives to some form or forms of cost sharing are few, and most of them unacceptable.

Conclusion

The increase in higher education costs for most low- and middle-income countries, where both the increasing size of the relevant age cohort and the expanding percentage of this rapidly growing cohort that wants and deserves access to some form of higher or postsecondary education, is both great and unrelenting. The resulting trajectory of continuously rising costs and revenue needs is almost certainly above the capacity of any country's tax revenues to meet (save perhaps some of the low population oil-rich countries of the Middle East). There are so-called solutions on the cost side in the forms of economies, but the easy ones (e.g., increasing class sizes and teaching loads) have already been met, and the more difficult ones (particularly shedding excess personnel, mainly nonteaching staff) tend to be exceedingly difficult. Efficiencies must still be sought, both because savings must be made in most countries and also because college and university administrations must be seen making the difficult internal decisions if the alternatives to such savings—that is, higher fees paid by students and/or families—are to be politically feasible.

However, cost sharing in the form of tuition and other fees is becoming accepted throughout the world, including developing (both low- and middle-income) and transitional (postcommunist) countries. Although opposition to tuition fees and other elements of cost sharing is virtually inevitable, a number of parents in all countries clearly can and will pay for some of the costs of higher education, as vividly demonstrated throughout the world by the growth of tuition-dependent private higher education (which is in most cases inferior in quality to that offered by the public universities and colleges), as well as by the growth of the privately funded tracks within the public universities. More parents and students, including those from low-income families, could afford a modest tuition fee and bear some or all of the costs of student living. The requirement will include available targeted, or means-tested, grants (nonrepayable) and generally available student loans, as well as grants and loans to increase access to higher education opportunities.

None of these funding patterns deny the need for governments to continue—and in fact to increase—their support of higher education. Parental and student participation must supplement, not supplant, the larger financial role in support of higher education, which must continue to be played by the state. However, it seems unlikely that enough additional resources devoted to higher education will meet the rapidly growing needs, given the enormous revenue needs of the public higher education system and the competition for additional revenues from such needs as elementary and secondary education, public health, public infrastructure, and all other social services. This emphasis on financial solutions on the revenue side also must not deter the government or the universities from continuing, as they have, to aggressively pursue financial solutions on the cost or efficiency side. Such measures should consider, for example, additional privatization of nonacademic services such as food and lodging, changes to teaching loads, and the ability of university management (with proper attention to employee rights) to shed less productive members of the faculty and/or staff.

Finally, these so-called solutions to the mounting financial problems of universities in the twenty-first century call for enlightened and courageous leadership at many levels, including not only rectors, presidents, and vice chancellors but deans, heads of departments and institutes, politicians, and citizen members of governing boards and councils.

References

Baumol, William J. and William G. Bowen (1966) *Performing Arts: The Economic Dilemma*. New York: Twentieth Century Fund.

Fjelstad, Odd-Helge and Lise Rakner (2003) *Taxation and Tax Reforms in Developing Countries: Illustrations from Sub-Saharan Africa*. Bergan, Norway: Michelsen Institute.

Herbst, Marcel (2006) *Financing Public Universities: The Case of Performance Funding*. Dordrecht, Netherlands: Springer.

International Comparative Higher Education Finance and Accessibility Project Web site. Available: http://www.gse.buffalo.edu/org/IntHigherEdFinance (accessed November 2009).

Johnstone, D. Bruce (1986) *Sharing the Costs of Higher Education: Student Financial Assistance in the United Kingdom, the Federal Republic of Germany, France, Sweden, and the United States*. New York: College Entrance Examination Board.

—— (2004) "The Economics and Politics of Cost Sharing in Higher Education: Comparative Perspectives," *Economics of Education Review*, 20 (4): 403–10.

—— (2006) *Financing Higher Education: Cost-sharing in International Perspective*. Chestnut Hill, MA: Boston College Center for International Higher Education; and Rotterdam: Sense.

Johnstone, D. Bruce and Pamela Marcucci (2010 forthcoming) *Financing Higher Education in International Perspective: Who Pays? Who Should Pay?* Baltimore, MD: Johns Hopkins Univ. Press.

Marcucci, P. and D. B. Johnstone (2007) "Tuition Fee Policies in a Comparative Perspective: Theoretical and Political Rationales," *Journal of Higher Education Policy and Management*, 29 (1): 25–40.

Shen, Hua and Adrian Ziderman (2009) "Student Loans: Repayment and Recovery: International Comparisons," *Higher Education*, 57: 315–33.

World Bank (2002) *Constructing Knowledge Societies: New Challenges for Tertiary Education*, Washington, DC: World Bank.

—— (2008) *Madagascar: Financing and Governance of Tertiary Education*, Washington, DC: World Bank.

4

Unlocking the Benefits of Higher Education through Appropriate Governance*

DAVID E. BLOOM AND HENRY ROSOVSKY

The second half of the twentieth century did not constitute a propitious period for higher education in the developing world. Painting with a broad brush, one can show that the postindependence elites who took power when the Europeans departed—and the international donor agencies on which they depended—did not grant this sector high priority. Tertiary education remained the preserve of the few. The reasons were practical but also grounded in theory.

At the time, in poor countries, only a low proportion of the population succeeded in graduating from secondary schools, and the supply of students prepared for higher education was small. This inadequate provision was matched by capacity: few functioning tertiary institutions existed in the developing world. These facts prevailed during much of the second half of the twentieth century and were reinforced by a view, widely espoused by policymakers, that the benefits of expensive higher education—almost always requiring substantial state support—accrued primarily to the few graduates themselves and contributed little to the nation as a whole. Thus, the government subsidies of tertiary education helped the affluent but created greater income inequality.[1]

These attitudes were undoubtedly formed or influenced through findings widely accepted by influential economic theorists and shared by the larger community of economic-development specialists. Calculations performed with international data sets showed a higher private rate of return on investment in primary and secondary schooling than from investment in tertiary education, and more crucial from the point of view of government policy, the same rankings of rates of return persisted when public benefits were included.[2] Little evidence seemed to convince policymakers who guided national development to favor higher education. Defining rates of return forms an important process:

* The authors thank Philip Altbach, Roberta Bassett, David Dapice, Rick Hopper, Salal Humair, Marija Ozolins, Harry Patrinos, George Psacharopoulos, Robert Putnam, Larry Rosenberg, William Saint, and Sidney Verba for helpful discussions, comments, and assistance.

The private rate of return reflects the direct cost to individuals of their schooling (i.e., out-of-pocket costs of education plus earnings forgone while in school) and the increases in earnings that can be attributed to having received education. . . . The social [public] rate of return compares the full costs to society of more schooling, including public subsidies, with the benefits to the entire society of having a better educated populace.

(Bloom, Hartley, and Rosovsky 2006, 295–96)

Using these concepts, the empirical results indicated that given out-of-pocket expenses and opportunity costs (with income forgone while in school) an individual's earning premiums declined as one moved up to higher levels of education. For example, completion of primary school conferred a greater proportionate lifetime income gain than did completion of a first university degree for a secondary school graduate.

If the value of education were confined to private gain it would make sense to favor primary and secondary at the expense of higher education in poorer countries. Proponents of higher education argued that its value to society was not exhausted by private gain, and an evaluation needed to include public and social benefits, categories in which tertiary education was believed to bring especially significant gains (see table 4.1). This required the analysis to move beyond private gain and also to take account of the so-called "spillover effects." (See the discussion in the "Economic Benefits" section, later.) The majority of development specialists remained skeptical. Compared to individual returns, public benefits were hard to measure and remained far more speculative. Policies of the World Bank reflected these uncertain attitudes, and its loans to low- and middle-income countries concentrated largely on the primary and secondary sectors.

Table 4.1 The Array of Higher Education Benefits

Benefits	Public Sector	Private Sector
Economic	• Increased tax revenues • Greater productivity • Increased consumption • Increased workforce flexibility • Decreased reliance on government financial support	• Higher salaries and benefits • Employment • Higher savings levels • Improved working conditions • Personal/professional mobility
Social	• Reduced crime rates • Increased charitable giving/ community service • Increased quality of civic life • Social cohesion/appreciation of diversity • Improved ability to adapt to and use technology	• Improved health/life expectancy • Improved quality of life for offspring • Better consumer decision making • Increased personal status • More hobbies, leisure activities

Source Institute for Higher Education Policy 1998.

Today, at the beginning of the twenty-first century, higher education remains a luxury in most of the world. Home to roughly 85 percent of global population, low- and middle-income countries house only about half of the students engaged in higher education. While the gross tertiary enrollment ratio[3] in North America and western Europe is 70 percent, this is below 30 percent in most of the rest of the world: only 9 percent in South Asia and a mere 5 percent in sub-Saharan Africa.

The problems go beyond numbers: the quality of the product in the developing world stands at a frequently low level.[4] It is difficult and sometimes misleading to generalize, but we can easily enumerate commonly encountered quality problems. Outdated facilities and teaching methods emphasizing rote learning represent common infrastructures. Curricula all too often are not suited for the demands of modern societies; and nepotism, bribery, and other forms of corruption defeat merit in the selection of students and faculty. Faculty tend to be poorly paid and often moonlight, diluting the quality of their efforts. Politicians often exert undue influence in university matters, sometimes curtailing the basic exercise of academic freedom. In many areas of the world, unregulated, for-profit private colleges have left students vulnerable to the schemes of unscrupulous providers.

Yet there have been positive signs of change in the last 20 years and especially in the last 10 years. Enrollment rates are rising (see tables 4.2 and 4.3), and the recent increases are to some extent seen as reflecting recognition by policymakers—including the World Bank—that higher education confers benefits beyond private gain. The public benefits provided by tertiary education are increasingly perceived as key drivers of national development in the twenty-first century. Improving the quality of higher education at present raises general concern among the leaders of the developing world, and the World Bank now shares this anxiety. To give a concrete example, an evaluation of a recent World Bank publication on higher education in Africa states that the report "further liberates the continent from the yokes of the imposed . . . and . . . *flawed intellectual discourse* that gripped the system for a long time" (World Bank 2009, emphasis added). The report declares, "Neglecting tertiary education could seriously jeopardize sub-Saharan Africa's long-term growth prospects, and slow progress towards Millennium Development Goals many of which require tertiary training to implement." And the reviewer—Damtew Teferra, coordinator of the International Network for Higher Education in Africa—adds: "This is indeed a major turnaround from the time when higher education was declared a luxury the continent could ill-afford" (Teferra 2009, 15). UNESCO has also recently issued a statement that summarizes its recent conference and argues in many different ways about the importance of higher education. The conference communiqué states:

> The past decade provides evidence that higher education and research contribute to the eradication of poverty, to sustainable development and

Table 4.2 Task Force on Higher Education Data on Gross Tertiary Enrollment Ratio, 1965–95

	1965	1975	1985	1995
World	9	14	13	18
Low and middle income	4	7	7	10
Sub-Saharan Africa	1	1	2	3
East Asia and Pacific	5	5	4	7
South Asia	4	7	8	6
Europe and Central Asia	9	14	13	32
Latin America and Caribbean	4	13	16	18
Middle East and North Africa	3	7	11	15
High income	20	33	37	58

Note: The regional categories are based on World Bank definitions, but this chart includes only low- or middle-income countries. While not listed in this table, Japan and the countries of western Europe are included in "high income." East Asia and the Pacific encompasses, among others, China, Indonesia, Vietnam, and all of the island nations of the Pacific Ocean. Europe and Central Asia includes most of eastern Europe, Russia, and most of the other former republics of the Soviet Union, and Turkey.

Source Task Force on Higher Education and Society 2000.

Table 4.3 World Bank Data on Gross Tertiary Enrollment Ratio, 1991–2005

	1991	1999	2000	2005
World	n.a.	18	19	24
Low and middle income	n.a.	12	13	19
High income	n.a.	57	57	67
East Asia and Pacific	n.a.	10	11	20
Europe and Central Asia	32	36	39	51
Latin America and Caribbean	17	22	23	30
Middle East and North Africa	n.a.	21	21	24
South Asia	n.a.	n.a.	8	9
Sub-Saharan Africa	n.a.	4	4	5

Note: The countries included in these regions are the same as those in table 4.2, with the important difference that in this table, all countries—both developed and developing—are included in the regional data.
n.a. = not available

Source World Bank 2008.

to progress towards reaching the internationally agreed upon development goals, which include the Millennium Development Goals . . . and Education for All. . . . The global education agenda should reflect these realities.

(UNESCO 2009)

A recent article in the *Chronicle of Higher Education* (Labi 2009) quotes Andreas Schleicher, who leads production of the Organization for Economic

Cooperation and Development's annual report on education (OECD 2009): "In virtually every [OECD] country, the public benefits of higher education outweigh the costs."

Raising the quality of higher education, while expensive and difficult, involves some familiar requirements: well-prepared students and faculty, appropriate facilities, and sufficient and assured funding. We will argue that to unlock the full benefits of higher education also requires suitable and effective governance both for tertiary systems and individual schools.

Governance refers to the formal and informal arrangements that allow institutions of higher education to make and implement decisions. Management and decision making take place within a structure of governance and include all things that make an institution function: from strategic planning and resource allocation to promotions and curriculum. Our concept of governance indicates who decides what and how decisions are implemented.

A decade ago, while working on *Peril and Promise,* the report of the World Bank/UNESCO Task Force on Higher Education and Society (2000), we spoke with university leaders from many countries spread over five continents. Without exception, academic leaders told us that dysfunctional governance was the single-greatest obstacle they faced. Subsequent experiences have confirmed this finding, and it is not a simple issue. A university is (ideally) neither a commercial enterprise nor just another government bureaucracy. To function optimally the special and quite specific requirements of higher education should be—need to be—reflected in governance.[5]

In this chapter we will first elaborate the somewhat belatedly recognized relationship between higher education and public benefits, followed by suggestions for paths toward suitable governance, an essential aspect of achieving maximum national benefit from the tertiary sector.

Higher Education and National Development

Following the Institute for Higher Education Policy (see table 4.1), we divide the national benefits of higher education, somewhat imprecisely, into two categories: economic and social benefits. Both of these categories include private and public returns.

Economic Benefits

Economists have conducted hundreds of studies documenting the sizable return on investments in education. The robustness of this finding—across countries and over time—makes this one of the best-established empirical results in the field of labor economics. Until recently, most of these rate-of-return studies ranked higher education below primary and secondary education. However, a new generation of studies (e.g., Colclough, Kingdon, and Patrinos 2009) notably suggests that the rates of return on investments in higher education exceed those for primary and secondary education. Presumably, this change reflects the fact that economic systems have become more complicated and demand a new set of skills—ones that are typically acquired in the course of higher education.

A striking feature of the older and newer studies consists of their neglect of effects of higher education above and beyond the impacts on graduates who have received higher education (i.e., "spillover effects").[6] Higher earnings (in absolute terms) lead to higher savings, leaving resources for investment and job creation potentially benefiting workers with all different levels of educational achievement. Furthermore, college and university graduates are generally among the most productive workers in society, thereby contributing disproportionately to economic efficiency and growth.

For example, a 17-country data set compiled by the Center for Entrepreneurial Studies at Babson College (Reynolds, Bygrave, and Autio 2003) also showed that tertiary graduates were involved in the creation of more new firms or start-ups, and entrepreneurs with higher education created more jobs than those with less education.

These spillover effects accrue to broad segments of the population or to the economy as a whole. Their existence for higher education has been verified in a variety of studies, several of which have demonstrated the positive effects of higher education on national productivity. For example, looking at individual US states, we found that, controlling for age, sex, race/ethnicity, marital status, educational attainment, industry, occupation, and state, the earnings of high school dropouts and high school graduates were higher in states with greater shares of college graduates, implying that both graduates and nongraduates benefited (Bloom, Hartley, and Rosovsky 2006). Moretti (2004) reported that an increase in the share of college graduates in cities raised the wage level of both high school dropouts and high school graduates who did not pursue further schooling. (Although we do not know of any studies of this phenomenon outside the United States, we have no reason to believe that these results would not apply to other countries. Such studies would be useful.)

The effects of globalization, though less quantifiable, magnify the importance of spillover benefits provided by higher education. For developing countries, globalization creates encounters with unfamiliar industrial, agricultural, and management technologies and opportunities. To take full advantage of increasing contact with the world economy requires entrepreneurs capable of appreciating innovations and adapting and implementing them in local contexts. The East Asian "Tigers" (Hong Kong, Singapore, South Korea, and Taiwan) did this in the 1970s and the 1980s, and they were joined more recently by India and China. These nations all possessed highly educated cadres who could lead the process; indeed, they have succeeded in transitioning from profitable adoption to innovation. Indian information technology (e.g., WIPRO and Infosys) and pharmaceutical companies (e.g., Ranbaxy and Cipla) have moved from copying technologies to creating original products. WIPRO, for example, created its own computers and developed customer-specific business software. Cipla manufactures low-cost medicines for a variety of diseases. Similarly, the "Tigers" have also become world leaders in new technologies. For example, the Taiwanese company, Acer, has become the world's third-largest maker of personal computers. Singaporean companies excel in the production of integrated circuit chips, and Singapore is a world leader in port-management efficiency technology. More broadly, East Asian countries have moved toward the extensive use of robotic manufacturing. If developing countries are to reduce their traditional dependence on primary products, thereby lessening the chance of being victimized by fluctuating world prices and associated economic insecurity, they will need highly educated adopters, adapters, and innovators. Modern economic history leaves no doubt about this conclusion.

Social Benefits

National development is not confined to the economy: the term includes economic and social development. While difficult to separate without ambiguity, social development focuses more on improving a broadly defined quality of life. Relevant indicators include the quality of government and civic life, social cohesion, control of crime, improvement of health, and others. Higher education is a major—though sometimes unrecognized—contributor to these social benefits. Students may seek education primarily to improve their own material lives. Teachers may also think that the task is mainly to prepare students for employment. While higher education produces private economic advantages that result in beneficial spillovers (higher overall wages, more enterprise, etc.), it also creates social benefits for the nation that strengthen economic growth.

Using data from 130 countries contained in the International Country Risk Guide, we examined the association between higher education and good government (Bloom, Hartley, and Rosovsky 2006). We found a positive and statistically significant correlation between enrollment rates and the rule of law, the absence of corruption, the quality of the bureaucracy, the absence of ethnic tension, and low risk of governmental repudiation of contracts and public appropriation. None of these prove causality, but they do suggest a strong connection between tertiary schooling and improved quality of life.

Along the same lines, in a study of the United States, Robert Putnam (2001) established that higher education increased societal political awareness and civic engagement. He demonstrated that tertiary graduates were more politically and socially engaged, voted more, joined more clubs, and volunteered more than those with less-advanced education. We do not believe that Putnam's study has been duplicated elsewhere, but it seems likely that his observations will have broad international applicability. At the very least, it is clear that a considerable body of evidence testifies to the relationship between higher levels of education and civic engagement.[7]

* * *

So far, we have argued that expanding and improving higher education may help promote development and national goals. Next, we turn to the importance of governance (both external and internal) in realizing those benefits. The potential benefits that higher education can convey do not automatically come into being. We therefore focus on a particular set of conditions relevant to governance that can help transform the promise of higher education into clear benefits for a country.

The Role of Governance

All institutions benefit from forms of governance that encourage and allow them to fulfill their missions. However, dissatisfaction with governance is common in business, government, and other forms of association. Both the needs and dissatisfactions apply to academic institutions, but colleges and universities face special and unusual problems that other sectors of society may fail to appreciate. Society at large is more likely to have some familiarity with the practices of government, business, and primary and secondary education than with customs and requirements of relatively more recent systems of higher education.

What makes higher education unusual from the perspective of governance?

1. Higher education is frequently wholly publicly financed or, at least, subsidized. Compared with lower forms of state-financed education, however, universities often ask for special privileges: to name just a few, academic freedom especially in research, control of instructional content, and workloads that may appear excessively permissive to outsiders.

2. Compared with most institutions, universities have extremely horizontal authority structures: the proportion of skilled senior staff is far greater than in other organizations, presenting major problems of control. Instead of a single unified voice for an institution, a more likely outcome will be a cacophony of voices and incessant dissonance.

3. The nature of quality higher education makes it a source of new ideas and criticisms: that is the inevitable result of faculty engaged in research and teaching and students involved in learning and questioning. Neither the new ideas nor criticisms of the status quo may be welcomed by the authorities. They may be equally offensive to large segments of public opinion. Universities often are societal irritants.

4. It is especially difficult to evaluate the performance of institutions of higher education. Various valuable metrics exist and are used, but

compared with business and the public sector there is no clear bottom line or control afforded by existing periodic elections, respectively.

University governance can be divided into two categories: external and internal. *External* refers to relations between the institution and the body to which it is accountable: the state or a group of trustees representing the state or the private sector. *Internal* refers to the lines of authority and management arrangements within an institution.

External governance in most countries involves supervision by a ministry— generally the ministry of education—and contentious issues frequently relate to the degree of ministerial control. In developing countries, ministerial micro-management is a particular problem.[8] For example, in China and Saudi Arabia, state authorities mandate ideological or religious content in the curriculum. In Korea, the Ministry of Education controls the selection of administrative personnel in public universities: "university staff are considered as public officials" (OECD 2007). Instead of confining itself to setting general research priorities, the Vietnamese Ministry of Science and Technology defines precise research topics—95 in 2006—that will receive financial support and then selects individuals through whom the funds will be disbursed. It is an excellent example of ministerial overspecification. In a similar vein, the government-mandated curriculum "demands too many core courses, utilizes out-of-date content, and draws few connections between related fields, contrary to the standards of modern engineering courses" (Chirot and Wilkinson 2009, 13).

In Pakistan, universities have suffered from the appointment of retired army generals as vice chancellors and from political appointees providing jobs for their party's supporters (Hussain 2005). These and similar policies hamper quality improvement.

Malaysia offers another example of problems that can arise when external authorities improperly intervene in university governance. The government has mandated an affirmative action policy in admissions to the University of Malaysia that favors Malays over other ethnic groups, mainly Chinese and Indians. This preference has aided Malays and, given their relatively low socio-economic status in the country, affirmative action may well be an essential and legitimate means of addressing the debilitating consequences of long-term interethnic inequality. Yet, this policy has significantly lowered the share of ethnically Chinese in the student population (from 56 percent to 29 percent, between the early 1970s and the late 1980s). The restrictive admissions policy has led many Chinese and Indian students to seek education elsewhere and, given the brain drain, has deprived the country of at least a portion of their potential contributions (Salmi 2009). A World Bank (2007) study finds that "the attainment of world class status by Malaysia [sic.] universities hinges, in part, on keeping a fine balance between two competing objectives: expanding the system and improving quality." The study notes the importance of ensuring that lower-income students can attend universities and "[ensuring] the match of the most academically qualified students to the best programs while simultaneously recognizing the value of diversity." Some observers think that, in actual practice, this program went too far: its main effect was not primarily to help a disadvantaged majority population but rather to exclude the better-off Chinese and Indian minorities.

A not uncommon form of external intervention occurred in 2002/03, when the Ethiopian government stepped directly into the process of evaluating faculty at Addis Ababa University and appointed new leadership when the previous leaders resigned in protest. Student and staff protests have also occasioned government intervention, leading William Saint (2004) to ask, citing Human Rights Watch (2003) (The latter events took place in 2001):

> Will new courses in civics prepare students for democratic practice when student government is suspended, when the student newspaper is banned, when security forces are stationed on campus, when student admissions and placement are directed by the Ministry of Education, when union organising among staff is prohibited and when freedom of the press is circumscribed? Will new courses in ethics produce more responsible citizens when student protests of the above impositions are met with slaughter, mass arrests, and torture?
>
> (Saint 2004, 109)

In the long history of higher education, students have frequently played a role that has led to governments being cautious about universities. It has certainly precipitated external intervention. The role of student rebellions has been highlighted as helping to topple or severely challenge governments, from the Middle Ages to events of the last 70 years in Argentina, China, Czechoslovakia, Hungary, Indonesia, Japan, Pakistan, Poland, South Korea, Venezuela, and Vietnam (Glaeser, Ponzetto, and Shleifer 2006). Indeed, student political unrest may be one reason why some of the worst governments in the developing world have resisted the expansion and improvement of higher education. The frequent suspicion with which governments view higher education often led to interference. More benignly, interference may express a genuine belief on the part of government officials that they know best how to run universities. In either case, excesses prevail.

Internal governance practices, in contrast, sometimes suffer from excessive participatory democracy in the form of undesirable faculty controls. Elections of deans and president/rectors are one possible example, for transformational academic leaders rarely emerge as winners in those contests. At Quaid-i-Azam University in Pakistan, faculty recently voted to exempt all applicants for faculty positions, at any level, from having to present a public seminar or lecture as part of their application process. They also unilaterally and significantly lowered the standards for receiving a PhD from the university, to well below international levels (Hoodbhoy 2009). According to Pervez Hoodbhoy, the exemption from public presentations is part of a long-term lowering of standards; the university's Academic Council deemed open lectures to be "illegal, unjust, and a ploy for victimizing teachers" (2009, 9). Hoodbhoy contends that the lower standards for PhDs are driven by greed, since professors who take on more PhD students earn more money. He also points out that the faculty are now making promotions much easier to obtain, so that they can take advantage of the much higher salaries that come with higher rank. All the aforementioned issues are examples of excessive and unaccountable faculty authority and a perverse incentive structure.

As a practical matter, governance arrangements are best evaluated on a case-by-case basis. Formal rules and more informal realities vary widely. Practical possibilities for reform need to go beyond theories and have to take account of history and culture. Under these circumstances, an attempt to list general principles is of limited usefulness but could provide a good beginning for discussion between the governors and the governed. What follows may appear quite obvious; this is because the difficulties lie less in the principles than in their implementation.

Principles of Good Governance

Academic freedom, the first principle, is "the right of scholars to pursue their research, to teach, and to publish without control or restraint from the institutions that employ them" (Columbia University Press 2001). It is a crucial principle for the exact reason that makes universities problematic from the perspective of governance. Incubators of new ideas and innovations, vital as drivers of socioeconomic progress, these institutions are bound frequently to displease the public authorities or other centers of power. However, the price of stifling intellectual liveliness is high.

Academic freedom is not an unlimited right and applies primarily to the professional activities of faculty and other scholarly workers. Obviously, there are reasonable differences of definition and interpretation. How are professional activities defined? Does academic freedom apply when teachers speak outside of their professional competence? Are certain restrictions permissible in institutions with religious sponsorship? Many other questions are possible; nevertheless, the finest universities in the world all benefit from enormous academic freedom. Shanghai Jiao Tong University (2008) world rankings do not list a single school in the top 100 in which this right is even a remote question, and there exist very few questions about the second 100. Academic freedom is not a sufficient condition for excellence. Perhaps it is not even a necessary condition.[9] But the association between academic freedom and excellence, as a matter of empirical observation, is very strong.[10]

Two traditional tools of governance have been used to safeguard the principle of academic freedom. The first consists of some form of security of employment for academicians. Sometimes this exhibits lifetime tenure after a probationary period. It could also take the form of long-term contracts. The purpose is the same: to protect intellectual workers from seemingly inevitable forms of political and other forms of arbitrary interference occasioned by their professional activities.

Similar protection should also be provided by governing boards or other forms of trusteeship that stand as a buffer between the institutions and external bodies to which they are accountable: state and private organizations, both civil and religious. Of course, to perform this task effectively requires an understanding and appreciation of the importance of academic freedom both by the boards and by bodies to which they are accountable. That can be a formidable obstacle.

Shared governance is also known as cooperative governance and is a necessity. This second principle arises from the concept of relative expertise and aims to ensure that decisions are devolved to those who are best qualified to make them. At the system level, it entails giving institutions or their advocates a role in shaping national higher education policy. At the institutional level, it ensures that faculty is given a meaningful voice in determining policy. This applies particularly to educational policy and especially to curriculum development and academic appointments (Task Force on Higher Education and Society 2000).

Shared governance is a matter of degree: shared yes, but shared with whom? And who determines what is to be shared? Historically, many constituencies have made claims: trustees, funders, faculties, students, staff, and the public. The list could be lengthened. The rights of those who pay the bills and their trustees are rarely questioned and appear self-evident. If an institution's budget is supplied by the state, it is understood that the government will—within limits—"call the shots." Even without supplying resources, the entitlement of the public sector to regulate aspects of education is generally understood. But the words of Harvard President Charles Eliot written just a century ago still make a great deal of sense:

> Trustees need above all 'good judgment' and . . . should 'always maintain a considerate and even deferential attitude towards the experts whom they employ' given that they 'are not themselves expert in any branch of the university teaching, and they are not experts in the policy or discipline of a university' and 'many of the things [a trustee] has learnt to value in his business experience he will have to discard absolutely in contributing to the management of a university, because they are inapplicable.
> (cited in Palfreyman 2005, 19).

In most cases these thoughts would apply with equal force to representatives of ministries. To be sure, Eliot may have been a bit self-serving, but in essence he was simply attempting to draw lines that recognized professional qualifications and academic function. And, of course, deference and respect do not mean trustee or ministerial laissez-faire.

The role of professors, however, is much more uncertain, and so is the function of students and staff in this process. Both become clearer when we consider some realities of well-functioning universities based on our own observations.

Not everything is improved by making the environment more democratic, or to put it less provocatively, a participatory democracy is an inefficient form of university administration. There are simply too many interest groups with different time horizons. Students are in school for comparatively brief periods. Senior faculty are likely to enjoy some form of security of employment and have a much longer time horizon. Probational faculty, research employees, and staff fall in between these extremes. The point is that it is wise to reflect length of commitment to the university in the rights and responsibilities given to a member of the community.

Length of commitment is not the only factor pointing to a leading role for faculty, especially senior faculty. In a university, those with knowledge should be entitled to a greater say. This does not apply to general knowledge, or knowledge irrelevant to the academic mission of the university. It does apply to judgment and understanding about the core intellectual activities of higher education—necessarily sophisticated and specialized—and those describe the faculty.

Length of commitment and knowledge suggest a special place for faculty in the application of shared governance. But governance is not an end in itself. One of its main justifications is to improve the institution's performance in teaching, research, and service. Too many administrative duties can harm the education mission, and this does not apply only to faculty. Student politicians are not usually the most devoted to their studies.

Excessive administrative burdens can have adverse and unintended consequences. Saudi Arabia has a regulation that permits only its citizens to be departmental chairs, deans, and rectors. Inevitably, Saudi higher education relies on a large number of expatriate faculty whose role in governance is severely limited by state regulation. As an unintended consequence, young Saudi scholars, in their prime research years, are diverted from core tasks and forced into using rather than creating intellectual capital. Shared governance exacts a price from all who participate.

There also have to be limits imposed by those who delegate decision-making authority: principally, ministries and trustees. Two levels of delegation are involved: the authority delegated by a state or private body to the chief of the university and that which is delegated to others—mainly faculty—as a group. It is a good idea to delegate issues in which academic competence is essential. Curriculum development and academic appointments—the choice of colleagues, always subject to higher review—suggest reliance on the faculty. Both require professional competence. (As we have noted in the case of Pakistan, even when appropriate delegation of responsibilities has taken place, there is no assurance that those responsible will make reasonable decisions.) It would be inconceivable, however, to delegate to a faculty the power to set their own salaries or the authority to commit the university to multiyear capital projects. In universities, as in other institutions, the quality of decisions is improved by preventing conflict of interest.

Vexing questions are frequently associated with shared governance. Should faculties elect their own leadership? This scheme remains the practice in much of Europe where rectors and deans are elected to relatively short, renewable terms. By contrast, the North American practice follows appointing presidents who are chief executive officers (CEOs) responsible to trustees or government bodies. Provosts, deans, and department chairs are also appointed. The developing world appears to have adopted the model that incorporates strong executive authority—the American model. We favor this because it improves the chances for long-term effective leadership at all levels.

A crucial question pertains to the role of students, other staff, technicians, janitors, guards, and others in governing a university. Both this and the former question relate to democratic practice. Why should not all stakeholders share power? Putting aside issues of knowledge and length of commitment—namely, the difference between the transients who are learners and the more rooted who are teachers—an analogy to democracy in political life is also, we believe, false. There are basic differences between the rights of citizenship in a nation and the rights that attach to voluntarily joining a community for a specific purpose—such as teachers, students, and those who support these efforts. Anyone who doubts the aforementioned proposition should think of the student unrest of the 1960s and the accompanying European experiments with parity governance. Those reforms resulted in decisions within some universities with roughly equal representation for faculty, students, and workers. Few, if any, institutions failed to decline under these regimes, and almost none of these arrangements have survived.

An equitable hierarchical system of governance requires explicit and extensive mechanisms of consultation and accountability. Everyone should be able to appeal a decision to a level above an immediate supervisor. A professor should be able to seek redress above the level of a dean and a student above the level of the instructor. Formal grievance procedures and sometimes specific *advisory* powers should also be given to representatives of other groups within the institution. This would include students, staff, and other personnel. As a final check against the arbitrary or otherwise unreasonable exercise of authority that can easily evolve in any hierarchical system, a university should consider an ombudsperson to field complaints that a petitioner believes have not received a just or adequate hearing and response. The exact rules that govern the ultimate power of such an ombudsperson may vary from one institution to another, but the idea is to offer an independent voice to weigh in on significant matters of university governance.

Mechanisms of appeal introduce the third principle: *accountability*. This is of much broader applicability and is difficult to summarize. Accountability includes obligations to ministries, boards, and taxpayers. It also includes transparent operations at all levels. Open standards of performance and regular evaluations should permeate the university. Students need to realize the definition of success, and faculty need to share some common understanding concerning academic evaluation. Similarly, the university "CEO" must work with clear goals reached in agreement with an overseeing authority. The rights and responsibilities of individuals and institutions should be precise enough to clarify the detection of failure. This approach is especially relevant for faculties, boards, and ministries. Combining teaching and research with the vital rights of academic freedom can easily lead to vague and self-serving notions of professorial obligations. Boards and ministries, by way of contrast, may have an insufficient appreciation of the legitimate differences between the "real world" and the academy. Both groups would benefit from formal instruction prior to assuming their duties. For example, requiring a seminar explaining professional conduct to all new academic hires is an excellent and all too rare practice. The discussion would focus not on academic discipline mastered merely as part of getting an advanced degree but on the obligations of citizenship in a university. A similar seminar could easily be designed for those about to become trustees.

It stands to reason that *meritocratic selection*, the fourth principle, is a necessary component of rising quality. The statement would be almost trite were it not for the fact that the principle is too often honored more in word than deed. We are referring, of course, to the selection of faculty (and also administrators and students) based on proven accomplishment or, in the case of young people, on promise. Why, then, is the application of the merit principle so problematic? Let us take for granted that measuring merit is an imperfect science and also admit the possibility of honest differences of opinion about specific candidates.

Selections based on merit create hard and unpleasant choices vis-à-vis friends, relatives, political authorities, and others. Some traditional cultures are particularly affected by this problem. Choices are further complicated by the horizontal authority structure of universities. Close association of colleagues stretching over many years does not welcome major and highly consequential differences of opinion. In addition, many institutions lack the data on which to base sound decisions.

A good first step in finding merit is to establish realistic and operational standards that meet the needs of a particular (developing) country and institution. Merely copying the practices of older and wealthier research universities are not effective because the attraction of "world-class" examples can exert pressure in the wrong direction. A candidate eagerly courted by Yale or Oxford or the Sorbonne—even if available—may not represent the wisest choice for a much newer university in a developing country. For example, a scholar of great research accomplishments in an esoteric subject and with no particular inclination to offer instruction might be an adornment for Oxford but a poor investment for Makerere University in Uganda. To achieve the greatest effectiveness in terms of societal or national needs is the task. This may call for a balance between teaching and research that differs from some "world-class" models. Perhaps another requirement involves a choice of instructional and research topics focused more on national needs and less on the latest fashions within the world community of scholars. It could extend to preferences for the citizens of one's own country, because they will be the institution builders.

Making hard choices is immensely aided by external—especially peer—review, which represents the critical and unending quest for disinterested and neutral evaluations. Especially when appointing senior scholars with a presumed record of achievement, peer review becomes the very foundation of meritocratic selection. It is a crucial tool because judgments made within the institution can or will be seen as tainted. But peer review is only advisory. The final decisions are internal, local, and should take account of particular institutional priorities.

Hard choices are also assisted by some version of probationary appointments for faculty, sometimes colloquially described as "up-or-out" policies. At the end of the probationary period the individual is either promoted to a senior position with security of employment or terminated. The decision depends on performance during the probationary period (and on available positions). This policy forces institutional choices that otherwise are too easily postponed and, sometimes, altogether avoided. Giving lifetime or long-term contracts to the unproven, as is the case when academics are treated as civil servants, will tend to decrease quality. A higher proportion of institutional disappointment is inevitable since such selections are based on much less and usually inadequate information.

Finally, are data adequate for making valid decisions? The needs will vary from place to place, but it may be instructive to list some of the elaborate metrics used by King Fahd University of Petroleum and Minerals (KFUPM), the highest-rated tertiary institution in the Arab world (*Times Higher Education Supplement* 2008). KFUPM measures teaching effectiveness by analyzing student completion rates, student evaluations, success in graduates obtaining employment, and—after an interval—employer satisfaction. University and professorial research performance is assessed annually by output in refereed and Institute for Scientific Information (ISI) journals and book publications. In addition, citation indexes are analyzed and external research support studied. The proportion of research addressing local problems is examined as a separate category. Selected international universities are surveyed for PhD candidates potentially employable by KFUPM. In addition to the usual evaluation of curriculum vitae, candidates are interviewed in their home countries. In 2008, KFUPM sent three different teams headed by senior academics to North America in search of talent. The results were considered excellent and resulted in quality-enhancing appointments.

Excellence has to be recognized not only at time of entry but also throughout a working career, and that strongly suggests market- and/or merit-oriented compensation that rewards superior performance. This process can be a controversial and even an impossible goal. Higher faculty achievement can be measured by external recognition. It can equally consist of internal institutional accomplishments, of which teaching and administration are major components. In either case, differentiated compensation permits the university to reward the most effective academics and staff. The enemy of market efficiency is bureaucracy, systems in which rewards and advancement are based entirely on seniority. Sometimes these are sarcastically referred to as "escalator systems"—that is, you go up slowly, with brief pauses and eventually and inexorably reach the top. From the point of view of quality, these methods are the least desirable for providing security of employment.

Our discussion has touched on both principles and tools of good governance. Few of these policies can be put into practice without the assurance of financial stability; without it, strategic planning and quality operations become impossible. Developing countries are repeatedly the victims of economic instability, and some of their tertiary institutions have made sensible attempts at income diversification. The public Makerere University in Uganda, for example, has reduced its reliance on fluctuating government funding by introducing student fees, running some for-profit services (a bookshop and bakery), and introducing evening classes to generate revenue. These actions have helped Makerere to retain academic staff and to improve facilities. Private universities have achieved greater stability by using philanthropic endowments and high tuition fees. Neither diversification nor endowments will provide adequate protection from economic cycles. Most important is that the need for financial stability be recognized by policymakers. Stability makes better governance possible, which in turn will assist in unlocking the private and public benefits of higher education.

In our title we used the words "appropriate governance"—appropriate primarily with respect to academic requirements for excellence—and these will not be the same for all countries and in all types of institutions. We have focused on research universities and they are the apex of the higher education pyramid. Such institutions are not, however, the whole system, which may include regional universities, polytechnics, teacher-training colleges, and others. Appropriate governance suggests adjustments of different types of educational missions and national traditions. A research university oriented toward creating top scholars may require slightly different types of governance arrangements than one whose mission is providing education to a large number of students. Specific governance arrangements are best carried out at the local level.

Before concluding, we must note that the best governance practices are sometimes undermined by a lack of trust: in particular, governing authorities, even when they are nominally operating under the principles enunciated here, sometimes act in ways that earn them the distrust of other constituencies within a university. Faculty and others can on occasion rightly feel that governance structures are successfully subverted by those wielding real power and that the decisions that matter are made outside of the agreed-upon governance framework. Hence, the principles of good governance, although essential, are not in themselves sufficient for guaranteeing good governance. The broader interplay of trust, power, and governance is a complex and vexing issue.

Conclusion

The two large topics discussed in this chapter—higher education and national development as well as governance of higher education—may seem disparate, but that is not the case. Recognition of higher education as a driver of development makes the performance of universities a matter of high national priority. Their nature and needs have to be understood by the political and economic leaders of society. Most of the needs of higher education are relatively easily understood: resources, buildings, teachers, students, among others. Less clear is the case with governance, where optimal practice is consequential, unfamiliar, and for some policymakers, uncomfortable. Systems and practices of governance that fail to recognize idiosyncrasies of the academy will diminish the opportunities of national development.

Notes

1. See Milton and Rose Friedman (1980).
2. See Psacharopoulos and Patrinos (2004), and the references therein to earlier studies they have conducted that summarize the literature on the rate of return on investments in education.
3. The gross enrollment ratio is defined by the UNESCO Institute for Statistics (2009) as "Total enrolment in a specific level of education, regardless of age, expressed as a percentage of the eligible official school-age population corresponding to the same level of education in a given school year. For the tertiary level, the population used is that of the five-year age group following on from the secondary school leaving." For example, if a country has 200,000 higher education students (irrespective of age) and 1 million people aged 18–23 (which would be the relevant age group if secondary education typically ends at age 17), its gross enrollment ratio will be 0.2.
4. Hanushek and Woessmann (2009) find that the low quality of education in Latin America is directly related to that region's relative inability to benefit from

relatively high enrollment rates. Note, however, that the authors do not distinguish between education levels.

5. A recent study of the importance for Vietnam of creating effective, top-tier universities (Chirot and Wilkinson 2009) focuses on improved governance as central to achieving this goal.

6. This concern also applies to estimates of rate of return on investments in primary and secondary school.

7. Glaeser, Ponzetto, and Shleifer (2006) review this evidence, which is generally consistent with the Putnam view. They find a high correlation between democracy and greater levels of education and offer some explanations for this correlation.

8. Until recently this was a worldwide problem, but trends have shifted in the direction of greater flexibility in both western Europe and East Asia.

9. In considering the link between academic freedom and academic excellence, the former Soviet Union and its satellites inevitably come to mind. There certainly existed centers of scientific excellence—though not in the field of modern biology—but the humanities and social sciences suffered greatly.

10. In a study of European and US universities, Aghion et al. (2009) find a high correlation between university outputs (measured as patents obtained and international research ranking) and autonomy. For European universities, the authors measure autonomy (and also competition and governance) via a questionnaire sent to university leaders. The topics covered included control of curriculum, selection of students and professors, wage-setting practices, government approval of the university's budget, government funding, and funding from competitive research grants. For US universities, the authors use "a combination of administrative data and existing surveys."

References

Aghion, Philippe, Mathias Dewatripont, Caroline M. Hoxby, Andreu Mas-Colell, and André Sapir (2009) "The Governance and Performance of Research Universities: Evidence from Europe and the US," *NBER Working Paper* no. 14851, April.

Bloom, David E., Matthew Hartley, and Henry Rosovsky (2006) "Beyond Private Gain: The Public Benefits of Higher Education," in James J.F. Forest and Philip G. Altbach (eds.) *International Handbook of Higher Education*, vol. I, Dordrecht, Netherlands: Springer.

Chirot, Laura and Ben Wilkinson (2009) "The Intangibles of Excellence: Governance and the Quest to Build a Vietnamese Apex Research University," unpublished report, New York: New School, June.

Colclough, Christopher, Geeta Kingdon, and Harry Anthony Patrinos (2009) "The Pattern of Returns to Education and its Implications," Cambridge, UK: Research Consortium on Educational Outcomes and Poverty, Policy Brief no. 4, April. Available: http://recoup.educ.cam.ac.uk/publications/pb4.pdf .

Columbia University Press (ed.) (2001) *The Columbia Encyclopedia*, 6th ed., New York: Columbia University Press.

Friedman, Milton and Rose Friedman (1980) *Free To Choose: A Personal Statement*, New York: Harcourt Brace Jovanovich.

Glaeser, Edward L., Giacomo Ponzetto, and Andrei Shleifer (2006) "Why Does Democracy Need Education?" *National Bureau of Economic Research Working Paper*, 12128. Available: http://www.nber.org/papers/w12128.

Hanushek, Eric A. and Ludger Woessmann (2009) "Schooling, Cognitive Skills, and the Latin American Growth Puzzle," *National Bureau of Economic Research Working Paper*, 15066. Available: http://www.nber.org/papers/w15066.

Hoodbhoy, Pervez (2009) "How greed ruins academia," *Dawn*. Available: http://www.dawn.

com/2009/02/09/op.htm#2 ; reprinted in *International Higher Education*, no. 56, Summer 2009, 8–9 (accessed February 9, 2009).

Human Rights Watch (2003) *Lessons in Repression: Violations of Academic Freedom in Ethiopia*, London: Human Rights Watch.

Hussain, Faheem (2005) "The Theoretical Physics Group at Quaid-e-Azam University: Lessons for the LUMS SSE." *Science and Engineering Education, the LUMS SSE Newsletter*, June. Available: sse.lums.edu.pk/documents/opednewsletter2005Jun.pdf.

Institute for Higher Education Policy (1998) *Reaping the Benefits: Defining the Public and Private Value of Going to College*. Washington, DC: Institute for Higher Education Policy.

Labi, Aisha (2009) "Across 30 Nations, Public Spending on Higher Education Pays Off, Report Says," *Chronicle of Higher Education*, September 8. Available: http://chronicle.com/article/Across-30-Nations-Public/48323/.

Moretti, Enrico (2004) "Estimating the social return to higher education: Evidence from longitudinal and repeated cross-sectional data," *Journal of Econometrics*, 121: 175–212.

OECD (Organization for Economic Cooperation and Development) (2007) "Korea: Progress in Implementing Regulatory Reform," *Reviews of Regulatory Reform*, Paris: OECD.

—— (2009) "Education at a Glance 2009: OECD Indicators." Available: http://www.oecd.org/document/24/0,3343,en_2649_39263238_43586328_1_1_1_37455,00.html.

Palfreyman, David (2005) *Oxford Magazine*, no. 239: 19.

Psacharopoulos, George and Harry Anthony Patrinos (2004) "Returns to Investment in Education: A Further Update," *Education Economics*, 12 (2) (August): 111–34.

Putnam, Robert D. (2001) *Bowling Alone: The Collapse and Revival of American Community*, New York: Simon & Schuster.

Reynolds, P.D., W.D. Bygrave, and E. Autio (2003) *Global Entrepreneurship Monitor. 2003 Executive Report*. Babson Park, MA: Babson College; and London: London Business School. Available: http://www.gemconsortium.org/download.asp?fid = 356.

Saint, William S. (2004) "Higher education in Ethiopia: The vision and its challenges," *Journal of Higher Education in Africa*, 2 (3): 83–114.

Salmi, Jamil (2009) *The Challenge of Establishing World-Class Universities*. Washington, DC: World Bank.

Shanghai Jiao Tong University (2008) *Academic Ranking of World Universities 2008*. Available: www.arwu.org/rank2008/EN2008.htm.

Task Force on Higher Education and Society (2000) *Higher Education in Developing Countries: Peril and Promise*, Washington, DC: World Bank.

Teferra, Damtew (2009) "The World Bank's Perspective on African Higher Education," *International Higher Education*, 54 (Winter).

Times Higher Education Supplement (2008) Available: www.topuniversities.com/worlduniversity-rankings/results/2008/overall_rankings/fullrankings/.

UNESCO (2009) "Communiqué, 2009 World Conference on Higher Education: The New Dynamics of Higher Education and Research For Societal Change and Development," July 8. Paris. Available: http://www.unesco.org/fileadmin/MULTIMEDIA/HQ/ED/ED/pdf/WCHE_2009/FINAL%20COMMUNIQUE%20WCHE%202009.pdf.

UNESCO Institute for Statistics (2009) Glossary, Gross Enrolment Ratio (GER). Available: http://www.uis.unesco.org/glossary/Term.aspx?name = GROSS%20ENROLMENT%20RATIO%20(GER)&lang = en.

World Bank (2007) *Malaysia and the Knowledge Economy: Building a World-Class Higher Education System*. Report No. 40397 – MY. Washington, DC: World Bank.

—— (2008) *World Development Indicators 2008*. Washington, DC: World Bank.

—— (2009) *Accelerating Catch-up: Tertiary Education for Growth in Sub-Saharan Africa*. Washington, DC: World Bank. Available: http://siteresources.worldbank.org/INTAFRICA/Resources/e-book_ACU.pdf.

5

Mission-Driven Higher Education in Emerging Academic Systems

PEDRO ROSSO

Some universities have a specific purpose that drives them beyond the traditional mission of education, research, and innovation. They are called "mission-driven" universities and are created with religious, patriotic, social, or cultural motivations. For example, in the context of European colonialism and the growing influence of Western culture, some Buddhist and Hindu leaders decided to create universities to educate the new generations and to nurture in them pride for their own culture and adherence to their religion (Wyatt 1984; Renold 2005). In countries where Muslims were, and still are, a minority religious group, Islamic universities were established to provide an educational experience inspired by the tenets of the Islamic faith (Hardy 1972). Christians, particularly Catholics, founded universities in "mission countries" to educate the elites converted to their religion but also to contribute to the social and economic progress of those nations. In the second half of the nineteenth century, however, reacting to the progressive secularization of traditionally Catholic countries and the laicism of public universities, the Church created a significant number of universities in Europe and Latin America (National Catholic Educational Association 1973).

Mission-driven universities offer comprehensive education programs where faith is an important component and determines the institutional ethos. Thus, by promoting certain values and attitudes, they seek to contribute to a personal spiritual and moral development modeled by an ideal. In Buddhist universities, education aims at imparting the principles of the written tradition or *Dhamma*, which contains the truth taught by Buddha in his first sermon after reaching Enlightenment. The goal is to teach the students to appreciate the positive virtues that Buddha's teaching represents: kindness, honesty, chastity, truthfulness, and mental sobriety (Santina 1984). Christianity is a religion centered on the life and teachings of Jesus Christ. Therefore, Christian education tries to enrich the students' lives with the fullness of Christ's message of hope, love, and universal brotherhood (Second Vatican Council 1965). For Hinduism, education represents an important means to achieve the four aims of human life: virtue, wealth, liberation, and devotion to God (Ramaswami Aiyar et al. 1965). In the Islamic tradition, persons are answerable to Allah for all their actions, and education must help people to use all the powers granted by God to mankind in accordance with His will. Thus, persons must live with a sense of responsibility, obedience, and humility (Hilgendorf 2003).

This chapter describes the general characteristics, contributions, and challenges confronting mission-driven universities in emerging academic systems, using four examples of this type of institution. The selected universities were the following: Aligarh Muslim University, Banaras Hindu University, Chulalongkorn University, and Pontificia Universidad Católica de Chile (Pontifical Catholic University of Chile). These universities share some common features such as: (1) located in a developing or middle-income country (gross domestic product per capita less than US$12,000); (2) medium size (10,000–25,000 undergraduate students); (3) strongly research oriented; and (4) striving to become "world class." Aligarh Muslim University, Banaras Hindu University, and Chulalongkorn University are public institutions with either explicit or implicit religious identities. In addition, Chulalongkorn University has a special liaison with the Thai royal family. Pontificia Universidad Católica de Chile is a private Roman Catholic university.

Aligarh Muslim University

> [W]e aim to turn this Muslim Anglo Oriental College into a University similar to that of Oxford or Cambridge. Like the churches of Oxford and Cambridge, there will be mosques attached to each College.
>
> Sir Syed Ahmed Khan[1]

Aligarh Muslim University (AMU) is located in Aligarh, a city of the Indian state of Uttar Pradesh, in northern India. With a population of over 190 million people, Uttar Pradesh is the country's most populous state—nearly 20 percent are Muslims. The remaining population consists of Hindus, representing 70 percent of the state's total, and various minorities such as Sikhs, Buddhists, Christians, and Jains.

AMU is organized in 89 departments and 12 faculties, including a Faculty of Unani Medicine, a type of traditional medicine that is very popular in the Muslim culture. It has approximately 1,500 faculty members and about 18,000 students, nearly 14,000 are enrolled in the undergraduate programs and over 3,500 in the graduate programs. Approximately 1,350 students are doctoral candidates; in 2008, AMU granted 197 PhD degrees. AMU does not select students on the basis of creed, religion, caste, or sex and tries to offer "a highly inclusive environment, nurturing the diversity of India." However, using the privileges of an institution serving a minority group, AMU can reserve up to 50 percent of its seats in the professional courses for Muslims students. The number of foreign students is over 300 and most of them come from Africa, West Asia, and Southeast Asia. Conceived as a residential university, AMU has 15 halls of residence, providing accommodation for approximately 11,000 students (Aligarh Muslim University 2008b).

During the 1999–2009 period, the AMU output of internationally indexed scientific papers amounted to 2,153 articles that generated 8,774 citations, thus, an average of 4.08 per paper. The most productive field was engineering, with 275 papers (Thomson ISI Web of Knowledge 2009).

AMU was established in 1875, as the "Mohammedan Anglo Oriental College," one of the first institutions of higher education created in India (Aligarh Muslim University 2008a). Patterned after Oxford and Cambridge universities, the college was the first significant response of the Indian Muslims to the challenges of the era that followed the 1857 Indian War of Independence. Its founder was Sir Syed Ahmed Khan, a social reformer who felt that Indian Muslims needed modern education without compromising Islamic values (Aligarh Muslim University 2009a). In 1920, an Act of the Indian Legislative Council granted the Mohammedan Anglo Oriental College the status of a Central University and it was named "Muslim University." Since then, AMU underwent a rapid expansion, giving rise to a new class of educated Muslims. Many of them were instrumental in bringing change not only in the Muslim communities but in all of India. Many prominent Muslims and Urdu writers and scholars have graduated from AMU, including—Khan Abdul Ghaffar Khan, a great political leader and close ally of Mahatma Gandhi; Zakir Hussain, who was India's president; Mohammad Hamid Ansari, current vice president of India and former vice chancellor of AMU; Ishwari Prasad, a noted historian; Sheikh Abdullah, who served as prime minister of Kashmir; and many other distinguished political leaders, scientists, scholars, businessmen, and artists (Aligarh Muslim University 2009b).

AMU is trying to rise to the historic challenge of contributing to the transformation of India, in one of the most competitive economies in the world. For this purpose, AMU vice chancellor, P.K. Abdul Azis declared 2008 as a year for the "academic rejuvenation" of the university (Abdul Azis 2008). During this period each professor was invited to publish at least one international research paper, a goal of 500 grant proposals was set, and candidates were encouraged to complete their doctoral programs within a three-to-five-year lapse. Additionally, a High Power Committee was appointed with the task of exploring the "potential of raising the international status of the Aligarh Muslim University in the field of teaching and research" (Aligarh Muslim University 2008c). *After* analyzing many aspects related to AMU governance, organization, teaching, research, and funding, the committee made specific recommendations in matters such as recruitment, promotions, admission, internationalization, study programs, infrastructure, and alternative sources of funding. AMU authorities also created an Expert Committee with the task of preparing a master plan for the restoration of the numerous heritage buildings on the campus, many of them more than one century old.

As part of its core mission of promoting the educational and cultural development of the Muslim community, recently AMU moved its Centre for Quranic Studies to a new and larger building and gave it the status of "International Centre." Also, in order to facilitate the integration of the Islamic religious schools (madrasas) with mainstream higher education, the university established formal links with some of the more prestigious madrasas in the country, recognizing the equivalence of their degrees for admission to various courses at the university. Also, the AMU Center for Promotion of Science has organized science courses for the teachers of these religious schools (Abdul Azis 2008).

Banaras Hindu University

> [I]t is my earnest hope and prayer that this center of life and light that is coming into existence will produce students that will not only be intellectually equal to the best of their fellow students in other parts of the world, but will also live a noble life, love their country, and be loyal to the Supreme ruler.
>
> Pandit Madan Mohan Malaviya[2]

Banaras Hindu University (BHU), located in Varanasi, one of the major cities of the state of Uttar Pradesh, in northern India, is considered the largest residential university in Asia. The BHU mission is to promote the study of the Hindu *shastras* or ancient and timeless body of knowledge and of Sanskrit literature. In addition, BHU strives to educate and conduct research in all branches of arts and sciences to promote indigenous industries and develop the material resources of the country; and to offer an educational experience inspired by Hindu religious values and ethics (Banaras Hindu University 2008b).

BHU is organized in 124 departments, 14 faculties, 3 institutes (Institute of Agricultural Sciences, Institute of Medical Sciences, and Institute of Technology), 4 interdisciplinary centers, a constituent college for women, and 3 constituent schools. It also has 6 centers of advanced studies, 10 departments under the Special Assistance Program and a number of research centers. Several BHU colleges—including engineering, agriculture, law, science, and medicine—and the faculties of science, commerce, and management are considered among India's best. However, the faculties that embody its institutional mission are the Faculty of Sanskrit Vidya Dharam Vijnan, for the preservation and development of the ancient and traditional languages and knowledge, and the Faculty of Ayurveda, created to integrate India's traditional medicine with modern medicine (Banaras Hindu University 2008c).

Currently, BHU academic staff includes 1,200 professors and lecturers. BHU offers 63 undergraduate study programs, 139 postgraduate programs, and 140 PhD programs. Total enrollment is approximately 15,300 students, including over 200 foreign students. Nearly 9,000 students are enrolled in the undergraduate programs and the rest in various postgraduate or diploma/certificate programs. BHU has approximately 800 doctoral students, and it is granting an average of nearly 200 PhD degrees per year (Banaras Hindu University 2008c).

During the 1999–2009 period, BHU faculty published 4,440 original articles in internationally indexed journals. The strongest field was physics with 670 papers, followed by material science, engineering, and clinical medicine. These publications generated 23,812 citations, an average of 5.36 citations per paper. The articles related to physics generated 10.15 citations per paper (Thomson ISI Web of Knowledge 2009).

The main BHU campus is approximately 526 hectare and features many buildings in the traditional Indian architectural style, surrounded by green areas where peacocks roam free (Banaras Hindu University 2008d). In addition to faculty housing and 55 residential hostels for students, including 3 for foreigners, the campus houses a Shiva temple that it is the tallest of its kind in India. Another significant building on the campus is the Bharat Kala Bhavan Museum, housing a vast collection of paintings, Hindu and Buddhist sculptures, and other materials of great archeological importance. The main campus also has a 927-bed hospital associated with the Medical College and an air field. BHU is building a second campus, the Rajiv Gandhi South Campus, covering an area of over 1,000 hectare, at Barkachha, in the Mirzapur district (Uttar Pradesh), about 75 km away from the main campus at Varanasi (Banaras Hindu University 2008d).

Founded in 1916 by Pandit Madan Mohan Malaviya, a great political leader, BHU grew and developed to become one of India's leading universities and an emblematic one for the role it played in Indian independence. Its founder had the active cooperation of many distinguished personalities, including Annie Besant, who conceived the new institution as the "University of India." Mahatma Gandhi attended the first stone-laying ceremony and delivered a provocative and unfinished speech (Renold 2005). Madan Mohan Malaviya's dream was a university that could offer to the new generations the traditional knowledge, wisdom, and spirituality of India and all the knowledge of modern sciences and technology (Banaras Hindu University 2008a). BHU has many distinguished alumni, including scholars, high-ranking politicians and statesmen, renowned artists, and businessmen.

Presently, BHU is trying to strengthen its research capacity and connections with the private sector to make an important contribution to the progress of India and its transformation into a knowledge-based economy (Banaras Hindu University 2008c).

Chulalongkorn University

> The university will serve not merely as a commemorative monument to the glory of H.M. King Chulalongkorn, our country's most beloved monarch, but also as one enduring educational institution for our country.
> King Vajiravudh[3]

Chulalongkorn University (CU) is located in Bangkok, Thailand. Regarded as the country's best and most selective research university, CU offers a large number of undergraduate programs. Its faculty staff includes nearly 3,500 professors and lecturers, and student enrollment is over 36,000 (approximately 22,100 undergraduate). Foreign students are close to 420, most of them enrolled in graduate programs. During 2007/2008, CU granted 275 doctoral degrees (QS Top Universities 2008). Over the last 10 years (1999–2009), the number of publications of its faculties numbered 4,959, with an average number of citations per paper of 5.67. CU's most productive area was chemistry, with 1,219 papers, followed by clinical medicine and plant and animal science (Thomson ISI Web of Knowledge 2009).

The university is organized in 20 faculties and schools, including the Sasin Business School, created with the active support of the Kellogg School of Management and the Wharton Business School, both from the United States (Chulalongkorn University 2008a).

CU campus is approximately 210 hectare, located in a prime area of downtown Bangkok. In its beautiful grounds, a variety of modern buildings contrast with others built in the traditional Thai architectural style. Besides the schools, faculties, and the main administration, the CU campus houses several museums, art centers, and a Dhamma Center—a place of worship where various religious ceremonies are performed. The Dhamma Center also offers daily lectures on Buddhism and coordinates a Moral Standard Awareness Program that promotes CU credo of professional ethics: "Knowledge with morality" (Chulalongkorn University 2008a).

Established in 1917, the first university created in the country, CU was named after King Chulalongkorn (Rama V), who decades earlier envisioned the possibility of creating an institution of higher education as an answer to the growing Western presence in Southeast Asia (Chulalongkorn University 2008b). The king founded the Royal Pages School, which later became Chulalongkorn University. Because of its regal origins, CU has a tradition of identity and closeness with the Thai royal family. In turn, the kings and other royal family members have actively supported the university. For many decades, graduation ceremonies were headed by the king himself, who in many occasions handed out the diplomas (Chulalongkorn University 2008b) Currently, the Royal Princess Maha Chakri Sirindhorn, who graduated from CU, performs some of these royal duties.

CU's mission is to produce graduates of "international caliber," with high ethical standards and leadership capabilities, create knowledge that benefits the Thai society, and preserve the country's arts and culture, including the country's religion. In the words of its president, Pirom Kamolratanakul, CU wants to be a "pillar of the kingdom," making a significant contribution to Thailand's social, economic and political progress (Kamolratanakul 2008). This mission implies a commitment to "work for society" and to wear proudly the university uniform, which was given by the founding king. In 2009, CU was ranked 138th in the world university ranking prepared by the London *Times Higher Education Supplement* (QS Top Universities 2009). This is the best standing for a Thai university. However, CU considers that it has many opportunities to improve and wants to focus these efforts on social sciences and engineering.

Pontificia Universidad Católica De Chile

> [W]e will consider that our efforts were deserving if Heaven blesses them, so that the Catholic University might contribute to increase the intellectual capital needed by our country.
>
> Monsignor Joaquín Larraín Gandarillas[4]

Pontificia Universidad Católica de Chile (UC) is located in Santiago de Chile. Pontifical universities are under the authority of the local Roman Catholic bishop, who serves as its chancellor (or great chancellor), and, ultimately, of the Holy See.

UC has 18 faculties, including theology, and it is organized in departments, institutes, and professional schools. In 2009, the colleges of arts and humanities, social sciences, and natural sciences and mathematics opened their doors. This was an important innovation for the Chilean higher education system, since college education was not available in the country (Pontificia Universidad Católica de Chile 2008).

UC has approximately 1,400 full time and 1,300 part time academics. Most members of the academic staff hold doctoral degrees granted by leading United States and European universities. Total student enrollment is about 23,000. Undergraduate students represent nearly 17,200, including 1,394 international exchange students (mostly coming from the United States and western Europe). Students enrolled in graduate programs are approximately 5,800, including 600 international students (QS Top Universities 2008). UC offers 29 doctoral programs, with a rapidly expanding total enrollment of nearly 800 candidates. In academic year 2008, 83 PhD degrees were granted. This represented a twofold increase with respect to the year 2000.

Students are selected and admitted through a national selection system based on school performance and the scores obtained by the candidates in a university entrance test. UC shares this selection system with a group of 24 public and private universities belonging to a Council of Rectors. Over the last 20 years, UC has recruited the very top candidates. For example, in the 2009 admission process, 55 percent of the top 1,000 candidates applied to UC—a staggering figure, considering that Chile has 59 universities.

During the 1999–2009 period, UC faculties published 5,758 internationally indexed papers, which generated 56,051 citations or an average of 9.73

citations per paper. The most productive field was clinical medicine, with 1,356 publications, followed by space science and chemistry. UC publications in the space science field average 25.23 citations per paper, an outstanding figure for a university located in a developing context (Thomson ISI Web of Knowledge 2009).

UC was founded by the Archbishop of Santiago in 1888, and it is the second-oldest higher education institution in the country. The Church's decision to create a Catholic University was a reaction to the government's explicit will of becoming the exclusive provider of education. Monsignor Joaquín Larraín Gandarillas, a prominent educator and humanist, was appointed as its first rector (Krebs, Muñoz, and Valdiviesco 1994).

UC's early years were extremely difficult ones. Plagued by financial and administrative problems, it hardly survived a suspicious fire, which shortly after the university's opening destroyed its facilities. Nevertheless, UC was able to overcome the initial difficulties and began to develop. In 1923, Monsignor Carlos Casanueva, its fifth rector, obtained financial help from the state. The state subsidies have been maintained ever since. In 1930, Pope Pius XI granted UC the honor of becoming a "Pontifical University." In 1967, following a period of student unrest and turmoil over academic reforms, the chancellor appointed a layman as rector (Krebs, Muñoz, and Valdiviesco 1994). All subsequent rectors have also been laymen.

The university's central administration, four faculties, and a 520-bed teaching hospital occupy a 1.8-hectare, densely built campus, dating from 1906, located in downtown Santiago. UC's second and largest campus, of approximately 38 hectare, is located 6 km away from downtown and has 12 faculties and a large outpatient health care facility. Finally, the two other campuses are used by the Faculty of Architecture and the Faculty of Arts, respectively.

UC's specific mission implies announcement and service. Announcement refers to the proclamation of the Gospel and bearing testimony of its Catholic nature. Consequently, following the Church's guidelines, UC tries its best to make sure that "Catholic ideals, attitudes and principles penetrate and inform university activities" (John Paul II 1990). The service component of its mission implies an institutional commitment to use knowledge for the good of society. Thus, UC defines its "third mission" as an active contribution to the social, economic, and cultural progress of Chile. Presently, UC participates in several projects in the fields of health care, low-income housing, and education of disadvantaged children, which have had a positive impact on public policies. Also, trying to contribute to the transformation of Chile in a knowledge-based economy, with the help of government's grants and the partnership of the industry, UC established a foundation that supports research on the sustainable use of natural resources and the creation of new companies, two successful business incubators, three technological consortia, and is helping small companies to increase their productivity.

In the 2009 world university ranking prepared by the London *Times*, UC was ranked 277, the third-best-ranked institution in Latin America (QS Top Universities 2009).

Special Challenges Faced by Mission-Driven Universities

Philip G. Altbach (2003) has pointed out that a world-class university status implies the capacity to excel in research, to have adequate facilities, academic freedom, an atmosphere of intellectual excitement, and a significant measure of internal self-governance. In addition, funding must be available to support research and teaching along with the other functions of the university. All these aspects represent challenges that mission-driven universities must face, but additionally there are some challenges inherent to their nature and others that mostly arise for their location in developing contexts.

Preserving the Original Identity

For religious universities, the progressive secularization of societies is an unavoidable fact. Secularization is a complex social phenomenon fostered by social diversity, especially in multiracial and multiethnic societies, where the separation of the state from the established religions becomes a necessary fact. It also reflects cultural evolution driven by an increasing number of nonbelievers and the acceptance of pluralism as a positive social value (Modak-Truran 2007). In Europe religion is slowly fading from the public realm, and many, self-defined, progressive people consider a religious institution "out of touch" with reality and the prevailing culture. Most academic communities feel that "modernity" and "progress" mean a scholarship without religious frameworks. The epitome of this attitude was the staunch opposition to the visit of Pope Benedict XVI to a Roman public university, in 2008 (*New York Times* 2008). Citing out of context a phrase of the pope's, the professors and students that staged the protest claimed that Pope Benedict XVI had defended the Inquisition's condemnation of Galileo.

In societies where religious feelings are abating, identity preservation is becoming increasingly difficult for religious mission-driven universities. The fate of some of the initially Protestant colleges and universities in the United States is often quoted as an example of how easily a mission-driven institution can abandon its original aim (Marsden 1994). Most of them had a strong Christian character, but in the first decades of the twentieth century they became totally secularized. One of the most eloquent cases is Harvard University, founded "for the provision of a learned ministry," whose original motto was *Christo et Ecclesiae*. Other institutions that underwent a similar evolution include Yale, Princeton, Chicago, Stanford, Duke, and Boston University. Most of them had clergymen presidents and the academic staff was recruited among

Christian believers. The curricula included faith-related subjects and students regularly attended religious services (Marsden 1994). Despite these century-old traditions, in the lapse of one generation most of those institutions lost their religious identity.

In developing countries, progressive secularization is also occurring, but the situation is not comparable to that of the Northern Hemisphere (Riesebrodt 2000). In Latin America, a traditionally Catholic region, the Church is suffering from dwindling vocations to priesthood and declining church attendance, but the vast majority of the people still define themselves as Catholics or at least as Christians (Hefner 1998). In fact, in some Latin American countries, including Brazil and Central America, a significant number of disaffected Catholics have joined other Christian denominations, thus leaving the Roman Catholic Church but maintaining basic Christian beliefs (Hefner 1998).

In Buddhist, Hindu, and Islamic societies, secularization is also taking place, but at a slower rate than in the Western countries. Thus, presently it does not pose a serious threat to the identity of religious mission-driven universities. Nevertheless, supporters of secularization have questioned what they consider unconstitutional privileges granted to some of them. For example, in 2006 a high court ruling deprived AMU of its minority privileges on constitutional grounds. This elicited a legal and political battle that finally was resolved by a Supreme Court ruling restoring the minority character of AMU (Anonymous 2006). A similar situation affected BHU in 1995, when the Banaras Hindu University (Amendment) Bill was discussed in the Indian Parliament. There was near unanimity concerning the desirability of modifying the university's present name on grounds that the communal element in its name was contrary to the principle of secularism. Several members suggested that the university should be named after its founder. Finally, the initiative was dismissed due to student unrest and opposition from other political forces (Anonymous 1966). On the other hand, in some mission-driven universities the hostility perceived against them by supporters of secularization has caused reactions. Particularly in Islamic institutions, more orthodox groups have taken a militant stance and reached greater visibility. In Indian universities there are also groups actively promoting a Hinduism "revival" (Hefner 1998).

Catholicism is the only organized religion that has officially expressed concern over the identity of its institutions of higher education. In 1990, during the Pontificate of John Paul II, the Church promulgated the Apostolic Constitution *Ex Corde Ecclesiae* (From the Heart of the Church) containing guidelines for Catholic colleges and universities and also norms aimed at preserving their identities (John Paul II 1990). In this constitution, the pope defined the mission of Catholic universities and encouraged them to preserve their identity and links with the Church. Despite stirring some debate related to academic freedom, at least in a few countries, *Ex Corde Ecclesiae* was well received by Catholic universities and colleges worldwide. Moreover, the Holy See's concern and guidance seem to be playing an important role in preserving the identity of many Catholic universities, particularly in the United States. Catholic institutions have been seen as resisting the secularizing trend because of the strength of their theological and moral tradition and the fact that Catholic intellectual life still maintains an outsider quality resisting complete assimilation (on issues such as abortion, euthanasia, war, social justice, and family planning) (Appleyard 1996). In addition, pastoral activities oriented to students and faculty's spiritual development and communitarian participation in worshipping are still an important part of life in most Catholic universities.

Faith and Science

Many people, including reputed scholars, believe that faith and science are separated by an unbridgeable chasm. However, from a religious perspective there is no conflict between faith and science. All the monotheistic religions of the world coincide in this aspect, and the reasons are well explained in the official Catechism of the Roman Catholic Church. With respect to this matter the Catechism states the following:

> Though faith is above reason, there can never be any real discrepancy between faith and reason. Since the same God who reveals mysteries and infuses faith has bestowed the light of reason on the human mind, God cannot deny himself, nor can truth ever contradict truth. Consequently, methodical research in all branches of knowledge, provided it is carried out in a truly scientific manner and does not override moral laws, can never conflict with the faith, because the things of the world and the things of faith derive from the same God. The humble and persevering investigator of the secrets of nature is being led, as it were, by the hand of God in spite of himself, for it is God, the conserver of all things, who made them what they are.
>
> (Catechism of the Church 1992).

As related in the *Kesaputtiya Sutra*, Buddha told the Kalamas, habitants of ancient Kesaputta, not to accept information, out of reverence, for a teacher or a given authority, or because it is written down; but to verify and test what has been heard, in the light of practical experience. Evidently, these teachings encourage verification through experience, which is a basic scientific attitude (Santina 1984).

From the perspective of *Bhagavad Gita*, one of the most important books of Hinduism, modern science is only a highly detailed analysis of the physical world. Consequently, its findings cannot conflict with the tenets of faith. On the other hand, science lacks a metaphysical perspective and does not investigate spiritual dimensions such as the soul or God himself. Instead, the *Gita* describes the oneness of a physical and a spiritual reality that is ultimately inseparable. Thus, from a Hindu perspective, modern science is a valid, but incomplete, path toward fully understanding reality (Ravindra 2002).

The view of Islam is somewhat similar, and the majority of faithful Muslims, including distinguished scientists, do not perceive contradictions between revelation and science. Furthermore, Muslim scholars have encouraged a re-interpretation of certain passages of the Quran, while stressing the fact that it contains scientifically validated information concerning astronomy, human reproduction, and other nature's phenomena discovered by empirical science only over the last century (Ahmad 2002).

Nevertheless, the interpretation of some of the sacred books by different religious schools of thought has motivated scientific controversy. For example, some Protestant denominations find deep contradictions between the Book of Genesis, if literally interpreted, and scientific cosmology, including the theory of evolution. Consequently, some higher education institutions in the United States, such as Liberty University and Temple Baptist College, teach the scientific theories alongside the biblical texts. There are Islamic schools that perceive similar, apparently insurmountable, differences between the Quran texts on creation and the scientific perspective on the origins of the universe and mankind. Something similar occurs in Hinduism, where the sacred Puranas describe a cosmology, which holds a geocentric view of the universe, with the sun located closer to the earth than the moon. However, most Hindu schools consider that Vedas cannot be interpreted literally, since they were only inspired by God to men conditioned by their time and culture.

Religions and science often clash over ethical issues. One conflict involves the use of human embryos as a source of biological materials. Buddhism, Hinduism, Catholicism, and some Christian denominations share the belief that human life is sacred from the moment of conception and that every embryo should be protected and given the opportunity to develop. On the other hand, there are Christian churches, such as the American Presbyterian Church, that consider research in human embryos acceptable if the goals cannot be reached in any other manner. Other Protestant and Evangelical denominations consider that research should be limited to embryos that cannot be used for reproductive purposes, and only within a 15-day lapse from fertilization. Based on the Quran texts relative to early human life, the Islamic view is that human embryos can be used for research and therapeutic purposes from conception up to the 40th day of development.

Because of the beliefs and moral convictions previously described, research in human embryos is banned in most religious mission-driven institutions. Additionally, in Catholic institutions in vitro fertilization, as well as other medical procedures involving human gametes and embryos, is not performed.

Managing and Financing Mission-Driven Universities

The decisive element that distinguishes good universities from world-class universities is their capacity to do relevant research (Altbach 2007). Thus, all mission-driven universities striving to become world class face only one goal: to excel in the quality and volume of their contributions to knowledge. Unfortunately, scientific research is very expensive. Therefore, the major challenges confronting the leadership of mission-driven universities located in developing countries are attracting suitable faculties and financing their research activities.

In developing contexts, finding essential funds to support competitive research can be an impossible task. AMU is a good example of this continuous struggle. Its total income in fiscal year 2007/2008 was approximately US$50 million (M.A. Khan, personal communication, 2008), a quantity that represents a small fraction of the research budget of some of the world's top universities.

BHU faces similar constraints and uncertainties. During fiscal year 2005/2006 its total budget was less than US$35 million (Banaras Hindu University 2008c). Lack of adequate financing also hampers BHU's possibility of recruiting talented faculty on a large scale and offering them competitive salaries and adequate infrastructure. To deal with the problem of inadequate funding, one of BHU's alternatives is to maximize the possibility to generate additional income through patenting, spin-offs, and industry-sponsored research projects. Some faculties and institutes have established already strong links with industries, and during the 2000–2005 period the additional income generated by these joint projects grew tenfold. However, total revenues from this source are still too small to make a difference (Banaras Hindu University 2008c).

In a different context and despite having a significant endowment, CU is also facing considerable financial limitations to improve its research capacity. Although Thailand's economy has been growing steadily, the country still has a gross domestic product per capita under US$10,000. Thus, it ranks midway in affluence in Southeast Asia, after Singapore, Brunei, and Malaysia. In addition, Thais are still trying to leave behind political turbulence and instability. The government has defined higher education as a national priority and reform of the system is underway. To transform Thailand into a knowledge-based society, drastic changes are being introduced in higher education governance, administration and funding (Ministry of Education of Thailand 2004). The objective is to get higher quality, efficiency, and effectiveness. The reform is providing universities with more administrative autonomy and, at the same time, closer supervision and assessment of their performance (Schiller and Liefner 2007).

Another challenge for CU and other Thai research universities is faculty salaries. Current ones are not competitive with those of the private sector and private universities (Bovornsiri 2006). Consequently, to improve their income many faculty members, including active researchers, seek complementary income through additional work off campus or through a greater teaching load. Obviously, this has a negative effect on scientific productivity and quality.

UC faces the same problems as its Thai peer. Despite Chile's accomplishments in free trade and export sales, total investment in higher education is only 0.3 percent of gross domestic product. Chile also has old-fashioned policies to promote scientific research and innovation. Presently, only 0.7 percent of its gross domestic product is devoted to research and development initiatives, most of the funds coming from the public sector. Over the last 10 years, despite official announcements that the country will increase research and development spending, progress has been slow and disorganized. In 2008, UC received approximately US$10 million in competitive research funds and fellowships for graduate students. This amount, mostly from government agencies, was complemented with approximately US$25 million, from its own resources, to cover indirect costs and faculty salaries. In Chile the National Science Fund does not cover the proportion of the investigators' salaries devoted to the project and does not allow overhead costs over 17 percent of direct costs.

Administrative Autonomy and Governance

Most universities with funding problems suffer permanent tensions and faculty rivalries over much-needed resources and budget priorities. Needless to say, this has a devastating impact on human relations, governance, and management. Some of the mission-driven universities included in the present chapter are familiar with these types of problems. For example, in 2007, AMU suffered the most turbulent and trying period in its history, including a student riot where the vice chancellor's home was burnt and other university property destroyed and looted. The crisis was attributed to a variety of disrupting facts, including mismanagement, political vendettas, overcrowding of the residence halls, and bitter feuds between professors (Rediffnews.com 2007).

BHU also must resolve several internal problems incongruous with its aspiration to a world-class status. The opportunities to improve, listed in its strategic planning report, include: an "ossified system of administration, management and recruitment of staff" (Banaras Hindu University 2008c). Other problems are related to weaknesses apparently deeply engrained in its institutional culture. However, many of its governance and administrative problems can be linked to the managerial style, bureaucracy, and political priorities of the Indian government. The chancellor, vice chancellor and other BHU key administrative leaders are either directly or indirectly appointed by the president of India (Banaras Hindu University 2008e). Consequently, their standing with the government officials in charge of higher education, particularly the Human Resource Development Ministry, is crucial for their appointment and permanence in office. This complex reality is reflected by the fact that BHU has had four vice chancellors in 10 years, certainly a disruptive leadership turnover for any university.

CU is establishing a greater degree of administrative and funding autonomy from the state, a process that its leadership describes as debureaucratization, not privatization. In Thailand, an autonomous university has the status of a government agency that is neither within the government bureaucracy nor a state enterprize (Bovornsiri 2006). The University Council can formulate rules and regulations for personnel administration, as well as stipulating staff welfare and benefits. With respect to budgeting and assets, the government provides a block grant that is considered as the university's own income. An autonomous university has its own budget systems, accounting, finance, and asset management. The State Audit Office will audit the accounts and follow up on the budget expenditures. In cases where the income generated is not sufficient to sustain the university's operations and funds cannot be procured from other sources, the government will allocate additional funds from the national budget. Aside from the state-allocated budgets, the income generated from other sources can be utilized to strengthen academic capacity. CU became an autonomous institution in 2007 and it is still in the process of implementing the various administrative and cultural changes brought about by the change of status.

UC has been recognized as an example of stable leaderships and managerial capacity (Clark 2004). Nevertheless, its current organizational structure is becoming obsolete, particularly its "Higher Council." This body seats all the deans, four representatives of the academic staff elected by their peers, and two students, are also elected by their peers. Presided over by the rector, this council approves all major academic and budgetary decisions with the votes of the deans and the academic staff representatives. Created more than 30 years ago, the council replaced a body that comprised deans, professors, administrative officials, and students. Despite the fact that, so far, no serious tensions have risen between the rector and the council, it appears self-evident that there is a conflict of interests inherent in the fact that deans approve a general budget that includes their own faculties' budgets. Also, academic communities tend to be self-centered and prone to "intellectual inbreeding." For these reasons if UC wants to increase the pace of its progress toward a world-class status, it should reorganize its governance structure and create a governing body with functions similar to those of a board of trustees.

Conclusion

In the international system of higher education, where the most salient characteristic is diversity, mission-driven universities occupy an undisputed niche. Few of them are research-oriented institutions and, in developing countries, even fewer have reached international recognition. Thus, the universities included in the present chapter are outstanding exceptions. Their main handicap is lack of adequate funding due to the status of the national economies and the rather low priority that higher education and science have in most developing and middle-income countries. Governance represents an additional challenge since most of them are still mired in the traditional paradigms of academic decision making.

What is remarkable in the mission-driven universities analyzed here is their ideals and commitment to the progress of their respective societies. All of them have a strong vocation for public service. This attitude is best reflected by the number and size of their outreach programs relative to their financial means. The same can be said about their efforts to promote the traditional culture of their nations. This spirit of service that stems from their original missions is being rekindled to face the challenge of transforming their countries into knowledge-based economies. The desire to reach this goal is their main motivation to become world-class institutions, certainly an elusive task unless some of their present problems are resolved.

Mission-driven universities face the additional challenge of preserving their identity. The success that they might have in this field will depend on the convictions and commitment of their leaderships and academic staffs. If either one weakens, the risk of losing their original identity would be very high. Thus, through adequate recruitment policies they must try to make sure that a "critical mass" of their faculties identifies with the original mission. This is a crucial aspect, since if the majority of the academic staff does not share a common faith or philosophical conviction, the educational environment of the university will become undifferentiated with respect to other institutions. In those circumstances, commitment to the original mission will become pure rhetoric.

But besides the religious and/or ideological alignment of their faculty, if mission-driven universities, especially the religious ones or those committed to national objectives, want to fulfill their founders' dreams, they must be socially relevant. This is the only element that can validate their proposition of certain values or their stance with respect to social, cultural, or ethical issues. If mission-driven universities want to be heard by society when they speak from the perspective of their deepest convictions, they must do so with the intellectual authority that only knowledge and academic excellence can provide.

Notes

1. Founder of Mohammedan Anglo Oriental College, later Aligarh Muslim University (Aligarh Muslim University 2008a).
2. Founder of Banaras Hindu University (Banaras Hindu University 2008a).
3. Founder of Chulalongkorn University (Chulalongkorn University 2008b).
4. First Rector of Pontificia Universidad Católica de Chile (Bravo 1992).

References

Abdul Azis, P.K. (2008) Address to the 58th Annual Convocation, *AMU News* Web site. Available: http://www.amu.ac.in/newamu/amunews.htm.
Ahmad, I. (2002) "The rise and fall of Islamic science: the calendar as a case study," presented at the conference on "Faith and Reason: Convergence and Complementarity," at al-Akhawayn University, Ifrane, Morocco, June 3. Available: http://www.minaret.org/ifrane.pdf.
Aligarh Muslim University (2008a) *Our Founder*. Available: http://www.amu.ac.in/index.asp.
—— (2008b) Available: http://www.amu.ac.in/index.asp.
—— (2008c) "Potential of raising the international status of the Aligarh Muslim University," AMU High Power Committee. Available: http://www.amu.ac.in/indexmain.asp?linkid = 69.
—— (2009a) *Sir Syed*. Available: http://www.amu.ac.in/index2.asp?sublinkid = 222.
—— (2009b) *Alumni of Aligarh Muslim University*. Available: http://en.wikipedia.org/wiki/Aligarh_Muslim_University.
Altbach, P.G. (2003) "The Costs and Benefits of World-Class Universities," *International Higher Education* no. 33, Fall, 5–9.
—— (2007) "Empires of knowledge and development," In P.G. Altbach and J. Balán (eds.) *World Class Worldwide*, Baltimore, MD: Johns Hopkins Univ. Press.
Anonymous (1966) "Disturbances at the Banaras Hindu University," *Minerva* 4 (3): 429–33.
—— (2006) "Minority for now. A reprieve for AMU," in, *The Tribune*, April 26. Available: http://www.tribuneindia.com/2006/20060426/edit.htm.
Appleyard, J.A., S.J. (1996) "The secularization of the modern American university," *International Higher Education* no. 4, Spring, 20–21.
Banaras Hindu University (2008a) *Founder's message*. Available: http://www.bhu.ac.in/.
—— (2008b) Objectives of the University. Available: http://www.bhu.ac.in/banaras.html.
—— (2008c) *Challenges & opportunities 2016*. Available: http://www.bhu.ac.in/VISIONdocument/Visionpar2.pdf.
—— (2008d) *BHU Home Page*. Available: http://www.bhu.ac.in/.
—— (2008e) *The Banaras Hindu University Act N° XVI of 1915*. Available: http://www.bhu.ac.in/bhuact/index.html.
Bovornsiri, V. (2006) "Thailand," in, *Higher Education in South East Asia*, Bangkok, Thailand: UNESCO Bangkok.
Bravo, B.L. (1992) *La Universidad en la Historia de Chile*, Santiago, Chile: Pehuén Editores.
Catechism of the Church (1992) *Faith and science,* chapter III, article 159.
Chulalongkorn University (2008a) Available: http://www.chula.ac.th/cuweb_en/.
—— (2008b) *A Brief History of Chulalongkorn University*. Available: http://www.chula.ac.th/chula/en/about/brief_en.html.
Clark, B.R. (2004) "The Catholic University in Chile. Lessons from South America," in *Sustaining Change in Universities*, Maidenhead, UK: Open Univ.
Hardy, P. (1972) *Muslims of British India,* Cambridge: Cambridge Univ. Press.
Hefner, R.W. (1998) "Multiple modernities: Christianity, Islam, and Hinduism in a globalizing age," *Annual Review of Anthropology*, 27: 83–104.
Hilgendorf, E. (2003) "Islamic education: History and tendency," *Peabody Journal of Education*, 78 (2): 63–75.
John Paul II. (1990) *Ex Corde Ecclesiae*. Apostolic Constitution on Catholic Universities.
Kamolratanakul, P. (2008) "Interview in *Bangkok Post*," October 27, 2008. Available: http://www.bangkokpost.com/271008_Business/27Oct2008_biz 34.php.
Krebs, R., M. Muñoz, and P. Valdiviesco (1994) *Historia de la Pontificia Universidad Católica de Chile*, Santiago, Chile: Ediciones Universidad Católica de Chile.
Marsden, G.M. (1994) *The Soul of the American University: From Protestant Establishment to Established Nonbelief.* Oxford: Oxford Univ. Press.
Ministry of Education of Thailand (2004) "Strategies and Roadmap for Higher Education Reform in Thailand." Office the Education Council. Available: http:// www.ksu.edu.sa/sites/KSUArabic/Strategy/Documents /strategy_Thailand_frum%202.pdf.
Modak-Truran, M.C. (2007) "Secularization, legal indeterminacy, and Habermas's discourse theory of law," *Florida State University Law Review* 35: 73–118.
National Catholic Educational Association (1973) "The Catholic University in the modern world," *College Newsletter*, 35 (3): 1–10.
New York Times (2008) "Pope cancels speech after protest at university," January 16.

Pontificia Universidad Católica de Chile (2008) *Home page.* Available: http://www.uc.cl/.

QS Top Universities (2008) *Chulalongkorn University.* Available: http://www.topuniversities.com/schools/data/school_profile/default/chulalongkornuniversity.

—— (2009) *Pontificia Universidad Católica de Chile.* Available: http://www.topuniversities.com/schools/data/school_profile/default/pontificiauniversidadcatolicadechile.

Ramaswami Aiyar, C.P., D. Nalinaksha, A.R. Wadia, M. Mujeeb, D. Pal, and Jerome D'Souza, S.J. (1965) "An introduction to Hinduism," *Gazeteer of India,* vol. 1, *Country and People,* New Delhi: Publications Division, Government of India.

Ravindra, R. (2002) "Science and the sacred," in *Science and the Sacred: Eternal Wisdom in a Changing World,* Wheaton, IL: Theosophical Publishing House.

Rediffnews.com (2007) *AMU to open, but problems remain.* Available: http://www.rediff.com/news/2007/nov/02amu.htm.

Renold, L. (2005) *A Hindu Education: Early Years of the Banaras Hindu University,* Oxford: Oxford Univ. Press.

Riesebrodt, M. (2000) "Secularization and the global resurgence of religion," presented at the Comparative Social Analysis Workshop University of California. Available: http://www.ssc-net.ucla.edu/soc/groups/ccsa/riesebrodt.pdf.

Santina, P.D. (1984) *Fundamentals of Buddhism,* Tullera, Australia: Buddha Dharma Education Association.

Schiller, D. and, I. Liefner (2007) "Higher education funding reform and university–industry links in developing countries: The case of Thailand," *Higher Education,* 54 (4): 543–56.

Second Vatican Council (1965) *Gravissimum Educationis.* Declaration on Christian Education.

Thomson ISI Web of Knowledge (2009) *Essential science indicators.* Available: http://search.thomsonreuters.com/search?q = Essential+Science +Indicators.

Wyatt, D. (1984) *Thailand: A Short History,* New Haven, CT: Yale Univ. Press.

6

Higher Education's Landscape of Internationalization*

PHILIP G. ALTBACH AND JANE KNIGHT

The international activities of universities have dramatically expanded in volume, scope, and complexity over the past two decades. This chapter examines the nature of internationalization, the motivations for it, and the international activities of universities worldwide. Internationalization, especially commercial cross-border education, is big business, earning considerable income for universities and other providers. International programs offer opportunities for students to study abroad and to learn about other cultures. International initiatives also provide access to higher education in some countries where local institutions cannot meet the demand for access.

While we provide a broad analysis here, we are cognizant that developing countries face special realities in the globalized higher education environment. Typically, developing countries must adjust to conditions created by the powerful academic institutions and systems of Europe and North America. International academic relations, like those relating to trade, the military, or diplomacy, tend to favor the powerful. Our goal here is to describe and analyze a reality that may place developing countries at some disadvantage, but which is nonetheless necessary for all to understand. As Thomas Friedman pointed out, the world may be flat, but it also has hills and valleys that may create difficulties for some (Friedman 2006).

International initiatives range from traditional study-abroad programs, branch campuses in other countries, franchised foreign academic programs or degrees, independent institutions based on foreign academic models in specific countries, and other models. Other approaches stress upgrading the international perspectives and skills of students on campus, enhancing foreign-language programs, and providing cross-cultural understanding. In this chapter, we are concerned with all of these aspects of internationalization—especially the cross-border provision of higher education programs and the commercialization of international higher education.

---

* An earlier version of this chapter appeared in Philip G. Altbach, *Tradition and Transition: The International Imperative in Higher Education.* Chestnut Hill, MA: Boston College Center for International Higher Education.

Globalization is often confused with internationalization (Altbach 2007). For our purposes, globalization means the economic, political, societal, and other forces that are pushing twenty-first-century higher education toward greater international involvement. These factors include the growing integration of research, the use of English as the lingua franca for scientific communication, the growing international labor market for scholars and scientists, and, especially, all aspects of information technology (IT). IT facilitates communication, permits efficient storage, selection, and dissemination of knowledge at all levels, and makes it possible to offer academic programs of all kinds through e-learning. The emergence of multinational publishing, technology, and communications firms has to some extent been exacerbated by the current wave of globalization.

Global capital has become interested in higher education and knowledge industries generally and has, for the first time, invested heavily in various aspects of education and training worldwide. The emergence of the "knowledge society," the rise of the service sector, and the dependence of many societies on knowledge products and highly educated personnel for economic growth are new phenomena (Castells 2000; Friedman 2006; Odin and Mancias 2004). These are some of the elements of globalization—the inevitable forces that are shaping the world of the twenty-first century—that underlie much of our analysis.

We will outline specific programs, institutions, innovations, and practices in higher education that academic institutions and systems, other organizations involved in the academic enterprise, and for that matter individuals create to cope with globalization and to reap benefits from this new environment. While globalization is a largely unalterable element of contemporary society, there are many choices involving internationalization.

Just as globalization has tended to concentrate wealth, knowledge, and power in the hands of those already possessing these elements, international academic mobility has favored already well-developed education systems and institutions. Significant elements of inequality exist in the expanding world of international higher education. Initiatives come largely from the North and are focused on the South. Ownership of knowledge, knowledge products, information technology infrastructure, and the like is almost exclusively in the hands of Northern institutions, corporations, and interests. Student flows tend to move from South to North. Other initiatives and programs flow mainly from North to South, although we are seeing increasing numbers of South to South activities, especially in Asia and Africa. While internationalization is much more than a one-way street and serves important needs in the developing world, it is largely controlled by the North.

We will stress the cross-border flows of students, academic personnel, and programs—including the flows of students from one country to another, the growing international market for academic and scientific personnel, curricular internationalization, cross-border academic programs and institutions, the growing influence of the new for-profit higher education sector in internationalization, and other trends. We will not focus on one key aspect of higher education—e-learning or the use of IT to deliver academic programs across borders. E-learning is, without question, one of the fastest-growing elements of internationalization and thus deserves a separate analysis.

The Free-Trade Context

International academic mobility is stimulated and facilitated by the contemporary stress on free trade. The World Trade Organization (WTO) exemplifies this trend and has considerable relevance for our analysis. The WTO is currently negotiating the General Agreement on Trade in Services (GATS). GATS will, when it is fully implemented and agreed to by WTO member countries, provide the parameters for international trade in education and other service-related industries. While this chapter will not discuss GATS and its implications in detail, it is worth noting the major targets of GATS because they correspond to many of the central themes of international mobility of higher education. The GATS framework includes the following:

> Mode 1: *cross-border supply.* This factor may include distance education (e-learning), franchising of courses or degrees, and other arrangements. This mode does not necessarily require the physical movement of the consumer or provider.
> Mode 2: *consumption abroad.* The consumer moves to the country of the provider. This element includes traditional student mobility from one country to another.
> Mode 3: *commercial presence.* The service provider establishes facilities in another country to provide the service. This phenomenon includes branch campuses and joint ventures with local institutions.
> Mode 4: *presence of natural persons.* This includes persons traveling to another country on a temporary basis to provide educational services, including professors, researchers, and others (OECD 2004, 35; National Education Association 2004).

We mention GATS and the WTO here because they are catalysts for current thinking about international higher education and because GATS will play a significant direct role in providing an international regulatory framework that encourages trade in education services. At present, GATS remains under negotiation, and individual countries have considerable leeway concerning what aspects of GATS they agree to in the formal negotiations.

The free-trade context is influenced by current thinking about higher education as a commodity to be freely traded internationally and the idea that higher education is a private good rather than a public responsibility. These powerful contemporary ideas place higher education much in the domain of the market and promote the view that commercial forces have a legitimate or even a dominant place in higher education (Kirp 2003; Altbach 2002).

The Motivations and Sources of Internationalization

There are many reasons for academic internationalization worldwide. By understanding the most important stimuli for internationalization, it will be possible to analyze the basic nature of the phenomenon.

Profits

Earning money is an important motivation for some internationalization projects. This aspect without exception involves the for-profit sector, as well as some traditional nonprofit universities that have sought to solve their financial problems by earning income from international initiatives. For-profit higher education providers such as Laureate Education (formerly Sylvan Learning Systems), Kaplan, Inc., the Apollo Group (the parent company of the University of Phoenix, now the largest private university in the United States), and others have entered the international market by establishing new institutions in other countries, purchasing existing institutions, and entering into partnerships with firms or educational institutions in other countries. Local private universities, some of them in the for-profit sector, with overseas links have also been started in many countries. Many of these institutions use an American, British, German, or other foreign curriculum, and many teach in English. They are in some cases accredited in other countries.

Traditional nonprofit universities have also entered the international market. According to a recent survey, the main motivations for internationalization are not financial gains but rather to enhance research and knowledge capacity, increase cultural understanding, as well as other related goals. But a significant number of universities, especially in countries whose governments have cut back on public funding and have encouraged international ventures (e.g., Australia and the United Kingdom). Among the initiatives are branch campuses, franchised degree programs, partnerships with local institutions, as well as others. Most of these efforts have been focused on developing and middle-income countries.

For many countries, the recruitment of international students is also seen as a way of earning profits, both direct and indirect. Many countries charge high fees for international students—including the United Kingdom, Australia, Canada, and the United States. International graduate students also provide much needed research and teaching services with modest compensation in some countries. International students also spend significant amounts of money in the host countries (Davis 2003). It is estimated, for example, that such students contribute some $12 billion to the US economy.

Quantifying the financial scope of academic internationalization in its many permutations is not possible. The sums are quite large. For a growing number of countries, knowledge industries now form a substantial part of the total economy, and higher education constitutes a significant element of that economy. It is also difficult to calculate the impact of international activities on academic institutions and firms actively engaged in them, but again the amount is large and growing rapidly.

Access Provision and Demand Absorption

A significant part of the provision of international higher education services relates to providing access to students in countries without the domestic capacity to meet the access demand. Higher education is everywhere much in demand. With the advent of mass higher education worldwide, the proportion of young people entering postsecondary education has expanded dramatically. Even in countries that still enroll relatively few young people (under 20 percent)—such as India, China, and much of Africa—demand is rapidly growing. Domestic institutions, both public and private, often cannot fulfill the demand. Access provision is related to the profit motivation for the most part.

Traditional Internationalization

Many universities have been engaged in international activities for decades and quite a few for a century or more, as a modest part of their traditional activities. In many countries these institutions, especially in the United States, use campus international programs as a way to provide an international and cross-cultural perspective to their own domestic students and to enhance the curriculum. Examples of initiatives include study abroad experiences, internationalizing the curriculum, and sponsoring students from other countries to study on campus. Colleges and universities that exercise this kind of internationalization tend to be the more prestigious and selective institutions, although programs are not exclusively limited to these schools. Campus-based internationalization can take many forms, including study-abroad programs, the enhancement of foreign-language instruction, the introduction of international studies majors or area studies, and others (Siaya and Hayward 2003). Traditional internationalization is not seen as a profit-making activity, except from the perspective that it might enhance the competitiveness, prestige, and strategic alliances of the institution.

European Internationalism

Related to the economic and political integration of Europe, academic internationalization has been actively pursued by European Union authorities for more than two decades. At first, the primary goal was to provide academic experiences outside the home country within the EU for university students, and programs such as ERASMUS were lavishly funded and promoted. Large numbers of European students studied elsewhere in the EU (Huisman and van der Wende 2005). Over the years, the scope of European regional integration expanded. Now, the Bologna process is harmonizing entire academic systems so that degree structures will be compatible, credits transferable, and academic qualifications equal throughout the EU. Students are still encouraged to study abroad within the EU. European internationalization focuses mainly on the countries of the EU, although several non-EU member states have joined as well.

An additional aspect of European internationalization involves efforts by the EU to expand Europe's international programs to other parts of the world. These efforts are particularly active in Latin America and the Asia Pacific regions. Regional and institutional linkages, scholarship programs, and other initiatives have been established.

Developing-Country Internationalization

Although they produce a large majority of the total flow of students worldwide, developing countries host only a small proportion of the world's international students. Some of these countries are seeking to attract foreign students to their universities for a variety of reasons—including improvement of the quality and cultural composition of the student body, prestige, and especially the desire to earn income. India and the Philippines, for example, are significant host countries for students from developing countries. India hosts more than 8,000 students from abroad, 95 percent from developing countries (Bhalla 2005). China, Malaysia, and India are developing strategies to attract students from other countries and to export educational programs and institutions.

Individual Internationalization

Often forgotten in the debate about the internationalization of higher education is the fact that individuals make many of the key decisions—and pay for it as well. Most of the world's more than 2 million international students are self-funded. Their academic work is paid for by the students themselves and their families—not by governments, academic institutions, or philanthropic sources. Students make the basic decisions on destinations and fields of study. With the constraints concerning immigration regulations, students decide whether or not to return home following their academic work or stay at home and enroll in the programs offered by foreign education providers. Students are the largest source of funds for international education.

Growth Areas for Cross-Border Higher Education

While international higher education initiatives exist in almost every country, the dominant forces that influence programs and institutions and the sources of international higher education services are in the developed countries—especially the large English-speaking nations and, to a lesser extent, the larger countries of the EU. Middle-income countries in Asia and Latin America and, to a lesser extent, the poorer nations of the developing world constitute the "buying" countries. A small number of developed countries reap the main financial benefits and control academic and other programs, given such factors as flows of international students, institutions or providers that franchise academic programs to foreign providers, countries that provide international accreditation or quality assurance, or controlling partners in "twinning" arrangements.

The markets for international higher education are varied and segmented. The largest programs may be called "demand absorbing"—initiatives that provide access to students who would otherwise not be able to attend a postsecondary institution. In most cases, lack of capacity to meet growing demand in many countries is the reason for this trend. In a few cases, such as Malaysia, government policies favoring particular ethnic groups over others play a role. Generally, demand-absorbing programs tend to be at the less-prestigious end of the higher education system. Foreign providers may link up with local providers—entrepreneurs or academic institutions in the public or private sectors—or may establish their own branch campuses. In almost all cases, the motivation for the foreign provider is to earn a profit.

Some international initiatives rank at the upper end of the hierarchy. Many top European and American institutions have set up branch campuses in Singapore and Qatar at the invitations of those countries. The University of Chicago business school was established in Spain (and recently relocated to the United Kingdom). These prestigious institutions offer degree programs that may include a period of study at the home campus, or they may offer the entire academic program offshore.

The market for international higher education initiatives thus attracts students who cannot otherwise obtain access at home and thus seek almost any means to study as well as high-quality programs carefully targeted at a small and able elite group. Some students from the North also seek an overseas cultural or academic experience as part of their undergraduate studies. While predominantly an American phenomenon—175,000 US students went to other countries—other industrialized countries also send significant numbers of their students abroad, both in the context of EU programs and through other means.

While we are mainly concerned here with the physical movement of students, programs, and providers—and to some extent academic staff—across borders, the internationalization of the curriculum and other efforts to provide an effective cross-cultural educational preparation for university students also constitute an expanding area. Initiatives, mainly in the industrialized nations, to prepare students for a globalized world, are a widespread phenomenon.

The Landscape of International Education

The increasing demand and call for international education is changing the face of internationalization and emphasizing the mobility of students, programs, and providers. It is not known to what extent the greater demand will result in student mobility, but clearly there will be significant growth in the movement of programs and education providers across national borders. New types of providers, forms of delivery, and collaborative partnerships are being developed to take education programs to students in their home countries.

A fascinating but complex world of international academic mobility is emerging. The last five years have been a hotbed of innovation and new developments. A review of some of the more interesting developments illustrates the variety of providers, both traditional private and public higher education institutions as well as the so-called "new providers"—commercial IT and media companies, corporate universities, professional associations, and international conglomerates—that are delivering education to other countries. Both face-to-face and virtual modes are being used to deliver programs through twinning, franchising, articulation, validation, and joint- or double-degree arrangements. Institutions and providers show more interest in establishing a physical presence through branch campuses, independent institutions, teaching and testing centers, and acquisitions or mergers with local higher education institutions.

This section outlines recent developments in program and provider mobility. The examples include all regions of the world and have been taken from the breaking news service of the Observatory on Borderless Higher Education, which tracks and reports trends in borderless education (Observatory on Borderless Higher Education 2004).

Only initiatives announced or established in the last two years are described here to illustrate the most recent developments. While examples from conventional higher education institutions outnumber those from commercial company providers or from corporate universities, the increase in initiatives from these new types of providers should not be underestimated in terms of volume, innovation, and impact.

Middle East

The diversity of new developments in the Middle East makes it a relevant region to examine. For example, Poland has been approved to establish a new private medical institute in Israel where students will study for three years before moving to the Medical University in Gdansk for an additional three years of clinical study and then returning to Israel for an internship. Saudi Arabia is in the process of establishing new private universities with the involvement of foreign institutions and investors. For instance, the Prince Sultan Private University is being established in cooperation with the University of Arizona and UNESCO. In addition, the Dar-Al-Faisal University is being founded in cooperation with the Stevens Institute of Technology in the United States and with financial investment from the Boeing Company and Thales, the French defense firm. It is also noteworthy that Harvard is planning to set up a branch campus in the United Arab Emirates.

In Bahrain, a new Euro University is being planned in affiliation with the University of Hanover (Germany). Egypt is home to the American University established more than 80 years ago. Since 2000, the German University in Cairo and the L'Université Française d'Egypte have been established, and a new British University is under development. Slightly different types of partnerships are being established between local and foreign partners, thus illustrating the creativity and diversity of new forms of collaboration. An interesting example is the franchise agreement through which the distance MBA program of Heriot-Watt University from the United Kingdom is being offered at the American University in Egypt.

Asia Pacific

Vietnam is an emerging center of activity, with the development of a fully foreign-owned branch campus of RMIT from Australia. The International College of IT and Management, established by Troy State University from the United States is another example of a foreign branch campus. The number of active partnerships between local and foreign institutions is steadily expanding. For instance, the University of Hue in Vietnam recently developed a franchised and joint-degree bachelor's program in tourism with the University of Hawaii. Hanoi University of Technology is currently offering master's and bachelor's degrees with higher education institutions from Belgium (1), France (8), Germany (1), Singapore (2), and the United States (1). The Vietnamese government recently announced the development of the "International University in Vietnam" as another initiative to increase the national capacity for higher education. It is expected that half the university teaching staff will be Vietnamese and the other half from foreign universities. The involvement of foreign institutions will build on and expand from the current links of Ho Chi Minh City National University.

Thailand is another country increasingly active in cross-border education and is an appealing destination for institutions and providers from Egypt, China, Australia, and the United States. For example, the Egyptian Al-Azhar University and Jinan University from China both planned to open a branch campus in 2005. Swinburne University of Technology (Australia) has been operating a branch campus since 1998, although it is changing its focus to industry training alone. Troy State University from the United States has a teaching site in Bangkok for its master of business administration (MBA) program, and students can transfer to the United States depending on funds and visa requirements. Other institutions operating in Thailand include the Thai-German Graduate School of Engineering as well as 13 Australian and 9 UK universities.

In Singapore, the University of New South Wales (Australia) established the first fully owned foreign university in 2007—it failed within a year due to low enrollments and was closed, with a large financial loss to the Australian sponsors. Other well-respected foreign institutions offering education and training programs in Singapore through joint ventures, exchanges, and branch-campus models include the University of Chicago Graduate School of Business, Shanghai Jiao Tong University, Stanford University, the German Technische Universität München, and the Technische Universiteit Eindhoven from the Netherlands.

It is also interesting to note the exporting activities of Singaporean institutions. For example, the National University of Singapore has developed a joint MBA with Fudan University, aimed at both Chinese and Singaporean students. It is also embarking on a new graduate school initiative for Chinese students to be located in Suzhou Graduate Town, which is part of the Suzhou Industrial Park.

Raffles LaSalle Ltd from Singapore is a publicly traded company active in providing programs in fashion and design in many Asian countries. It has a number of innovative partnership arrangements and spans many countries. It is described by the Observatory on Borderless Higher Education as:

> A remarkable instance of international partnership, combining a Singapore firm with branches in Australia, China, Malaysia and Thailand, accreditation from an Australian state and a Canadian province, degrees from an Australian and a UK university, and a number of in-county university and college partners.
>
> (Observatory on Borderless Higher Education 2004)

The speed of change and innovation in India's higher education sector is unprecedented and includes both the import and export of programs and services. One of the more interesting initiatives is the partnership between the Caparo Group—a UK firm with interests in steel, engineering, and hotels—and Carnegie Mellon University in the United States to set up a new campus in India.

Africa

While Africa, with the partial exception of South Africa, is the least-affected region in terms of international and cross-border initiatives, there is some activity. The Universiteit Nienrode (Netherlands Business School), a private institution, has recently established a new branch campus in Nigeria in partnership with the African Leadership Forum, a nonprofit organization founded in 1988. This is one of the first such initiatives on the continent outside South Africa. In South Africa, in the last few years, there have only been a handful of foreign institutions with branch campuses—including Monash and Bond from Australia, De Montfort (United Kingdom), and the Netherlands Business School. As a result of the recent review of all MBA programs offered in South Africa, three of the foreign institutions are leaving because of accreditation-related issues. Monash will remain (it does not offer an MBA program) as well as the British-based Henley Management College, which is primarily a distance education provider. South Africa is one of the countries that have experienced a decrease in the number of foreign programs offered, largely due to strict new government regulations and accreditation processes. Kenya is home to two private nonprofit universities. Pakistan's Aga Khan University opened a branch university campus in Kenya in 2002 that specializes in nursing education, and Alliant International University from the United States provides education in social sciences and the humanities.

Mauritius is taking some bold new steps as it tries to establish itself as a "cyber-island" by attracting foreign IT firms from the West and from India. A "knowledge centre," described as a world-class integrated education and training complex is a key aspect of its plans. To date, there are already more than 50 foreign universities and professional bodies offering programs locally. These programs tend to be at the diploma or certificate level and in specialized fields. The concept of attracting foreign education providers to support the education and training needs of a new cyber-island may have positive consequences in terms of stemming brain drain or even stimulating brain gain, but the impact on local education institutions is as yet unclear.

Europe

Russia is an example of a country undergoing major economic reform, with important implications for the higher education sector. Many higher education institutions—for example, the Moscow International Slavonic Institute and the Moscow State University of Industry—are operating programs abroad, such as in Bulgaria. However, Russia is not only a sending country, it is also a receiving country through joint and double degrees, twinning, and franchise arrangements. For instance, the Higher School of Economics has a double-degree program with the London School of Economics. The Stockholm School of Economics is operating in St. Petersburg and the University of Oslo's Centre for Medical Studies in Moscow. The British Open University is active through 80 business training centers across the country. The University of Southern Queensland is partnering with Far Eastern National University in Vladivostok for program delivery. The Pune (India)-based International Institute of Information Technology plans to offer its master's and PhD programs through the newly established Russian-Indian Centre for Advanced Computer Research in Moscow.

In Greece, the University of Indianapolis has been active for more than a decade, first through an articulation program whereby students would start their studies in Athens and then go to the United States for completion of the program. This model has now evolved into a campus in Greece called the University of Indianapolis Athens.

In terms of activities by private companies, Laureate Education owns a part of or all of the Universidad Europa de Madrid in Spain, Les Roches and Glion Hotel School in Switzerland, and the Ecole Supérieur du Commerce Extérieur de Paris in France. Apollo International is offering its courses in the Netherlands, and Raffles LaSalle from Singapore has recently signed an agreement with Middlesex University, in the United Kingdom, to offer their bachelor's and master's programs in fashion and design.

North America

To report on US-led cross-border activities is a challenge because of the volume, diversity of providers, and types of partnerships (de Wit 2002). A review of the previous regional sections shows that US colleges and universities and private companies are probably the most active and innovative in program and provider mobility around the world. One of the more interesting recent developments is that George Washington University is giving serious consideration to opening a branch in South Korea since the government of South Korea has changed its regulatory system to permit foreign providers. There are several examples of US program mobility into Korea through partnerships with local institutions and companies. For instance, Syracuse University, in conjunction with Sejong University in Seoul, offers a specially designed MBA program for Korean students. Duke and Purdue Universities are also offering MBAs in Korea, and Stanford University is delivering online graduate and postgraduate courses and uses alumni as local tutors. These types of cross-border activities from US higher education institutions can be found in many Asian countries— for example, China, Vietnam, Thailand, Malaysia, Singapore, Philippines, and more recently India as well as the Middle East. For instance, the University of Missouri at St. Louis has been involved in the establishment of the first private university in Kuwait—the Gulf University of Science and Technology— and has a similar relationship with the Modern College of Business and Science in Oman.

An important feature of the US cross-border activity involves private and publicly traded companies. The Global Education Index, developed by the Observatory on Borderless Higher Education, is a system of classifying many of the largest and more active publicly traded companies that are providing education programs and services. A scan of more than 50 companies shows that the United States is home to the majority of these companies (Garrett 2004). Some of the better-known ones include Kaplan (owned by the *Washington Post*), the Apollo Group, DeVry, Career Education Corporation, and Laureate Education. Kaplan owns 57 colleges in the United States and now owns the Dublin Business School—Ireland's largest private undergraduate institution. This is likely to be the first of many purchases of foreign institutions. The Apollo Group owns the University of Phoenix, now the largest American private university, and is aggressively seeking to broaden its foreign investments and holdings. Since 1995, Apollo has also owned Western International University, which runs a branch campus called Modi Apollo International Institute in New Delhi through a partnership with the KK Modi Group, an Indian industrial conglomerate. Through its three business schools in Beijing, the Canadian Institute of Business and Technology offers Western International University programs. Another smaller but nonetheless interesting initiative has been the establishment of Northface University by Northface Learning Inc., which offers degree programs in IT and business and has the backing of IBM and Microsoft. This will be a company to watch in terms of future international expansion. The University of Northern Virginia is another small private university offering programs in business and IT and has recently opened a branch campus in the Czech Republic and has created delivery partnerships in China and India. These are only a few examples of the hundreds of new initiatives that US higher education institutions and companies are undertaking to deliver education courses and programs to other countries of the world.

In early 2004, the Canadian International Management Institute, a private postsecondary institution that represents the recruiting interests of 10 Canadian universities and colleges, signed a memorandum of understanding with the Chinese Scholarship Council to offer a foundation and credit transfer program to students in China wanting to gain Canadian university degrees. It is a five-year program during which students will be based in China for foundation studies, cultural adjustment, and language training for the first three years. If students meet grade requirements, they can continue their studies either in Canada or China for the final two years.

The Al-Ahram Canadian University in Egypt is Canada's first and, to date, only example of Canadian universities directly supporting the establishment of a new foreign university. The Al-Ahram Organization is a large company that owns the Egyptian daily newspaper. It is cooperating with McMaster University, Ecole Polytechnique de Montreal, and the Université du Quebec in Montreal to establish a new private university that opened in 2005.

The Serebra Learning Corporation is a publicly traded Canadian company offering generic and tailor-made software plus more than 1,800 courses mainly in IT. Serebra is working with the Consortium for Global Education—a group of 45 Baptist higher education institutions in the United States to provide quality-assured IT training in the developing world. Serebra also played a key role in the creation of the Pakistan Virtual University.

Latin America

In Mexico, the University of the Incarnate Word, a private American institution in San Antonio, Texas, opened a new campus in 2003. Other American institutions with Mexican campuses include Endicott College and Alliant International University, as well as Texas A&M, which has a "university center" in Mexico City. In 2000, Laureate Education purchased the Universidad del Valle de Mexico and is expanding to Guadalajara. It also owns Universidad Interamericana, a private university with campuses in Costa Rica and Panama, and part of three private universities in Chile. Bologna University from Italy is one of the few foreign institutions with a branch campus in Argentina. In terms of exporting, the Technical Institute of Monterrey in Mexico is well known for its online education programs, especially the MBA, delivered to many countries in Latin America.

This section examined the diversity of educational activities by both conventional higher education institutions and new commercial providers. The initiatives demonstrate the range of countries and types of partnerships being formed to promote, exchange, link, and predominantly sell higher education across borders. Another trend is the domination of developed countries—especially Australia and the United States and the emerging interests of India and China. New opportunities and potential benefits and risks can be identified in this international tour of recent cross-border activities.

Quality Assurance and Recognition Issues

Several issues related to quality assurance and the recognition of providers, programs, and credits or qualifications at national and international levels warrant closer attention.

The first issue concerns the licensing or registering of institutions and providers who are delivering cross-border courses or programs. A fundamental question is whether the institutions, companies, and networks that are delivering award-based programs are registered, licensed, or recognized by the home (sending) country and by the receiving country. The answer to this question varies. There are many countries that do not have the regulatory systems in place to register or evaluate out-of-country providers. Several reasons account for this, including lack of capacity or political will. If providers are not registered or recognized it is difficult to monitor their performance. Usually, if an institution or provider is not registered as part of a national system, regulatory frameworks for quality assurance or accreditation do not apply. This is the situation in many countries around the world, and hence foreign providers (bona fide and rogue) do not have to comply with national regulations.

Numerous questions and factors are at play in the registration or licensing of foreign providers. For instance, do providers who are part of and recognized by the national education system in their home country face criteria and conditions that differ from those that apply to other types of providers? Does it make a difference if the provider is for-profit or nonprofit, private or public, an institution or a company? What conditions apply if in fact the provider is a company without home-based presence and only establishes institutions in foreign countries? How does one track all types of partnerships between local domestic institutions or companies and foreign ones? Clearly, there are challenges involved in trying to establish appropriate and effective national or regional regulatory systems.

The second issue addresses the quality of the courses or programs offered and of the academic experience of students. The increased provision of cross-border education by institutions and commercial companies has introduced a new challenge to the field of quality assurance. Historically, national quality-assurance agencies have generally not focused their efforts on assessing the quality of imported and exported programs, with some notable exceptions. Hong Kong, Malaysia, South Africa, and Israel as receivers of cross-border education have developed regulatory systems to register and monitor the quality of foreign education provision. The United Kingdom and Australia are sending countries that have introduced quality assurance for exported cross-border provision by their recognized higher education institutions. The higher education sector now must somehow deal with the expansion of cross-border education—in particular, from the new private commercial companies and providers that are usually not recognized by nationally based quality-assurance schemes.

The role of accreditation is the focus of the third issue. Market forces are highlighting the profile and reputation of an institution or provider and their programs. Marketing and branding campaigns are undertaken to earn name recognition and to increase enrollments. The possession of some type of accreditation is part of the campaign and assures prospective students that the programs and awards are of high standing. This situation is introducing an internationalization and commercialization dimension to accreditation practices.

It is interesting to note the increase in the number of bona fide national and international accreditation agencies that are now working in over 50 countries. For instance, the US national and regional accrediting bodies are providing or selling their services in over 65 countries. The same trend is discernible for accreditation bodies of the professions such as ABET (engineering) from the United States and EQUIS (business) from Europe.

Furthermore, self-appointed networks of institutions and new organizations engage in accreditation of their members. These are positive developments in terms of trying to improve the quality of the academic offer. However, some concern exists that these networks and organizations are not totally objective in their assessments and may be more interested in contributing to the race for more and more accreditation "stars" than in improving quality. Another related and more worrisome development is the growth in accreditation mills. These organizations are not recognized or legitimate bodies, and they more or less "sell" accreditation status without any independent assessment. They are similar to degree mills that sell certificates and degrees with no or minimal course work. Different education stakeholders—especially students, employers, and the public—need to be made aware of these accreditation (and degree) mills, which are often nothing more than a website and are therefore outside the jurisdiction of national regulatory systems.

The fourth issue addresses the recognition of the actual awards or qualifications offered for the goals of employment and further study. Specifically, students, employers, and the public need to be made aware of the quality and validity of the programs and awards provided. Mechanisms are required that recognize the academic and professional qualifications gained through domestic or international delivery of education. The key questions are who awards the qualification, especially in partnerships and network arrangements, whether the provider is recognized (and, if so, by what kind of accrediting or licensing body), and in what country that body is located? Given the importance of both student mobility and professional-labor mobility, within and between countries, the mechanisms for qualification recognition have to be national, regional, and/or international in nature and application

The fifth issue focuses on the need for a review of the policy and regulatory environments in which program and provider mobility is operating. Of current interest and debate is the question of whether national-level accreditation and quality-assurance systems (where they exist) are able to address the complicating factors of education mobility across countries, cultures, and jurisdictional systems. A fundamental question is whether countries have the capacity to establish and monitor quality systems for both incoming and outgoing education programs, given the diversity of providers and delivery methods. Should national quality-accreditation systems be complemented and augmented by regional or international frameworks? Is it advisable and feasible to develop mutual recognition systems between and among countries? Would an International Code of Good Practice be appropriate or strong enough to monitor quality? These are key questions for the education sector to address.

As the discussion moves forward it will be of strategic and substantive importance to recognize the roles and responsibilities of all the players involved in quality assurance—including individual institutions and providers, national quality-assurance systems, nongovernment and independent accreditation bodies, professional associations, and regional or international organizations. It will be important to work in a collaborative fashion to build a system that ensures the quality and integrity of cross-border education and maintains the confidence of society in higher education.

It would be wrong if one was left with the impression that these issues do not have implications for individual providers and especially higher education institutions. Quality assurance starts with the provider who is delivering the program—domestically or internationally. Many higher education institutions have adequate quality assurance processes in place for domestic delivery, but these processes do not cover all the aspects of delivering abroad. The challenges inherent in working cross-culturally, in a foreign regulatory environment and, potentially, with a foreign partner raise new issues. These include academic entry requirements, student examination and assessment procedures, workload, delivery modes, adaptation of the curriculum, quality assurance of teaching, academic and sociocultural support for students, title and level of award, and other issues. Quality issues must be balanced with the financial investment and return to the source provider. Intellectual property ownership, choice of partners, division of responsibilities, academic and business risk assessments, and internal and external approval processes are only some of the issues the higher education providers need to analyze.

The Future of Internationalization

Universities have, from their medieval European origins, been international institutions, attracting students and faculty from many countries. The rise of nationalism and the nation-state in the period following the Protestant Reformation focused academe inward. Later, the emergence of the Third World from colonialism in the mid-twentieth century also stimulated the establishment of national universities in these developing countries. Now, in the twenty-first century, academe is increasingly international in scope and direction. Information technology; the knowledge economy; increased mobility for students, faculty, programs, and providers; and the growing integration of the world economy all impel this internationalization. Without question, internationalism will continue to be a central force in higher education in the coming period.

Questionable Trends

Australian experts have argued that about 15 million students will study abroad by 2025—up from the current 2 million. This prediction might, however, be overly optimistic. Australia itself, after expanding the number of international students studying in the country dramatically for a decade, has experienced a certain decline. The United States, the leading host country, has also declined modestly in 2004—although totals again modestly increased in 2005 and 2006. While the basic trends are strong and stable, there are a variety of uncertainties that may affect internationalization.

Political realities and national security. Terrorism and the reactions to it in many countries may affect international higher education in significant ways. The tightening of visa requirements in the United States and other countries, national security restrictions on what subjects can be studied in certain countries, fear on the part of potential international students to come to some countries, and other problems may affect the flows of students across borders and other aspects of international higher education.

Government policies and the cost of study. Policies concerning the cost of tuition, fees for visas and other documents, and in general the changing policies of the host countries may affect international initiatives in different ways.

Expansion of domestic capacity. As countries build up their own local access to higher education, and especially as they develop master's and doctoral programs, there may be less interest in going abroad to study or in enrolling in international programs within a country.

English. The growing use of English as a medium of research and instruction, especially at the graduate level, may stimulate interest in international programs, offered by universities in English.

The internationalization of the curriculum. As the curriculum is harmonized worldwide—moving largely toward models developed in the United States and other large industrialized countries—students may find international programs useful.

The expansion of e-learning. As degrees offered through distance education expand and become more widely accepted internationally, these degrees are likely to grow in size and scope and become a more significant part of the higher education system worldwide. It is not clear if international e-learning degrees will become more widespread or if domestic e-learning programs will continue to dominate. It is worth noting that most of the largest distance-education universities are located in developing or middle-income countries.

The private sector. At present, private higher education is the fastest-growing segment of higher education worldwide. A small part of this sector is international. It is not clear if private higher education providers will find the international market sufficiently profitable—although it seems quite likely that there will be some expansion of private sector institutions in the international market.

Quality assurance and control. Quality assurance is a major concern within countries and it is even more of a problem internationally. It is as yet unclear how quality can be measured in international higher education programs. Many international programs have been criticized for low standards.

European policies. It is not yet clear how the Bologna initiatives and the harmonization of higher education in the EU will affect international patterns within the EU or between the EU and the rest of the world. Will the EU build walls to protect is own "European higher education space," or will it welcome students and programs from the rest of the world? Will tuition and other fees be imposed on non-EU students? The answers to these and other questions are largely unanswered.

* * *

Our focus in this chapter is to understand both the underlying motivations and patterns of international higher education and the landscape of international programs and institutions. We believe that international higher education will play an increasingly influential role in providing access in some countries and will become a "niche market" in others. At present, numerous uncertainties exist about both the realities and the future of international higher education. Our concern is to ensure that international higher education embodies a force for the public good and not simply a means for earning profits. We are at an international crossroads—the programs and practices that are emerging now will shape the realities of international higher education for years to come.

References

Altbach, Philip G. (2002) "Knowledge and education as international commodities," *International Higher Education*, no. 28 (Summer): 2–5.
—— (2007) "Globalization and the university: Myths and realities in an unequal world," in Philip G. Altbach, *Tradition and Transition: The International Imperative in Higher Education*, Chestnut Hill, MA: Boston College Center for International Higher Education.
Bhalla, Veena (2005) "International students in Indian universities," *International Higher Education*, no. 41 (Fall): 8–9.
Castells, Manuel (2000) *The Rise of the Network Society*, Oxford: Blackwells.
Davis, Todd M. (2003) *Atlas of Student Mobility*, New York: Institute of International Education.
de Wit, Hans (2002) *Internationalization of Higher Education in the United States of America and Europe: A Historical, Comparative, and Conceptual Analysis*, Westport, CT: Greenwood.
Friedman, Thomas L. (2006) *The World is Flat: A Brief History of the Twenty-First Century*, New York: Farrar, Straus & Giroux.
Garrett, Richard (2004) *The Global Education Index, 2004 Report*, London: Observatory on Borderless Higher Education, Association of Commonwealth Universities.
Huisman, Jeroen and Marijk van der Wende (eds) (2005) *On Cooperation and Competition II: Institutional Responses to Internationalization, Europeanization, and Globalization*, Bonn: Lemmens Verlag.
Kirp, David (2003) *Shakespeare, Einstein, and the Bottom Line: The Marketing of Higher Education*, Cambridge, MA: Harvard Univ. Press.

National Education Association (2004) *Higher Education and International Trade Agreements: An Examination of the Threats and Promises of Globalization,* Washington, DC: National Education Association.

Observatory on Borderless Higher Education (ed.) (2004) *Breaking News Stories Service 2002–4,* London: Association of Commonwealth Universities.

Odin, Jaishree K. and Peter T. Mancias (eds) (2004) *Globalization and Higher Education,* Honolulu: Univ. of Hawaii Press.

OECD (Organization for Economic Cooperation and Development) (2004) *Internationalization and Trade in Higher Education: Opportunities and Challenges,* Paris: OECD.

Siaya, Laura and Fred M. Hayward (2003) *Mapping Internationalization on US Campuses.* Washington, DC: American Council on Education.

7

Where the Quality Discussion Stands
Strategies and Ambiguities

LIZ REISBERG

Multiple factors have converged to provoke the current international preoccupation with quality and standards in education during the past several decades—the rapid expansion of tertiary education; the simultaneous shrinking of public subsidies for higher education; the knowledge explosion; the need for universities to acquire more expensive infrastructure; the mobility of professionals and researchers; and, finally, the increasing worldwide competition for prestige and often for the same funds, students, and faculty. Moreover, expectations of the output and achievement of higher education have become increasingly complex. At one time, the purpose of higher education might have been to provide a thorough grounding in classical knowledge or preparation for a few specific professions. In the recent past, a diverse public looks to universities as engines of development, social equalizers, professional training grounds, and centers of continuing education, among other things.

Universities are under pressure from many directions to reform long-standing traditions and pedagogy, account for their activities and use of resources, and address broad social agendas. National governments have implemented policies to diversify higher education, encourage greater operating efficiency, improve productivity, increase fiscal independence, and foster more competition between institutions (Clark 1998). Also, there is a growing demand for greater accountability to a new array of education "consumers." The challenges facing higher education to measure up against diverse and often ambiguously defined expectations are vast.

At the very least, most countries have now accepted the need for both greater accountability and for some formal process to assure multiple constituencies that higher education is being evaluated regularly in a transparent way. During the last decade, the discussion has moved beyond national borders as regional and international organizations endeavor to find comparability between degrees and congruency and harmony among the quality-assurance schemes now in effect.

Quality means so many different things to different people. Lee Harvey and Diana Green (1993) ask, "Whose quality?" It has become increasingly problematic that different stakeholders judge quality against divergent values and priorities. Nevertheless, the quality movement has moved forward, leaving many fundamental concepts and much vocabulary undefined.

The Changing Quality-Assurance Discussion

In its early stages, the quality-assurance movement was largely motivated by waning confidence in higher education. So many new types of institutions were awarding degrees to an expanding student population that concerned stakeholders were questioning the comparability of degrees. The general lack of information about the internal workings of universities and colleges became a cause for concern. "Opportunistic politicians" (Harvey and Newton 2004) exploited the uncertainty of students, taxpayers, and employers about growing public investment and the value of a university degree to impose new reporting obligations on higher education.

Since the 1980s, nearly every nation has introduced some kind of quality-assurance scheme in higher education. Typically, an intermediary agency is established to coordinate the information needs of government and individual institutions. In most cases, the process begins with standards or fixed criteria to structure internal and external evaluations that provide information to external stakeholders and identify opportunities for improvement to the academic community. Programs initially approach easily verifiable or measurable (quantifiable) criteria. In its earlier stages, the US system emphasized "inputs"—such as size of the library, number of professors with advanced degrees, faculty/student ratios, and rates of graduation. In the United States and elsewhere, measurable criteria have expanded to include faculty publications and citations, faculty awards, and grants secured. Increasingly, the pursuit of quality has led to the perplexing challenge of measuring the nonquantifiable characteristics and production of higher education.

There is a broad consensus that inputs alone do not guarantee the quality of the enterprise or, as Lee Harvey and Jethro Newton stated, inputs are as conclusive as "evaluating the quality of a football match for spectators by examining the stadium, the pitch, the team sheet, and the credentials of the coach" (Harvey and Newton 2004, 150). Recent trends have emphasized outcomes over "inputs" as institutions attempt to measure their impact. This approach is not easily accomplished since education is a slippery commodity to quantify. As Martin Trow (1998) points out, outcomes should be measured over the course of the graduate's lifetime so as to be measured accurately.

As institutions have begun to make peace with the relevance and inevitability of greater accountability, the discussion has moved to a deeper level. It is increasingly apparent that quality in higher education requires more than responding to standards. Now, scholars are insisting that quality must be imbedded in institutional culture, not regarding specific criteria, and that the process must be ongoing rather than just a periodic response to an audit or inspection. If the process of ensuring quality is to be ongoing, then the responsibility lies with individual institutions to integrate quality-assurance into all levels of activity. With many new layers of quality-assurance in place it is time for politicians and the larger society to again trust that universities can indeed determine and protect the quality of their work (Harvey and Newton 2004; Trow 1998).

The discussion of criteria, standards, measures, and validation continues to evolve. There are (in practice) two levels of quality management—one involves a sequence of procedures to document and report; the second requires the consideration of less-tangible aspects of higher education. With growing international experience, the discussion has become more nuanced with the recognition that the challenges of quality-assurance are ever more complex.

When confidence in colleges and universities wavered, new programs for external supervision were put into effect. The vocabulary that accompanies these new programs is daunting, mostly because the same or similar words are used without similar meanings: quality-assurance, quality management, quality control, and quality enhancement. The mechanisms to measure quality may include accreditation, audit, assessment, and external monitoring.

Countries may review entire institutions, specific degree programs only, or both. Systems are both voluntary and compulsory. Where accreditation is voluntary, there are usually incentives to participate. In the case of the United States, for example, accreditation is voluntary, but institutions must be accredited to receive funds from the national government for student financial aid or research. In most fields of study, US students must graduate from accredited degree programs to qualify for a professional license, likewise in Argentina. In Chile, the program of accreditation is voluntary but extremely useful as successful completion of the review provides programs and institutions with data to legitimize demands for additional resources (Lemaitre 2004).

The United States relies on two levels of accreditation, both managed by membership organizations. Regional membership associations certify the performance of colleges and universities, while nonprofit professional member organizations review and accredit individual degree programs. More often, accreditation, audits, and external reviews are coordinated by quasi-governmental agencies. Still, the process is generally the same—self-studies are conducted, teams of peer evaluators are evaluated, reports are compiled and reviewed, and some decision is taken.

The process requires an enormous commitment of time and resources. While the self-study itself is a serious undertaking, in theory it is an opportunity for an institution to step back from daily activity, assess strengths and weaknesses, build on the former, and resolve the latter. The value of the endeavor depends, to a large degree, on the extent to which the academic community is engaged. When quality-assurance is viewed as an external obligation, simply as accountability to an external audience, the process is easily delegated to a specific administrative office or an external consultant with limited impact; it becomes a bureaucratic exercise. When the process is viewed as an opportunity for honest reflection and includes a broad range of participants, the potential for improvement and development is much greater but so, alas, is the effort.

The literature returns over and over again to the ambiguous goals of this process and what it accomplishes. Of course, there are multiple goals—reassurance that public money is being spent wisely, that students are learning, that degree studies are relevant, that institutions are attentive to opportunities and necessities for improvement, that faculty are properly qualified, and many more. The processes of accreditation, audits, and assessment as currently followed lend themselves to measuring some things better than others. The impact of all of this effort has proven very difficult to measure.

What Does "Quality" Actually Mean in Practice?

One of the enormous challenges confronting the quality issue is defining quality in higher education. The quest for a broadly useful definition is ongoing. Quality is generally agreed to be desirable even if it is indefinable, but the ambiguity of its meaning complicates the design of systems to ensure it.

The fact that the quality-assurance discussion has moved to an international level adds linguistic challenges to the confusion over definitions. Distinctions made between words such as "assessment" and "evaluation" in English have no equivalents in many other languages (Vlasceanu, Grünberg, and Pârlea 2007).

Different constituents and stakeholders use different constructs for addressing quality in higher education. To complicate the discussion further, quality often becomes tangled with the related, but separate, issues. But as Bjorn Stensaker points out, we now have the "need to go beyond formalities and definitions of quality and pay more attention to good practice and how this can be demonstrated" (2008, 9). *Something* needs to be demonstrated and this is the challenge going forward.

As already stated, there are many approaches to ensuring quality, but the emphasis is often on evaluating without a clear idea of the objectives the process is meant to achieve (Harvey and Newton 2004). The ambiguity contributes to some degree of doubt about the value and impact of so many evaluations taking place today. Yogi Berra, an American baseball player as famous for his quotable comments as for his athletic achievement, once said "You've got to be very careful if you don't know where you are going, because you might not get there." This applies to much of the quality-assurance schemes operating today.

Regulation, Accountability, and Autonomy

In many cases, quality-assurance schemes arose from a general "need to know." As higher education expanded and diversified, governments were unable to provide the level of control or supervision exercised in the past. Nor was that level of national presence seen as desirable any longer. Yet an ongoing tension exists between government authority and institutional autonomy. Responsibility for quality-assurance sits at the fulcrum of that tension. Quality-assurance schemes unavoidably represent some level of external regulation, and these schemes can be contentious, depending on who establishes the procedures and measures and how they are implemented.

Does higher education need to be regulated or can it regulate itself? Are quality-assurance schemes a mechanism for external regulation or for keeping external regulation at bay? Guy Neave (1994) suggested that despite the appearance of greater autonomy, the devolution of responsibility for quality from the state to individual institutions was passed along with norms of performance still determined by governments or parastatal agencies, allowing the state to "hedge its bets." Or, as Harvey and Newton describe it, "establishing delegated accountability" (2004, 151).

Concerns are frequently raised about whether institutions can truly "police" themselves and whether doing so allows institutions to become too complacent. In the United States, despite a long history of self-management, the federal government has frequently expressed dissatisfaction with the level of performance expected of higher education institutions. As a result, the national government has made repeated attempts to use its funding clout to impose additional standards for institutional performance in areas not addressed by regional institutional accreditation. While the national government was not successful, many state governments have followed suit exercising greater control through performance-based funding. Indicators commonly added include time to degree, class size, student retention, and faculty workload (Dill 1997, 39). These easily quantifiable outcomes provide public reassurance, but it is not so clear whether they ensure academic quality.

The line between accountability and regulation is a fine one. Accountability means "coming clean" or revealing to external constituencies details deemed important. Institutions that receive public funds are understandably obligated to account for how those funds were used but to what end and with what results.

Trow (1998) suggests that accountability may indeed serve as an *impetus* for improving performance and therefore, perhaps, a component of quality-assurance. But reporting on performance does not represent assuring quality, and Trow warns that this activity might work against quality improvement if accountability pushes institutions to conform to external standards that constrain diversity or inhibit the autonomy institutions need to foment their own development. Accountability can too easily come down to responding to a checklist of predefined criteria established externally and passing an inspection at regular intervals (Stensaker 2008).

Yet institutions should be accountable for their performance. Institutions accept public and private funds to deliver a service and should be able to verify that good service (if not excellent) was indeed provided. There is a great deal at stake for participants, most importantly students whose personal and professional future opportunities are often shaped by this educational experience but for the larger society as well. The question is, of course, how to incorporate accountability usefully.

Standards and Accreditation

The concept of "standards" is in itself ambiguous and interpreted differently in various systems. In the United States, "standards" is used interchangeably with "criteria," although in Europe the meaning is different. Standards generally provide a critical reference point but may refer to minimum requirements, targets for performance, measures for comparison. Standards can be applied to academic content covered, intellectual abilities demonstrated, service provided, among other aspects (Vlasceanu, Grünberg, and Pârlea 2007). Despite the vast meaning(s) of standards, this concept generally serves as the basis of quality-assurance programs.

Dill (2007) suggests that from the public-policy perspective, academic quality requires the assurance of academic standards. But, whose standards? How specific? How high? How low? Different processes are followed to check or validate that some predefined standards have been achieved.

> Accreditation refers to a process resulting in a decision that warrants an institution or programme; audit explores internal processes; assessment passes a judgment (often with a grading) usually about the quality of a teaching or research subject area; and external examination checks standards (be they academic, competence, service or organizational).
>
> (Harvey and Newton 2004, 150)

The term "accreditation" is increasingly used in international discussions of quality. It is often viewed as a guarantee that standards have been established and honored. In their glossary compiled with support from UNESCO, Vlasceanu, Grünberg, and Pârlea offer the following definition:

> The process by which a (non-)governmental or private body evaluates the quality of a higher education institution as a whole or of a specific educational programme in order to formally recognize it as having met certain pre-determined minimal criteria or standards.
>
> (2007, 25)

The United States has the longest-standing system for institutional accreditation, a system unusual because of the absence of a national authority over higher education. Also unusual in the international context is the long experience with institutional diversity within this sector. Educational institutions in the United States belong to one of six regional membership associations, depending on where the institution is located. Despite some variations, the process of accreditation follows the same general pattern throughout the country—self-study, external review, agency recommendations, and decision. This process has been imitated by most quality-assurance programs around the world, with the difference that the coordinating agency (elsewhere) typically has some connection to government.

The other commonly followed pattern, also originated in the United States, is mission-driven evaluation. In other words, to accommodate the diversity of institutions and their objectives, an institution or program is often evaluated in terms of its success if meeting the goals it set for itself. This concept implies a great deal of elasticity within standards. While this flexibility offers many advantages, it also allows mediocre institutions to adjust their goals so that they can be easily fulfilled (Lemaitre 2004) or provides the opportunity for "manufacturing an improved identity" (Newton 2000).

It is still conceived as possible to apply carefully formulated standards across institution types, but as mentioned, this glosses over the less-attractive realities within higher education. External evaluators are expected to have the skill to adapt standards to each unique context. This places enormous faith and responsibility on peer evaluators who may have had little or no training for this kind of activity. The practice risks lax interpretation and at the same time the possibility of turning peers into inspectors (Westerheijden, Stensaker, and Rosa 2007).

How far can standards be adapted to diverse environments before they lose their value and utility? At what point do standards become simply a mechanism for certification? Is conforming to standards enough to guarantee a threshold for quality?

> The introduction of relative rather than absolute standards by which to "judge" institutions or courses raises issues of comparability. Quality as conformance to (relative) standards tells us nothing about the criteria used to set the standards. . . . For quality to be conformance to relative standards seems to undervalue the notion that quality implies something "above the ordinary" and the conformance standards set may seem rather ordinary and in no way exceptional.
>
> (Harvey and Green 1993, 13)

Standards, while important, are often overemphasized in quality-assurance programs. Standards can be written so that they are irrelevant or unrealistic in a particular environment. Conforming to standards without consideration of context accomplishes little (Gil Antón 2006). At best, standards can serve as a framework for organizing evaluations, not as well as precise measurements for comparison purposes. At their worst, standards function as a meaningless checklist and distract from a deeper consideration of quality. Yet, much credibility is placed on value of standards and accreditation as will be explored later in this chapter.

Prestige

Prestige is another characteristic often viewed as a reflection of quality. Prestige can be misleading, though as it emanates from a complex convergence of circumstances. Generally, prestige is highly correlated with the research productivity of a university's faculty (Dill 1997). It can also be a reflection of institutional wealth, difficulty of gaining admission, "star" faculty or, more recently, a position in one ranking or another. Correlating prestige with quality is risky as an institution's reputation so often results from one or more specific characteristics or activities and rarely reflects the broader performance of an institution.

Prestige also comes from less-rational public perception. Rankings have achieved considerable influence in the current "marketplace." Not only have rankings ramped up competition between institutions but also greatly shaped the perception of quality. Although few educators concede that rankings are an indication of quality, students, parents, and policymakers often do. Trow (1998) warns us that the rankings more often only affect how and what institutions report rather than encourage significant improvements in quality.

Rankings vary widely in the criteria they use; and despite being explicit about methods and meaning, the general public focuses more on an institution's placement in the rankings than how it got there. Rankings often rely on "reputational measures" (Dill 1997) that tend to be not only highly subjective but also self-perpetuating. Yet, rankings are widely popular, and their influence in the quality discussion cannot be overlooked.

Rankings are perhaps most seductive because of their ease of use. It is unrealistic to hope that "consumers" of higher education will review self-study reports or reports completed by external evaluators when comparing institutions. Rankings provide easy answers; they advise prospective students that a university ranked at 5 is better than a university ranked at 21—of course, with limited validity. Institutions are not so easily compared. A number of alternatives are being introduced to make better comparative data available. A new Web site, College Portrait, has been set up by the American Association of State Colleges and Universities and the Association of Public and Land-Grant Universities (to compare US schools. These organizations' effort to be fair to the diversity among institutions quickly opened them to criticism for their lack of precision (Lederman 2010). The Center for Higher Education Development in Germany publishes data to allow students to construct their own rankings, according to their needs (Thompson 2008). For now the rankings still have undue influence in the discussion of quality.

Competition and Markets as Driving Forces

A myth in vogue at one point was that a competitive higher education market would be a powerful incentive for institutions to improve the quality of their activities. This assumption has been debunked by a number of scholars. It is now recognized that competition may actually have perverse effects, diverting funds to investments that will enhance an image in the "marketplace" or in the dramatic rhetoric of an Organization for Economic Cooperation and Development report, "to throw their best assets overboard in the rash attempt to keep their university afloat" (OECD, 2010)

One of the fallacies in suggesting that competition will improve quality is assuming that people have access to good information and use it to make thoughtful and rational choices:

> It is assumed that the student has insufficient information about the quality of academic institutions or programs to make discriminating choices. If such information were to be provided, either by institutions under government mandate, or by independent quality-assurance agencies, it is assumed that subsequent student choices would provide incentives for institutions to improve their academic quality. . . . However, this logic rests upon a long and complicated causal chain, which assumes that reliable and valid measures of academic quality readily exist and that students will base their enrolment choices on this type of information.
>
> (Dill 1997, 37)

For most individuals, let alone teenagers, the official processes of quality-assurance schemes and accreditation are incomprehensible and, as a result, not terribly useful. Rankings provide data that are easily referenced. As a result, they are also appealing. Their growing influence has meant that many colleges are now focusing resources on investments that promise a better position (Labi 2008).

In a competitive market, it is important to keep in mind that nonacademic factors often sway an adolescent's college choice. Increasingly, colleges are using residential facilities and amenities such as luxury dorms with swimming pools (Fogg 2008) and double beds over the traditional twin (Strauss 2007) to compete for students. While market forces drive change and "improvement," the results may not have any bearing on the academic performance of the institution.

Institutions compete for top faculty as well as top students. Likewise, the competitive pressure may serve to focus resources on gains with limited impact on the quality of an institution as a whole. Dill (2007) asserts that in fact the competitive market for high-profile faculty only diverts attention from teaching and learning and concentrates resources on prestige:

[T]he indicators of academic prestige drown out the weaker signals of the quality of teaching and student learning, and the aggressive pursuit of prestige crowds out the activities associated with the improvement of academic standards. . . . [T]he dominance of the prestige goal in systems of mass higher education encourages all institutions to invest in cream skimming the student market, in building their research capacity, and in incentives designed to recruit and retain the most prominent scholars/ researchers. The pernicious effect of this competitive pursuit of academic prestige is that it diverts resources as well as administrative and faculty attention away from the collective actions within universities necessary to actually improve academic standards.

(Dill 2007, 65)

Dill goes on to warn that hiring well-known research faculty diverts attention from teaching and encourages "individual academic autonomy," in the hands of star research faculty, at the expense of "individual involvement in the collective quality-assurance activities of academic program planning and co-ordination" (Dill 1997, 39). In other words, competition tends to sidetrack resources that could well have had a broader impact on institutional quality. The pursuit of prestige tends to encourage focused efforts rather than deeper ones. Instead of investing in long-term strategies for institutional development, universities often leverage limited resources to draw attention through accoutrements such as star faculty, investments to improve ranking position, or more luxurious student amenities.

Refining the Discussion

In their early stages, quality-assurance schemes tend to pursue the most obvious strategies, validating the qualifications and workloads of professors, infrastructure and resources, preparedness, and progress of students. It was assumed that addressing the basic building blocks of higher education and responding to the external pressures for increased accountability and competition would produce better quality. However, there is no simple formula for quality-assurance. The lack of definition and ambiguity of objectives come back to haunt. Quality-assurance programs—accreditation, audits, or whatever—result in some level of institutional change. The question is what kind of change, and is it the desired change. At the very least, the requirements of accountability built in to most quality-assurance schemes have obliged institutions to do a better job capturing and organizing data. But that is not enough.

How quality in higher education is being considered and judged is shifting as nations acquire experience with evaluating institutional and program performance. There is increased attention to the "transformative" role that higher education should play in the development of their students (Harvey and Green 1993).

Alexander Astin asserts that quality is demonstrated by the impact that an institution has on its students, in particular on their personal and intellectual development (Harvey and Green 1993). Gil Antón (2006) asks whether improvement in student learning has occurred commensurate with raised standards applied to higher education. What will be required is further understanding of the impact of higher education on students, but to date both methodology and data are lacking.

Until recently, quality assessment has paid surprisingly little attention to the fundamental activities of teaching and learning—where, of course, institutions have the greatest impact on students. Yet, important as these activities are, they are not easily measured, compared, or benchmarked. The number of faculty publications, student examination results, graduates who work in their field of study or go on to advanced study are of only limited use in measuring quality when viewed from this perspective.

Assessment of Higher Education Learning Outcomes (AHELO), an ambitious new initiative of the OECD is proposing to develop meaningful measures of learning outcomes intended for use on an international scale. AHELO proposes to examine institutions on the basis of four categories—general skills (analytic reasoning, critical thinking, ability to generate ideas, the ability to apply theory, writing skill, leadership, etc.); discipline-specific skills (expertise in a field of study); learning environment (physical and organizational characteristics, student-faculty interaction, psychosocial attributes, behavior and attitudinal outcomes); and value added to the development of individual students. The usefulness of this kind of evaluation and data to quality development is indisputable. That OECD does not expect AHELO to be "up and running" before 2016 is a reflection on just how challenging this undertaking will be.

In the meantime, academic tradition may make it difficult to refocus evaluations and audits on the learning and pedagogy. Powerful trends work against the growing concern with teaching and learning by quality-assurance agencies. Prestige, rankings, and funding reward research more readily than excellence in teaching. Dill suggests that incentives encouraging a growing "faculty disengagement" from the classroom not only undermine the quality of teaching but also distract from "collective faculty activities such as curriculum development, teaching evaluation, and student assessment" (2003, 4). The emphasis on scholarship and productivity encourages faculty to work independently, yet improvements of academic programs require faculty to work collectively. Dill emphasizes the importance of "the internal transfer of new knowledge on improving teaching and student learning" (2003, 8) to support the pursuit of excellence. Developing processes for the assessment and improvement of student outcomes will require an integrated institutional engagement that will necessitate a shift in incentives and rewards to faculty and other members of the academic community.

What Have We Learned?

The challenge of how divergent ideas about quality and quality-assurance can be translated to higher education institutions is a difficult one. Despite all of the ambiguity, mechanisms for some level of quality-assurance and shared benchmarks have become essential. There must be a means of communication from inside higher education institutions to the outside.

Attempts to borrow concepts and processes from other sectors are problematic as quality in other arenas is more easily measured as specific outputs. Exactly what the output of education should be is a subject of contentious debate. Yet, quality should no longer be taken for granted, and there is a general need for a mechanism to validate that each institution provides something valued by the larger society.

Moreover, it has been learned that the interpretations of politicians, institutional administrators, faculty, and students about what reflects quality in higher education are different and that quality-assurance systems in use serve the needs of some constituents more than others.

Quality has been addressed in most countries through a now almost standard protocol for evaluating activities in higher education. This process involves obliging institutions to establish internal procedures for monitoring their success in achieving standards of quality, followed by a periodic external inspection to verify and expand on the results of the internal evaluation, all under the auspices of an agency with some official recognition.

Institutions are no longer permitted to "police themselves" without some kind of impartial external validation. Yet, self-regulation remains a critical piece of the quality-assurance process. What most national quality schemes accomplish today is to ensure that the evaluation sequence described earlier takes place. The external system that exists to ensure "internally propelled quality management" (Westerheijden 2007) is adequate. How effective the process is depends entirely on the level of institutional commitment and engagement, which, of course, varies from one institution to another.

> The crucial factor in a system of academic quality control, monitoring, and improvement lies in efforts to create an institutional culture marked by self-criticism, openness to criticism by others and a commitment to improvement of practice.
>
> (Trow 1998, 44)

For now, there really is no alternative to trusting institutions with primary responsibility for their own performance (Trow 1998). The activities of today's modern colleges and universities are too vast, too complex; ongoing external coordination and oversight is impractical as well as undesirable.

> No external agency, no accrediting body or coordinating council, can assess academic units with the accuracy and in the detail necessary to make good judgments and decisions. Nor can their assessments have the legitimacy for the institution and its units that internal reviews carry with them when they are done properly.
>
> (Trow 1998, 46)

External control will always have limited impact on quality improvement and possibly could work even to the detriment of improvement rather than its enhancement depending on the way the control is exercised. For now, periodic evaluations or inspections can be best used to ensure that procedures are in place for ongoing self-assessment and improvement and for verifying the content of evaluation reports. Considering that most external evaluators are on site for only a few days, they rely on the information presented to them; the knowledge they gain about an institution cannot go very deep.

> Regardless of how eminent, distinguished, and important the members of expert panels may be, data gathering, information processing, and strategic considerations could for a priori reasons constitute the Achilles heel of these models.
>
> (Blackmur 2007, 31)

Institutional leadership and culture of an institution are key to the pursuit of quality. Quality-assurance has to be fully integrated into institutional management and operation. By engaging broad participation in a commitment to quality, an institution will always be attentive to weaknesses and opportunities to improve. This type of engagement will promote the "collegial connections and communication of academic norms that will lead to quality academic programs" (Dill 1997, 39). Most institutions are still learning how to do this.

The Internationalization of Quality

The mobility of students, scholars, and programs has contributed to the urgency of pushing the quality discussion to an international level. While established international organizations—OECD, UNESCO, and International Standards Organization—are addressing the implications of increasing cross-border activity, many new organizations are assuming a role as well.

There is a growing trend toward international cooperation to achieve mutual recognition of the degrees and diplomas awarded by member countries. Quality-assurance is inevitably a prerequisite to international recognition.

Since the early 1990s, new organizations have created international forums where national quality-assurance agencies can pursue agreements and collaborations. One example is RIACES, an organization whose members are national agencies for quality-assurance in Latin America. Among its many objectives is an agreement on comparable criteria used by the diverse accrediting agencies in the region to facilitate the comparability of degrees and institutions (González Enders 2010). The International Network for Quality-assurance Agencies in Higher Education (INQAAHE) brings together national agencies and members of regional organizations into a larger organization with a broader international reach for similar purposes. In addition, INQAAHE contributes to the development of accrediting agencies in a number of ways, including disseminating information about "good practice" in quality-assurance, providing training materials, and by facilitating the sharing of information and experience internationally (Woodhouse 2004; INQAAHE 2010).

In addition, new supranational agencies are engaging in accreditation activities in different countries. The European Quality Improvement Scheme (EQUIS) is an example of this. EQUIS accredits business and management programs throughout the world, creating a single measure of quality for programs in this area.

Clearly, when local accreditation provides international validity important benefits are received by many sectors. Although much international activity and discussion are taking place and accelerating at great speed, the agreements being made and considered are all based on whether participants can be confident of shared vocabulary, shared values, and shared objectives. Currently, the discussion tends toward "we will recognize what you recognize." With the ambiguity that hangs over the understanding of quality and standards in higher education, the process of mutual recognition seems to rest on a house of cards.

Conclusion

The discussion of quality will always be complicated by the lack of consensus about what quality means in higher education. Many attempts have been made to define it; most of the literature acknowledges the elusiveness of a useful definition. Harvey and Green offered different views of quality in their often-quoted 1993 essay—[quality] as exceptional, as perfection (or consistency), as fitness for purpose, as value for money and as transformative (1993, 11). As noted in this chapter, quality is often confused with a competitive position in the marketplace, star faculty, and prestige. Quality, to a large degree, remains in the eye of the beholder, and different perspectives will respond to different measures of it.

UNESCO's compiled glossary (Vlasceanu, Grünberg, and Pârlea 2007) is an important attempt to align the shared vocabulary of quality. For the short term, the same words and phrases will continue to be understood differently by various actors, with, in some cases, agreements signed on the basis of misunderstandings about those meanings. Regional agreements have been signed that recognize degrees as comparable as long as they are "accredited" in the country where they were awarded, without fully exploring the ways in which accreditation might be conducted or whether it fully meets the needs of all parties.

The diversity of higher education has made the problem even more complicated. Because quality is expected regarding *all* higher education institutions, quality-assurance programs must accommodate the enormous range of missions and resources that these institutions now represent—nationally and internationally. The question remains as to how usefully the same criteria can be applied to this growing diversity. Much care needs to be exercised before standards are applied from one country to the performance of another, a trend evident as national accrediting bodies are beginning to validate programs and institutions beyond their borders.

It needs to be known that faculty credentials, research, student/faculty ratios, institutional facilities and other factors can be easily documented. Learning about the performance of academic institutions and programs seems to defy easy measurement. There are too many variables that cannot be quantified. Often numerous variables combine to produce results making measurement even more difficult. Different institutions operate within the constraints of realities that must be factored in to the way their activities are assessed (Gil Antón 2006). Certain conventions have been achieved but no one seems entirely satisfied with them.

There are national, regional, and increasingly international agencies that provide oversight to quality-assurance processes. In most cases, these organizations rely on standards and/or criteria that reflect input as the basis of quality assessment, although there is increasing attention to outcomes. The oversight that these intermediary organizations can provide is limited. In the end, external agencies only guarantee some degree of attentiveness to quality. The critical work of quality-assurance and quality improvement must be conducted locally. Essential to success is "encouraging colleges and universities to become 'self-developing' organizations—institutions continually seeking improvement in their teaching and learning processes" (Dill 1997, 36).

As a result of the implementation of so many new quality-assurance schemes, quality is now a part of institutional management and planning everywhere. There is still limited research on the outcomes of all of the increased attention to quality (Stensaker 2008; Lemaitre 2004). At the very least, institutions now do a better job of collecting information and data. All of this evaluation is producing a lot of reports and making the internal activity of higher education a little more transparent. The quality of institutional management is certainly better as a result (Stensaker 2008).

Likewise, more attention is needed to be focused on teaching and learning, the impact of postsecondary study on students, and the relevance of academic programs to a globalized socioeconomic environment. More attention is needed on whether the incentives and rewards distributed within higher education contribute to the greater quality of its principle activities.

The key issue left unresolved is what purpose all of this attention to quality is meant to serve. Is quality-assurance or quality improvement being pursued? Has it been demonstrated that standards, whatever they mean, are being met or that performance is improving (Harvey and Newton 2004)? Many quality-assurance schemes attempt to do both. Yet, without the ability to define what quality is, perhaps the best policy is to engage in an ongoing process of improvement.

Although "globalization" and the resulting mobility of individuals, institutions, and activities underscore the growing importance of international benchmarks and standards for higher education, quality management has to remain a largely local endeavor. Context and culture are important factors in the consideration of quality. External agencies have provided an important impetus, ensuring that the pursuit of quality remains at the top of the higher education agenda. To receive benefits from the many evaluations now taking place, a broad range of participants within each higher education institution needs to recognize value in the process and participate in earnest. Quality-assurance is truly more of a process than a result and requires the cultivation of institutional cultures where all actors are open to self-criticism and attentive to opportunities for improvement.

References

Blackmur, Douglas (2007) "The public regulation of higher education qualities: Rationale, processes, and outcomes," in D.F. Westerheijden, B. Stensaker and M.J. Rosa (eds.) *Quality-assurance in Higher Education: Trends in Regulation, Translation and Transformation*, Dordrecht, Netherlands: Springer.

Clark, Burton R. (ed.) (1998) *Creating Entrepreneurial Universities: Organizational Pathways of Transformation*, London: Pergamon.

Dill, David D. (1997) "Accreditation, Assessment, Anarchy?" in John Brennan, Peter de Vries, and Ruth Williams (eds.) *Standards and Quality in Higher Education*, London: Jessica Kingsley.

—— (2003) The "Catch 22" of Academic Quality: Implications for Universities and Public Policy. Chapel Hill: University of North Carolina.

—— (2007) "Will market competition assure academic quality: An analysis of the UK and US experience," in D.F. Westerheijden, B. Stensaker and M.J. Rosa (eds.) *Quality-assurance in Higher Education: Trends in Regulation, Translation, and Transformation*, Dordrecht, Netherlands: Springer.

Fogg, Piper (2008) "Dorm therapy," *Chronicle of Higher Education*, March 7.

Gil Antón, Manuel (2006) "¿Cómo arreglar un coche? De los indicadores a la calidad, o de la calidad a los indicadores," ponencia presentada en el Foro Nacional sobre Calidad de la Educación Superior.

González Enders, Ernesto (2010) Las políticas de evaluación y acreditación de la calidad de la educación superior en América Latina y el Caribe: Una nueva agenda para la integración regional. *Boletín IESALC informa de educación superior* (203). Available: http://www.iesalc. unesco.org.ve/index.php?option = com_content&view = article&id = 1702%3Alas-politicas-de-evaluacion-y-acreditacion-de-la-calidad-de-la-educacion-superior-en-america-latina-y-el-caribe-una-nueva-agenda-para-la-integracion-regional-&catid = 6%3Aeditorial&Itemid = 729&lang = es.

Harvey, Lee and Diana Green (1993) "Defining quality," *Assessment & Evaluation in Higher Education* 18 (1): 26.

Harvey, Lee and Jethro Newton (2004) "Transforming quality evaluation," *Quality in Higher Education* 10 (2): 149–65.

INQAAHE (International Network for Quality-assurance Agencies in Higher Education) (2010) *INQAAHE 2010*. Available: http://www.inqaahe.org (accessed March 4, 2010).

Labi, Aisha (2008) "Obsession with rankings goes global," *Chronicle of Higher Education*, October 17.

Lederman, Doug (2010) "Imperfect Accountability," *Inside Higher Education*. Available: http://www.insidehighered.com/news/2010/03/02/voluntary.

Lemaitre, Maria José (2004) "Development of external quality-assurance schemes: An answer to the challenges of higher education evolution," *Quality in Higher Education* 10 (2): 89–99.

Neave, Guy (1994) "The politics of quality: Developments in higher education in Western Europe 1992–94," *European Journal of Education* 29 (2): 115–34.

Newton, Jethro (2000) "Feeding the beast or improving quality: Academics' perceptions of quality-assurance and quality monitoring," *Quality in Higher Education* 6 (2): 153–63.

OECD (Organization for Economic Cooperation and Development) (2010) *OECD Feasibility Study for the International Assessment of Higher Education Learning Outcomes*. Available: http://www.oecd.org/document/22/0,3343,en_2649_35961291_40624662_1_1_1_1,00.html (accessed March 2, 2010).

Stensaker, Bjorn (2008) "Outcomes of quality-assurance: A discussion of knowledge, methodology and validity," *Quality in Higher Education* 14 (1): 3–13.

Strauss, Valerie (2007) "Students can rest easy now: Demand has colleges ditching twin beds for doubles," *Washington Post*, September 18.

Thompson, Lyndon (2008) "Breaking ranks: Assesssing quality in higher education," in V. Lafon (ed.) *Institutional Management in Higher Education*, Paris: OECD.

Trow, Martin (1998) "On the accountability of higher education in the US," in W.G. Bowen and H.T. Shapiro (eds.) *Universities and Their Leadership*, Princeton, NJ: Princeton University Press.

Vlasceanu, Lazar, Laura Grünberg, and Dan Pârlea (2007) *Quality-assurance and Accreditation: A Glossary of Basic Terms and Definitions*, Bucharest, Romania: UNESCO.

Westerheijden, Don F. (2007) "States and Europe and quality of higher education," in D.F. Westerheijden, B. Stensaker, and M.J. Rosa (eds.) *Quality-assurance in Higher Education: Trends in Regulation, Translation, and Transformation*, Dordrecht, Netherlands: Springer.

Westerheijden, Don F., Bjorn Stensaker, and Maria Joã Rosa (eds.) (2007) "Conclusions and further challenges," in *Quality-assurance in Higher Education: Trends in Regulation, Translation and Transformation*. Dordrecht, Netherlands: Springer.

Woodhouse, David (2004) "The quality of quality-assurance agencies," *Quality in Higher Education* 10 (2): 77–87.

8

Global University Rankings and their Impact

NIAN CAI LIU AND YING CHENG

University rankings, which compare universities by uniform criteria, can generate simple and useful information on universities' conditions and performance, arousing considerable interests among stakeholders of higher education. Prospective students and their parents can use rankings to shortlist the universities to attend; governments and funding agencies, to inform funding decisions; employers, to recruit capable graduates; and universities, to position themselves, set strategic goals, choose partners, and enhance marketing activities. Therefore, university rankings seem to be here to stay and become more popular, causing leaders of universities to take them seriously. However, there are "uses" and "misuses" of rankings:

> The world seems to be obsessed with rankings in every walk of life. Countries are ranked for their performance in all possible domains, from the Olympics to the quality of life. Even Mozart's musical pieces are being ranked as the planet celebrated his 250th birth-year anniversary.
>
> (Salmi and Saroyan 2007, 58)

The History of Rankings

The *US News & World Report*, which began to publish the ranking of American universities in 1983, is usually recognized as the origin of university ranking (Usher and Savino 2007; Van Dyke 2005). In 1983, 1985, and 1987, the *US News & World Report* rankings were based on a survey of university presidents alone, and since 1988 *America's Best Colleges* was published and statistical data were used together with a reputation survey (Morse 2008). Now, the *US News & World Report* ranking not only provides the most important ranking in the United States but also probably the most influential national ranking throughout the world. University rankings are offered in almost all developed countries, and this trend is growing rapidly in less-developed areas of the world as well—such as eastern Europe, Latin America, Asia, and the Middle East (see Salmi and Saroyan 2007, for a list of university rankings). Some countries possess a dozen or more university rankings, ranging from the more sophisticated ones to the amusing ones. The publishers of university rankings include news-papers, magazines, companies, independent research institutions, government agencies, and individual researchers. While some rankings cover universities as a whole, others conduct the comparison on the school, department, and/or program level, or in terms of discipline and field.

A ranking system is built based on a set of indicators. Several reviews of indicators are used in university rankings. The ranking indicators can be categorized either by evaluation factors such as quality of academic staff, students, programs, and other aspects (Van Dyke 2005) or from a dynamic perspective involving input, process, and output (Dill and Soo 2005). An analysis of 18 rankings found hundreds of individual indicators and that some rankings use different indicators, thereby indicating a significant range of quality definitions (Usher and Savino 2007).

Traditionally, ranking indicators are weighted and then aggregated into a composite index. While such a method is understandable and has been applied by most rankings, it was often criticized because of the arbitrary or subjective allocation of weights by ranking publishers (Brooks 2005). As a response, the Center for Higher Education Development in Germany initiated a new approach to rank German university departments (Federkeil 2002). This ranking does not weigh individual indicators, leaving such decisions to users. By means of interactive web interfaces, one can select items of interest from an indicator set and weigh them freely to create customized rankings. Many ranking publishers offer such an option as complements of their formal rankings—among them, the Complete University Guide in the United Kingdom (Jobbins et al. 2008) and *Maclean's* ranking (*Maclean's* 2007) in Canada.

University rankings have faced heavy criticism since their emergence—with regard to inherent flaws in individual indicators and their weak correlations with quality, their faulty indicator sets and weighting schemes, and their dangerous directions, with misleading results and negative impacts. The extreme reactions were the boycotts of universities. In 2007, a dozen US college presidents wrote a public letter claiming they would not participate in the annual reputation survey of *US News & World Report's* ranking and would not cite ranking results in their promotional materials. This letter was later signed by a total of 61 US college presidents, who "disengaged from *US News & World Report's*" rankings. Yale University hosted a conference sponsored by the Education Conservancy on developing alternative ways to compare colleges, in 2007 (Education Conservancy 2007). A similar response occurred in Canada in 2006. The object concerned the *Maclean's* ranking, and the boycotters were the leading research universities—such as the University of Toronto, McMaster University, University of British Columbia, and Université de Montréal (CBC News 2006). In Asia, the regional university ranking by *Asiaweek* magazine had experienced the noncooperation of many prestigious Asian universities—

including the University of Tokyo, a flagship university in Japan listed top in the first two years of the ranking. However, in 2000, the magazine ceased its ranking, three years after its initiation (Cohen 2001).

Global University Rankings at a Glance

Due to the accelerated globalization of higher education, world-university rankings have grown in influence in recent years. Up to now, nearly a dozen global rankings of universities have been published.

Academic Ranking of World Universities

The first multi-indicator ranking of world universities was the (Shanghai) Academic Ranking of World Universities, published in June 2003 and then updated annually (Institute of Higher Education of Shanghai Jiao Tong University 2003). Although the initial purpose of this ranking project in Shanghai was to find the global standing of Chinese top universities, it attracted a great deal of attention from universities, governments, and public media worldwide. The Academic Ranking of World Universities used six objective indicators to rank world universities—including the number of alumni and staff winning Nobel Prizes and Fields Medals (10 percent weight for alumni and 20 percent weight for staff), highly cited researchers selected by Thomson Scientific (20 percent), articles published in two journals—*Nature* and *Science* (20percent), articles indexed in the Science Citation Index-Expanded and Social Sciences Citation Index (20 percent), and per capita performance with respect to the size of an institution (10 percent). More than 1,000 universities were actually ranked by the Academic Ranking of World Universities every year, and the top 500 were published on the web site.

World University Rankings

In November 2004, the *Times Higher Education Supplement* (2004) published its "World University Rankings." From 2005 to 2009, the ranking was copublished by *Times Higher Education* and the Quacquarelli Symonds company every year (http://www.topuniversities.com/worlduniversityrankings/). The *Times Higher Education* ranking intends to provide a global comparison of universities' success by recognizing their multiroles. The ranking indicators include an international opinion survey of academics and employers (40 percent weight for academics and 10 percent weight for employers), student faculty ratio (20 percent), citations per faculty member (20 percent), and proportions of foreign faculty and students (5 percent weight for each).

Global University Rankings using Bibliometrics

Bibliometrics studies the patterns and impact of publications. The bibliometric indicators have been widely used to measure research productivity and performance at all levels, and several global university rankings were made through this approach. The Higher Education Evaluation and Accreditation Council of Taiwan conducted the "Performance Ranking of Scientific Papers for World Universities," based on the analysis of paper publications of universities (Huang 2007). The indicators used included the number of articles in the last 11 years, articles in the current year, citations in the last 11 years, citations in the last 2 years, average number of citations in the last 11 years, h-index (i.e., the Hirsch index that provides the scientific output of a researcher) of the last two years, highly cited papers, papers in high-impact journals, and excellent fields. Twenty percent weight is assigned to the h-index of the last two years, and each of eight other indicators obtains 10 percent weight. Other globally bibliometric comparisons of universities include the International Champions League of Research Institutions, by the Centre for Science and Technology Studies at Switzerland (Centre d'études de la science et la technologie 2002), the "Bibliometric Rankings of World Universities" (Moed 2006), and "World Top Universities" by the Research Center for Chinese Science Evaluation of Wuhan University (2006). It should be noted that all indicators calculated in these bibliometric rankings are derived from citation indexes produced by Thomson Scientific.

Global University Rankings Using Web Metrics

The rapid development of information science and technology leads human society to a new era, and the Internet becomes an important source for learning and research. Some rankings try to measure and compare the web presence and visibility of world universities. The "Ranking Web of World Universities" presented by Cybermetrics Lab of CSIC (2004) used a series of web indicators to rank 16,000 universities worldwide. These indicators included the number of web pages (20 percent); rich files such as Adobe Acrobat, Adobe PostScript, Microsoft Word and Microsoft Powerpoint (15 percent); papers in Google Scholar (15 percent); and the total number of unique external links received (50 percent). Another web metrics ranking—"The G-Factor International University Ranking" (Hirst 2006)—used the number of links to a university's web site from other universities' sites as the only indicator to rerank the top 300 universities in the (Shanghai) Academic Ranking of World Universities.

Other Global University Rankings

Newsweek has provided a ranking of the top 100 global universities (*Newsweek* 2006), based on a combination of selected indicators in the Academic Ranking of World Universities and the *Times Higher Education* rankings and based on library holdings (number of volumes). A French higher education institution, École des Mines de Paris (2007), published the "Professional Ranking of World Universities" by calculating the number of alumni among the chief executive officers of the 500 leading worldwide companies. Besides global rankings, there were several regional rankings such as Leiden Ranking of European universities by the Center for Science and Technology Studies of Leiden University (2008) and the already ceased *Asiaweek* ranking.

Methodological Problems of Global University Rankings

Inadequate Reflection of University Functions

Global rankings have different purposes, and they only measure parts of universities' activities. Bibliometrics-based rankings focus on research output in Thomson Indexes; the Academic Ranking of World Universities also heavily emphasizes the research dimension of universities. The fundamental roles of universities—teaching and their contributions to society—are neglected in these systems. The compilers of the Academic Ranking of World Universities thought that it was impossible to compare the education quality worldwide due to the huge differences among higher education systems (Liu and Cheng 2005). Although the *Times Higher Education* ranking attempts to recognize and measure the multifaced universities by combining indicators of different activities—including some proxies of teaching quality—its practice hardly convinced others and the ranking was viewed as about reputation and "not about teaching and only marginally about research" (Marginson 2007). Thus, none of the current global ranking systems can provide a complete view of universities. Engaging any single ranking as a standard to judge a university's whole performance is improper. In addition, the popularity of research indicators in global ranking systems may encourage universities to devote too much to research regardless of their own traditions and features.

Pitfalls of Indicators

Currently, none of the ranking indicators can be viewed as perfect. Some seem practically acceptable, but others have serious flaws. The so-called academic peer review, used by the *Times Higher Education* ranking, might be the most heavily criticized indicator. First, it is just an expert opinion survey rather than a typical peer review in the academic community; the respondents, even though they are experts, can hardly make professional judgments regarding large entities due to cognitive distance (Raan 2007). Second, as an opinion survey, the results were affected by some psychological effects such as "halo effect" (Woodhouse 2008) and "leniency effect" (Van Dyke 2008). Thus, given a bias toward well-known universities and the respondents' universities, these effects may be further amplified by the disproportionally geographic distributions of respondents. Third, some technological problems in conducting a survey have arisen, such as low response rates. These issues make the reliability and validity of the indicator very questionable. The correlation coefficient between the score on experts' judgments in the *Times Higher Education* ranking and the citation-analysis-based results was found to be close to zero (Raan 2007), which is not consistent with the earlier empirical evidence that significant correlation exists between citation-based indicators and peer-assessment results.

The bibliometric indicators such as publications and citations (with or without normalization) were relatively credible in measuring research performance of large entities. Yet, some problems and shortcomings still occur when these indicators are used to compare universities worldwide (Raan 2005; Moed 2006; Zitt and Filliatreau 2007). Almost all global rankings chose Thomson Citation Indexes as their bibliometric sources; therefore, only publication output and work published in indexed journals are taken into account. This approach inevitably leads to some bias against universities with strong humanities and social science and universities from non-English-speaking countries. In addition, the correct identification and attribution of publications of universities from the Thomson Citation Indexes are by no means an easy task. For example, many universities have several variations of names, and overlooking one of these variations means some papers are missed out.

The teaching-related indicators such as student-faculty ratio and percentage of international faculty and students were also criticized, mainly because they cannot be used to adequately measure the teaching quality (Marginson 2007). Some indicators can be seen as proxies of teaching output—for example, the number of alumni among chief executive officers of top 500 companies and the number of alumni who receive Nobel Prizes or Fields Medals. However, the measured objects were restricted within a tiny group, which thus reveals little about the general quality of teaching output.

Other Aspects

Some general criticisms of ranking practices can also hold true for global rankings. A common phenomenon in global ranking is the arbitrary decision of the weights of indicators. Another question is that among universities with dissimilar global ranks, the difference between their scores may in fact be statistically insignificant. Moreover, due to technical difficulties, some major characteristics of universities, such as teaching quality, cannot be properly measured and are hence omitted from existing global rankings (Altbach 2006).

Ranking is an information tool, but global rankings simply provide information on a small number of universities. Even a list of 500 universities can only cover less than 3 percent of all 17,000 higher education institutions in the world. The number is reported in the International Association of Universities' World Higher Education Database 2008 (see http://www.unesco.org/iau/directories/index.html). The majority of countries are entirely absent from rankings. Therefore, when these excellence rankings consolidate and strengthen the prestige for universities on the lists, they may weaken the global visibility of other universities. Failure to be included in global ranking lists may bring additional difficulties to universities in enhancing their international activities.

The Impact of Global University Rankings

Although they can attract prospective students and employers, global university rankings obtain most attention from governments and universities.

Governments

With the emergence of the knowledge-based economy, research universities are expected to play a key role in building the core competiveness of countries. Therefore, national governments are eager to learn the strength and weakness of their universities in the world, but such information was not readily available until the appearance of global rankings. The global rankings provide comparative information on universities' performance in different countries, which helps governments realize the international standings of their universities. While some nations were satisfied with the global ranks of their universities, more nations began to feel a crisis. For example, the European Commissioner for Education said to the media, "If you look at the Shanghai index, we are the strongest continent in terms of numbers and potential but we are also shifting into a secondary position in terms of quality and attractiveness" (Blair 2007). In many countries, including France, global ranking has even become part of national debates about higher education and research policies: "France's poor showing in the Shanghai rankings—it had only two universities in the first top 100—helped trigger a national debate about higher education that resulted in a new law, passed last month, giving universities more freedom" (Enserink 2007). Nowadays, clearly more and more nations reveal their ambitions of having a certain number of universities within the top tier of the world in the future, regardless of the current standings of their universities.

Governments used global rankings not only to judge universities in their own countries but also to qualify foreign universities for different purposes. The authorities in Mongolia and Qatar restricted their "study abroad" scholarships for students admitted by highly ranked universities (Salmi and Saroyan 2007). Recently, the Dutch government introduced a new immigration rule allowing foreign students with a degree from the top 150 universities (in the *Times Higher Education* ranking or the Academic Ranking of World Universities) to apply for a Dutch residence permit even if they do not have a job offer (Expatica

2009). However, the authors think people should always be cautious with the direct use of ranking as determinative criteria, given the methodological limitations of rankings.

Universities

Whether or not universities admit their outlook, they do care about rankings. For better-placed universities, global rankings are effective tools in building and maintaining reputations, which attract talent and resources and extend support from the general public. A number of universities have been observed citing their global ranks in their campus news, annual reports, and promotional brochures. On the contrary, universities' poor performance (as compared with expectations) and absences in global rankings may have negative impacts. Because of the great influence of global rankings, climbing up on the lists has become a common desire among universities. A survey of leaders and senior managers of higher education institutions in 41 countries found that 82 percent of respondents wanted to improve their international position and 71 percent to be in the top quarter of the world (Hazelkorn 2008). At the same time, over 56 percent of respondents said their universities had established a formal internal mechanism to monitor rankings and their own performance, and 63 percent had already taken strategic, managerial, or academic actions in response to rankings.

One of the features of internationalized higher education consists of varied forms of collaboration among universities in different countries. The global rankings are then used by universities to inform their choice of partners in other countries. The international survey shows 57 percent of respondents thought rankings were influencing the willingness of other universities in conducting partnerships with them, and 34 percent thought rankings were influencing the attitude of support by other universities when they applied for a membership of academic or professional organizations (Hazelkorn 2008).

Trends in Global University Rankings

Ranking systems, resulting from strong market demands, are here to stay and unlikely to disappear in the foreseeable future. Global university rankings are even more vital because of the lack of other internationally comparable information on universities.

In May 2006, a guideline document for ranking—the Berlin Principles on Ranking of Higher Education Institutions—was endorsed by a group of ranking compilers and scholars, and was expected to support the improvement of ranking systems over time (Institute for Higher Education Policy 2006). The Berlin Principles consist of 16 descriptive principles covering four aspects: the purpose and goal of ranking, the design and weighting of indicators, the collection and processing of data, and the presentation of ranking results. The Berlin Principles reflect what a good ranking should do and were seemingly accepted by major ranking compilers. However, the Berlin Principles are considered not to have impacted the existing ranking practices, with most principles steering clear of the key problems of rankings; some principles being worthy but impractical, and others being so pious and obvious that no one would oppose them regardless of their actual operation (Marginson 2007). Significantly, the fifth principle is directly related to global rankings, stating that cross-national ranking should "specify the linguistic, cultural, economic, and historical contexts of the educational systems being ranked" (www.che.de/downloads/Berlin_Principles_IREG_534.pdf). Like other principles, this one may seem right, but the reality is that none of the global rankings have initiated practical approaches. In fact, an actual improvement in ranking methodology is not easy to achieve. Currently, based on the Berlin Principles, publishers of global rankings can make their ranking methodology—including data collection and processing—as transparent as possible and include adequate warnings with their ranking results, to prevent misuse.

At the end of 2008, the European Commission issued a call for tenders to design a multidimensional global university ranking system, and the CHERPA-Network consortium—led by the Centre for Higher Education Policy Studies of the Twente University in the Netherlands and the Centrum für Hochschulentwicklung (Center for Higher Education Development) in Germany—was finally selected to carry out a feasibility study (European Commission 2009). The primary purpose of this project, expected to finish in May 2010, is to develop a global ranking system over the various missions of higher education institutions—such as education, research, innovation, internationalization, community outreach, and employability. The project plans to select 150 higher education and research institutions worldwide as pilot institutions. The selection will be based on voluntary participation with consideration of institutions' geographical spread and different types of institutions.

The project's prospective achievement will depend on its progress regarding two aspects. First, it was frequently expressed that institutions' performance in teaching and other functions beyond research should be included in global rankings, but little has been accomplished up to now. The main goal of this project is to build a multidimensional ranking system. Therefore, a set of globally valid indicators for the teaching/learning and the service mission are expected to be produced. Second, because the project executes a feasibility study testing around 150 institutions, the possibility of applying its developed method to institutions all over the world in the future represents a crucial problem. In fact, there have been many good evaluation practices such as the Teaching Quality Assessment/Subject Review in England and the Assessment of Research-Doctorate Programs in the United States. However, it is almost impossible to carry out similar rigorous practices at a global level, given the workload and expenses. Undoubtedly, people do not anticipate a ranking system that can hardly be put in practice.

Obviously, global university rankings are born in the era of the global market. Their great influence derives from increasingly fierce competition in attracting excellent students, prominent researchers, and money among higher education institutions in different countries. Thus, while the number of global rankings will increase, the most influential ones no doubt will need to effectively measure institutions' global competence. The preferable global rankings should emphasize institutions' performance in areas where global competition exists. For example, the number of an institution's graduates who hold jobs abroad would be more valuable to a global comparison than a simple employment rate. The proportion of foreign students and professors, as well as resources from foreign bodies, contributes to institutions' global success.

Conclusion

The Pros and Cons of Rankings

The main feature of global rankings is measuring institutions' global competence and internationality. Thus, this procedure should not be a concern among all types of higher education institutions, especially teaching colleges that focus on addressing local needs. As a large majority of institutions in the world, teaching colleges are funded by local governments and do not carry out research. Their students mostly come from their own regions or countries, and their primary commitment involves cultivating the necessary talents and workforce. For institutions of this type, global rankings will serve as an almost pointless operation.

Some universities that hope to earn international influence or to enhance their international activities may be vexed by their absence or unsatisfactory positions in global rankings. However, before taking any special actions, those universities should carefully evaluate whether progress in certain global rankings would signify real improvements in global competence, whether such improvements would be consistent with universities' core values, or the financial burden. In addition, one should recognize the fact that the number of chairs for global scholars is always limited and the common expenditure of universities with good positions in global rankings is unaffordable for most universities. Therefore, the blind pursuit of global standings could be dangerous and harmful, especially for universities in less-developed countries.

Rankings' Methodologies and Shortcomings

Rankings are adopted for various purposes and often use different indicator systems, which could result in an alteration in ranks for the same university. Therefore, one should carefully examine ranking methodologies before looking at the results. The existing global rankings show a range of indicators to define quality. The Academic Ranking of World Universities mainly uses indicators of research performance; the *Times Higher Education* ranking gives high weight to reputation survey; other global rankings rely on either bibliometrics, Web metrics, or other special measurements. Because of the variations in ranking indicators, it is not surprising that different lists are generated by global rankings. For instance, only 63 universities are ranked among the top 100 in both the Academic Ranking of World Universities and *Times Higher Education* 2009 rankings, and only two of the universities received the same ranks (Shanghai Ranking Consultancy 2009; *Times Higher Education*-QS 2009).

Since all rankings have their limitations, university leaders should be aware of the possible bias caused by immature ranking methods. As introduced in previous sections, none of the existing global rankings can be seen as a comprehensive comparison of universities, because the learning output of students is hardly considered and universities' contributions to the economy are always ignored. Therefore, having earned high positions does not mean those universities are good in all terms, whereas low-ranked universities might do quite well in teaching or technology transfer.

The pitfalls of ranking indicators should also be analyzed while interpreting ranking results. Universities with strong life science departments and medical schools are favored by bibliometric indicators based on Thomson Citation Indexes, while universities' performance in humanities and social science are often underestimated when the bibliometric comparison is undertaken for the entire institution. Survey-based indicators could be distorted by uneven distributions of respondents; universities from particular countries would be ranked well if a disproportionately high percentage of respondents come from these countries. Some indicators are meaningful by themselves but not closely related to institutions' quality. For example, the percentage of international students can represent universities' success in global education markets, but this aspect has little to do with universities' attraction to the best students in the world or their teaching quality. Many global rankings indicators are measurements of gross performance of an institution, which may lead to bias against small institutions. Indicators of per capita performance may not equal reliability, due to technical difficulties in obtaining globally comparable data. For instance, the number of faculty members is often used as the denominator for normalizing institutions' gross performance. However, the definition of "faculty member" varies in different higher education systems, and the data were often collected without a unified standard.

Improvement of Strategies and Institutional Quality

An earlier-mentioned survey (Hazelkorn 2008) shows that most university leaders want to improve their institution's global positions. Thus, they need to know their environment and how to do better, and global university rankings assist them in considering and answering these questions. University leaders can form more rational views based on their global standings.

Global rankings not only generate ranks, but provide globally comparable data on universities. University leaders can use such information to identify their relative strengths and weaknesses more specifically, which is often helpful to universities' strategic planning. As Salmi and Saroyan suggested, universities should "look at specific indicators in order to understand better the determinants of their performance and work towards improving the quality of teaching, learning and research as may be the case" (2007, 30). For instance, the Academic Ranking of World Universities shows that in recent years top Chinese universities have realized a rapid growth in the total number of papers indexed by the Thomson Citation Databases, and some of them have already been ranked among the world's top 50, based on this metric. However, their number of publications in two prestigious journals—*Nature* and *Science*—remain mostly unchanged, implying an ongoing lack of creative studies. This information could help leaders of top Chinese universities realize that in the future special attention should be paid to encourage original research and innovation.

University leaders should be careful about making decisions toward improving ranking positions, for that practice may have a negative impact on institution quality. For example, the higher proportion of international faculty and of international students is enticed by the *Times Higher Education* ranking, but universities should be cautious about setting different standards for foreign candidates during the recruitment of academic staff and students. Although global rankings have many limitations, they can be used to think about new directions and chart innovative strategies.

References

Altbach, P.G. (2006) "The dilemmas of ranking." *International Higher Education*, 42: 1–2, http://www.bc.edu/bc_org/avp/soe/cihe/newsletter/Number42/p2_Altbach.htm (accessed 15 August 2007).

Blair, A. (2007) "Asia threatens to knock British universities off the top table." *Times* (21 May 2007). http://www.timesonline.co.uk/tol/life_and_style/education/article1816777.ece (accessed 30 December 2008).

Brooks, R.L. (2005) "Measuring university quality." *Review of Higher Education*, 29(1): 1–21.

CBC News (2006) "Eleven universities bail out of Maclean's survey" (14 August 2006). http://www.cbc.ca/canada/story/2006/08/14/macleans-universities.html(accessed 18 December 2008).

Center for Science and Technology Studies of Leiden University (2008) "The Leiden Ranking 2008," http://www.cwts.nl/ranking/LeidenRankingWebsite.html (accessed 15 December 2008).

Centre d'études de la science et la technologie (2002) "La Suisse et la Champions League international des institutions de recherche 1994–99." http://www.cest.ch/Publikationen/2002/CEST_2002_6.pdf (accessed 20 December 2008).

Cohen, D. (2001) "Asiaweek cancels controversial university survey." *Guardian.co.uk* (1 August 2001). http://www.guardian.co.uk/education/2001/aug/01/highereducation.uk(accessed 18 December 2008).

Cybermetrics Lab of CSIC (2004) "Ranking web of world universities." http://www.webometrics.info/index.html (accessed 20 December 2008).

Dill, D. and Soo, M. (2005) "Academic quality, league tables, and public policy: A cross-national analysis of university ranking systems." *Higher Education*, 49(4): 495–533.

École des Mines de Paris (2007) "Professional ranking of world universities." http://www.mines-paristech.fr/Actualites/PR/Archives/2007/EMP-ranking.pdf (accessed 20 December 2008).

Education Conservancy (2007) "The sixty-one college presidents withdraw from the college rankings system—Yale to host conference on developing alternative ways to compare colleges" (9 August 2007). http://www.educationconservancy.org/presidentsPR.html (accessed 18 December 2008).

Enserink, M. (2007) "Who ranks the university rankers?" *Science*, 317(5841): 1026–28.

European Commission (2009) "Commission launches feasibility study to develop a multi-dimensional university ranking" (2 June 2009). http://ec.europa.eu/education/news/news1416_en.htm (accessed 15 August 2009).

Expatica (2009) "Changes in Dutch immigration law 2009" (27 January 2009). http://www.expatica.com/nl/essentials_moving_to/essentials/Dutch-immigration-update-2009-.html (accessed 31 January 2009).

Federkeil, G. (2002) "Some aspects of ranking methodology—The CHE-ranking of German universities." *Higher Education in Europe*, 27(4): 389–97.

Hazelkorn, E. (2008) "Learning to live with league tables and ranking: The experience of institutional leaders." *Higher Education Policy*, 21(2): 193–215.

Hirst, P. (2006) "The G-Factor International University Ranking." http://www.universitymetrics.com/node/3#What (accessed 30 December 2008).

Huang, M.H. (2007) "2007 Performance ranking of scientific papers for world universities." http://ranking.heeact.edu.tw/en-us/2007/Page/Background (accessed 15 December 2008).

Institute for Higher Education Policy (2006) "International partnership issues groundbreaking principles on ranking of higher education institutions" (30 May 2006). http://www.ihep.org/press-room/news_release-detail.cfm?id = 145 (accessed 10 January 2009).

Institute of Higher Education of Shanghai Jiao Tong University. (2003) "Academic Ranking of World Universities—2003." http://ed.sjtu.edu.cn/rank/2003/2003main.htm (accessed 20 May 2008).

Jobbins, D., Kingston, B., Nunes, M., and Polding, R. (2008) "The Complete University Guide—A new concept for league table practices in the United Kingdom." *Higher Education in Europe*, 33(2/3): 357–59.

Liu, N.C. and Cheng, Y. (2005) "The Academic Ranking of World Universities." *Higher Education in Europe*, 30(2): 127–36.

Maclean's (2007) "17th Annual *Maclean's* Rankings 2007." http://oncampus.macleans.ca/education/2007/11/08/our-17th-annual-rankings/ (accessed 5 March 2008).

Marginson, S. (2007) "Global university rankings: Implications in general and for Australia." *Journal of Higher Education Policy and Management*, 29(2): 131–42.

Moed, H.F. (2006) "Bibliometric Rankings of World Universities." http://www.cwts.nl/hm/bibl_rnk_wrld_univ_full.pdf (accessed 25 June 2007).

Morse, R.J. (2008) "The real and perceived influence of the US News ranking." *Higher Education in Europe*, 33(2/3): 349–56.

Newsweek (2006) "The complete list: The top 100 global universities" (13 August 2006). http://web.archive.org/web/20060820193615/http://msnbc.msn.com/id/14321230/site/newsweek/ (accessed 18 December 2008).

Raan, A.J. van (2005) "Fatal attraction: Conceptual and methodological problems in the ranking of universities by bibliometric methods." *Scientometrics*, 62(1): 133–43.

——(2007) "Challenges in the ranking of universities," in J. Sadlak and N.C. Liu (eds.) *The World-Class University and Ranking: Aiming beyond Status*, Bucharest: UNESCO-CEPES.

Research Center for Chinese Science Evaluation of Wuhan University (2006) "World Top Universities." http://apps.lib.whu.edu.cn/newbook/sjdakypj2006.htm(accessed 30 December 2008).

Salmi, J. and Saroyan, A. (2007) "League tables as policy instruments: Uses and misuses." *Higher Education Management and Policy*, 19(2): 24–62.

Shanghai Ranking Consultancy (2009) "Academic Ranking of World Universities—2009." http://www.arwu.org/ARWU2009.jsp (accessed 28 December 2009).

Times Higher Education-QS (2009) "World University Rankings." http://www.topuniversities.com/university-rankings/world-university-rankings/2009/results (accessed 28 December 20098).

Times Higher Education Supplement. (2004) "World University Rankings 2004." http://www.

timeshighereducation.co.uk/hybrid.asp?typeCode=194&pubCode=1&navcode=120 (accessed 20 December 2008).

Usher, A. and Savino, M. (2007) "A global survey of university ranking and league tables." *Higher Education in Europe*, 32(1): 5–15.

Van Dyke, N. (2005) "Twenty years of university report cards." *Higher Education in Europe*, 30(2): 103–25.

——(2008) "Self- and peer-assessment disparities in university ranking schemes." *Higher Education in Europe*, 33(2/3): 285–93.

Woodhouse, D. (2008) "University rankings meaningless." *University World News* (7 September 2008). http://www.universityworldnews.com/article.php?story=20080904152335140 (accessed 30 December 2008).

Zitt, M. and Filliatreau, G. (2007) "Big is (made) beautiful: Some comments about the Shanghai-ranking of world-class universities," in J. Sadlak and N.C. Liu (eds.) *The World-Class University and Ranking: Aiming beyond Status*, Bucharest: UNESCO-CEPES.

9

Fund-Raising as Institutional Advancement

KAI-MING CHENG

Mobilization of nongovernment resources has become an issue that looms high on the policy agenda of many countries. Most systems of higher education are seeking various reforms. Such reforms almost inevitably involve higher education enrollment, "world-class" elite universities, improved student learning experiences, learning qualities, student support systems, physical and technological infrastructure, as well as internationalization. All such reforms lead to increased spending in higher education and create a felt need everywhere to seek more resources outside public revenues.

Thus, mobilization of nongovernmental resources becomes a key issue for every system to tackle—with a focus on three areas. The first issue handles the legitimization of private institutions, where tuitions are the major sources of income. The second issue involves the collaboration of public institutions with the private sector, often in the form of sponsors or commissions by the private sector, sales of research products, or other spin-off income-generating activities by the public institutions. The third issue indicates donations from private philanthropists to both public and private institutions. This chapter concentrates on the emergence and trends of philanthropy in higher education, and the impact on higher education development as demonstrated in some systems. Two dimensions of philanthropy are addressed: government policies and institutional undertaking.

Resource Strategies

While governments cannot afford to spend more on higher education, support from society at large can be expected. Of course, public revenues do not represent the full extent of community resources. To develop higher education to a new level, the totality of community resources has to be taken into consideration. This procedure is no longer a theory but is becoming a reality in many systems of higher education. Numerous governments are now shifting their thinking from purely depending on public funding to actively utilizing community resources in developing higher education. Revised resource strategies are required to face a new era of higher education development. This is perhaps the first step in a paradigm shift.

In this context, the notion of public-private partnership provides a useful overarching conceptual as well as policy framework. The critical issue in establishing a public-private partnership is the notion of a partner, where the government includes the private sector in its plans for higher education.

Understandably, appropriate to their respective histories and cultures, governments have a range of commitments to public-private partnership. On one end of the spectrum, the government may allow minimal participation of the private sector, such as allowing private institutions to exist only under stringent control. At the other end of the spectrum, as is the case in Pakistan, the government is keen to breed elite private institutions and includes private-sector representatives in formulating its higher education blueprint.

Most countries are in the middle in terms of policies regarding the private sector. Private institutions could be treated as a nuisance, a necessary evil, indifferent companions, strategic partners, or champions for spearheading developments (Cheng 2009). In general, governments are adopting encouraging attitudes toward the private sector, and the private sector is increasingly being included in the strategic plans of higher education development.

Given the increasing involvement of the private sector, the policy agenda of public-private partnership may include:

1. Creating legislation to facilitate the establishment of private institutions; as is the case in China, where a *Law for the Facilitation of Non-Government Education* was enacted in 2002.
2. Formulating a policy framework in order to accommodate development of private institutions, which may include land granting and subsidy for capital constructions.
3. Providing subsidy to students in private institutions, as a matter of legitimizing the role of the private sector; this might include subsidizing teachers' salaries, as a measure to enhance the quality of teachers in higher education institutions.
4. Including private institutions in the competition for funding in areas such as science research, policy consultancy, technology enhancement, or other funding for special purposes.
5. Establishing mechanisms for accrediting credentials offered by private institutions, thereby recognizing such credentials in the recruitment of civil servants.
6. Introducing "cost-recovery" or "self-financing" elements in public institutions, mainly in the realms of teaching programs; encouraging public institutions to engage in all kinds of income-generating activities, sometimes with tax exemptions.
7. Allowing public institutions to enter into partnerships with private enterprises in research, training, and consultancy, in an attempt to generate incomes beyond government funding; the typical case is Japan,

which in 2002 started "corporatizing" higher education institutions and allowing them to enter partnership as an independent legal entity.

8. Establishing mechanisms for government matching funds to encourage private philanthropic donations to higher education, as is the case in Singapore and Hong Kong, which will be discussed further later in this chapter.

Many other policy measures may facilitate the participation and growth of the private sector. The healthy development of such policy measures requires a critical mass of governments' genuine sincerity and long-term commitment—so that the private sector is treated as governments' equal partners and not perceived only as an expediency to supplement the shortage of government funding. There is also the necessity to reconstruct a system of accountability that transcends pure administrative control. In this latter dimension, it is always a learning exercise for governments to respect the principles and mechanisms of the market.

Wealth and Commonwealth

The most visible dimension of public-private partnerships highlights private institutions. It is common knowledge that, around the world, many systems of higher education include a substantial sector of private institutions. Most of such private institutions are financed through tuitions charged to the students. In quite a few systems of higher education, private institutions constitute the major sector (Levy 2008). In such systems, students are willing to pay, in anticipation of higher lifelong income because of the education they receive. In typical economics of education jargon, individuals invest in higher education for private return.

Private institutions are now often seen as a solution for expansion, without public funding, or for diversity beyond the civil service bureaucracy. In the case of private institutions, nongovernmental community resources are mobilized. First, the students pay from their household resources. Second, the private operators contribute with their investments or, in cases of charitable bodies, through student subsidies and scholarships. Likewise, as a matter of public-private partnership, some governments also provide subsidy, either means-tested or merit-based, to students. In exceptional cases, governments also subsidize teachers' salaries in private institutions.

However, private institutions are not seen to be helpful in facing issues of equity. Accompanying the expansion of higher education is the problem of disparity that all systems have to tackle. Many private institutions operate on a commercial basis. The finance of higher education has dug into the private household purse. Thus, while this line of development provides some solution to the massive expansion of higher education, it creates problems of inequity and hence barriers for social mobility. Often, young people from poor families are deprived of opportunities in public institutions, and they are less likely to be able to pay for private tuition.

Hence, if the equity dimension is factored into the higher education financing formula, private institutions provide at most a partial solution. This trend might, meanwhile, exacerbate problems of disparity. In other words, private institutions have helped expand higher education when public funding is not widely available for more students. They have widened the access to higher education but not for students who lack the means to pay the tuition. The private sector gives opportunity to people who could afford to invest but not those who could not. In other words, the private institutions are mobilizing only minimal resources from the household wealth; they do not mobilize the substantial wealth in the community to help the deprived.

How can we most effectively mobilize the wealth in the community to help the deprived in the realm of higher education? This issue is covered in the book *Wealth and Our Commonwealth*, by William Gates, Sr.—the father of Bill Gates and an entrepreneur turned philanthropist (Gates and Collins 2003). The title succinctly argues for the case of mobilization of resources in private wealth for the common good. With the exception of primitive tribal communities, he argued, there is disparity in people's wealth in all societies—the rich and the poor and "concentrated wealth" in a few. William Gates, Sr., in a speech he made at the Council for Advancement and Support of Education in 2004, said that in America, every person has the opportunity to become rich, and he proposed that it is only fair for the rich to share some of their wealth with the "commonwealth," so that more people would enjoy similar opportunities.

In many developing countries I visited, I asked, typically in a national conference, three questions. The answers echoed the aforementioned proposition. (1) *Do you want a strong higher education system?* The normal answer is a unanimous "Yes." (2) *Do you think the government can afford it?* The normal answer is a unanimous "No." (3) *Do you have rich people in the country?* Often the assembly pauses for a few seconds, and then answers unanimously, "Yes."

The three questions and answers are perhaps a good summary of the situation in almost all countries. Regardless of the economic status of the nation, there are always people with different degrees of wealth in the nation. It is a matter of how some of the wealth among the richer could also benefit public good. In a way, William Gates, Sr. is not only making a proposition about resources but also about people and about how the entire community could best use the totality of resources to benefit public good, in this case higher education.

William Gates, Sr. was arguing very much on the justification for taxation. However, the argument could go well beyond taxation and indeed *should* go beyond contributing to the public revenues. That is, there is also the issue of how community resources could directly benefit higher education.

Philanthropy and Public Funding

How does philanthropy feature in this general situation? Tax systems are a means to redistribute wealth, so that the poor would not be deprived of their basic rights. Such rights include food, water, health, accommodation, and among others, education. However, even if a nation that is rich, can afford high taxes, and possess a wealth of resources in the public coffer, there are limitations to how much general revenues could help develop higher education.

First, in most jurisdictions, public revenues could hardly go beyond supporting subsistence, and higher education can hardly be identified as a basic subsistence need. Even in systems with an oversupply of higher education—Taiwan and Korea serve as examples where the systems of higher education have exceeded the number of high school graduates—the enrollment ratio in higher education stands only around 85 percent. Higher education is yet to become universal or compulsory as is the case with basic education. If higher education is not seen as a commitment to the entire population, fundamental problems hamper the allocation of public money to higher education.

Second, government appropriation often provides public institutions the mere means to support teaching (i.e., teacher salaries). There are systems in developing countries—for example, in Latin America—where public funding is not even sufficient to support teachers' salaries and they have to survive on moonlighting. In such systems, it would be hard to anticipate support on research or other developments from government funding. Even in more affluent systems like Hong Kong and Singapore, where government funding is generous, only limited pools of public resources exist for development in new ventures. To tap the resources from such pools would usually entail tedious procedures and fierce competition.

Third, public funding often emerges with public accountability, which could easily present bureaucratic, mechanistic, and quantitative measurements that are averse to academic undertakings. Public funding tends to favor programs or projects that could bring about immediate results, yield measurable outcomes, respond to urgent questions, or supply simple conclusions to complicated issues. As such, it is difficult to expect the government to fund scopes of higher education development unable to provide quick visible results.

In this context, philanthropy is generally realized as donations, although the term *donation* could take on different meanings in different cultures, as will be seen later. Philanthropy in higher education materializes as support from private resources, often to benefit individual institutions or individual students. Donations seem to be able to compensate for the aforementioned limitations of government funding.

Hence, it could be perceived that most of these donations are intended to help facilitate and enhance excellence in higher education. Departments or professors in higher education receive donations because the donors appreciate their contributions and endorse their missions and hence are glad to become a partner in a meaningful course. Donations in higher education do not come forth to an ailing department or a deteriorating discipline. Hence, in the end, the respective areas of excellence are supported by additional resources without disturbing the public system of resource allocation.

By the same token, private donations support higher education as a distinguished sector, rather than as a rescue for the deprived. Donors are dedicated to a prominent institution, look forward to more distinguished graduates, support distinguished research undertaking, or seek to improve the buildings and facilities. Thus, in higher education philanthropy, "making the rich richer" is a general pattern.

Donation also allows ventures that could not easily reach the usual public agenda. Such funding would assist pioneering or experimental studies or programs that do not promise immediate success. Other motives would include allowing creative and innovative ideas to emerge, while the outcomes are not always predictable. Donations, dependent on the donors' endorsement, could also facilitate the testing of new concepts that would otherwise be seen as too futuristic or idealistic.

In general, private donations seldom undertake recurrent expenditures, which largely go to teaching. Recurrent expenditures in public institutions are often viewed as the responsibility of government funding. For private institutions, recurrent expenditures are often supported by student tuitions. This is understandable, because regular budgets are long-term commitments not related to the nature of private donations.

In this context, public and private funding often become intertwined. Private institutions may receive government money through competitive application of government grants. In increasingly more systems, private institutions could receive government funding through these channels. On the other hand, public institutions receive private funding directly on various projects and indirectly through student scholarships due to private donations. Indeed, many systems that witness emerging trends of philanthropy toward higher education do not experience any shortage of public funding. Private donations enable institutions to go the extra miles.

Thus, a sound higher education system could not survive only on private money (tuitions and donations), but likewise, it could not excel only on public money.

Philanthropy and Autonomy

Donations are often also called gifts in philanthropy literature. Donors provide gifts to higher education institutions for a reason. Seven faces of philanthropy have been identified, referring to the motives for private donations (Prince and File 1994): (1) giving makes sense, where donors may take a rational approach and think they should share their wealth with society; (2) giving is God's will, so that people donate as part of fulfilling their religious beliefs; (3) giving is good business and some donors calculate the returns to donation in terms of fame, status, or connections or for tax benefits; (4) giving is fun, where donations cause happiness when one's own money is seen put into good use; (5) giving feels good, where giving up some of one's wealth gives the person an unusual relief; (6) giving in return, for example, to the alma mater where the former student completed study on donations; and (7) giving as a family tradition.

We could easily add two more categories: giving as an obligation, responsibility or mission, as individuals, family foundations, and corporations increasingly see donation as part of their commitment to society; and giving as a way of presenting a challenge to the conventional and the mediocre or as a way of offsetting dissatisfaction. People may donate to a new type of school or educational venture to challenge the public sector, to create new frontiers of excellence, or to test new ideas.

The list illustrates that donors' motives often differ from purposes and missions in higher education. Therefore, it is not possible, or necessary, to expect total alignment of donors' motives with the institutional visions and values. A useful examination covers the issue of institutional autonomy or academic freedom vis-à-vis private donations. In other words, it is legitimate to ask, are there always "strings attached" with private donations?

Donations could come from corporations or from individuals. Those from corporations often represent some collective decision and therefore tend to be more exact and scrupulous in the granting and use of the donation. The style of private donations varies, often from a private or family foundation.

Donations could be "restricted" ones, which are earmarked for specified purposes agreed between the donor and the institution. They could be "unrestricted" ones, where the institution has the discretion to utilize the money in ways that it prefers. A large part of donations to higher education are "restricted" in nature, because many donors would like to know how the money they provide could make a difference.

Donations could become an "endowment," where the funds are set up as a foundation and the institution draws upon the interests generated from the capital. Otherwise, donations form money that will be spent within a certain period of time or by the end of a project.

The relationship between the donor and the institution may encounter a spectrum of possibilities, with different degrees of "exchange," and that pertains to institutional autonomy. At one end of the spectrum are donations in their pure form. Money is given to the institution for agreed purposes, and the donor should have no interference whatsoever in the practical disbursement of the money, given that the agreed purposes are served. In cultures where philanthropy has a long history, such as the United States, a mature legal system embraces donations. The donors enjoy substantial tax benefits because of their contribution to education, but in return donors are not allowed to participate in the practical disbursement of the funds. That is, the money provided no longer belongs to the donor. Under these conditions, academic autonomy is protected by law, notwithstanding the positive contributions the donations may bring about.

At the other end of the spectrum, donation is seen as a transaction, and the donors receive privileged benefits from the institution because of the donation. This is the situation at some institutions in mainland China. There are cases where the donor is given a "list of privileges," so that with the donation they will enjoy benefits based on the amounts they donate. Such benefits include priority admissions of their recommended student applicants, space for advertisement, contracts for purchase or services, or even membership in the governing board. Such practices in China or other countries could be seen as a rather serious infringement of academic integrity in other cultures, and the donations not seen so much as "gifts."

Most systems lie somewhere between the two ends. Some of the issues are handled differently in different cultures—for example, the issue of the extent to which a scholarship donor should participate in the selection of the scholarship recipient. Another controversy is over naming rights—such as, the conditions under which a building or an institution should be named after the donor.

The crux of the issue is to what extent the donation should affect institutional autonomy—for instance, affecting the discretion of the institution in making decisions related to its academic affairs. Given that the concept of academic autonomy bears different meanings in different societies, indeed no definitive rule binds the institutions in their positions toward the donors. Nonetheless, regardless of the culture and the definition of academic autonomy, unambiguous guidelines should cover the relationship between the donor and the institution, and mechanisms should make sure such guidelines are observed.

However, advocates of higher education philanthropy would see the positive impact of donations regarding institutional autonomy. They would argue that with donations, institutions and donors work as preferred partners to each other. As such, the institutions negotiate with the donors over areas or projects. Institutions also have the freedom to choose the preferred areas of strategic importance to institutional development. Before the donations are actually made, the institutions have the freedom to negotiate the conditions and terms of the donation. In the end, donations could relieve the institutions from bureaucratic requirements inherent in government funding.

Institutions with substantial endowments would be able to launch new programs that are outside the categories expected by public funding. At the University of Hong Kong, for example, donations have enabled one-third of each student cohort to enjoy exchange-study abroad, for one year or one semester. At the same university, donations have created a "first-of-family" scholarship for first-generation university students, as an encouragement to high school graduates.

The institutions need to define their boundaries of academic freedom and to guard this freedom against possible concessions due to the donation. In the worst case, the donations may come forth because of substantial surrender of academic integrity and may receive criticism or objection from the community, for example, the alumni of the institution. Quite a few recent controversial cases of donations from pharmaceutical corporations to medical schools in the United States belong to this category. However, in many cases donations are rejected by institutions either because they are against some consensual principles (for example, against the tobacco industries) or because the donor's proposal does not fit into the institution's strategic plan.

In a way, self-confidence and self-esteem go hand in hand with fund-raising. It is only self-respect that enables an institution to negotiate with the donors and persuade the donors to respect the integrity of the institution. Most donors have no intention to intrude on academic territory. It is up to the institutions to align the donors' motives to loftier goals.

Whatever the cultural environment could be, a distinction should be made between donations and commissions. A commission consists of the institution being urged by a sponsor to carry out a project where the sponsor has a say in the process. The end product of the project normally belongs to the donor or is shared between the institution and the donor, on agreed terms. In some cases, the commission is similar to a purchase of the institution's service as an outsource facility. Donations, however, are made on condition that the disbursement of the donation is left to the institution. The spirit of this arrangement is that institutions do not attract donations by any sacrifice in their academic autonomy. All these issues perhaps demonstrate that higher education will never be as neat and simple as when it is either supported purely by public funding or with the mere support of tuitions.

Government and Philanthropy

With the general awakening to the importance of private participation, quite a few governments have pioneered schemes aimed at inducing private donations and creating a philanthropic culture. As an example, in 1997 the Singapore government started a scheme of "a matching fund" to foster a culture of higher education philanthropy. As per this scheme, the government would match every dollar from private donation with three dollars. The effort to cultivate a culture of philanthropy was so successful that the scheme was soon modified to a dollar-to-dollar matching, because of the enthusiasm for donations aroused by the scheme.

Hong Kong started a similar "government matching grant" scheme in 2003, ironically at the bitter economic downturn due to the epidemic SARS. It started with a dollar-to-dollar matching which evolved into a one-to-two matching, whereby the government would match every two dollars of donation with one dollar. In four rounds over five years, the government contributed 4 billion Hong Kong dollars (around US$500 million) in matching donations to the tune of more than 11 billion (around US$1.4 billion), almost three times the government contribution, which is equivalent to the government's budget for a year for the entire higher education system in the jurisdiction.

Unlike the Singaporean scheme, which is the government's perpetual commitment, the Hong Kong scheme is offered as a one-off chunk in each round, and there is no promise of continuation. Despite the admission that the stronger institutions will benefit more by the matching scheme, some equity element has been built into the Hong Kong scheme. A "ceiling" is formed for each institution, so that no one institution can have monopoly, as well as a "floor," where even the weaker institutions will be protected for a minimum. Following a similar model, the United Kingdom started a matching fund scheme in 2008 where the government put aside £200 million for three years to attract private donations.

The matching grant schemes worked miracles and have created totally new sources of funding for higher education. The government matching has convinced the community that the government is not shirking its responsibilities. It has also given the donors the opportunity to double or increase (in the case of less than one-to-one matching) the value of the money they give. The matching grants scheme has also motivated institutions to engage in fund-raising as a necessary part of their operation. Institutions started development offices, and academics learned to develop their dreams and explain their contributions to the laymen in the community. It is almost a revolution in its own right, as will also be examined later in this chapter.

The matching scheme in Hong Kong also induced an Alumni Challenge scheme established in 2005 by Stanley Ho, the casino tycoon in Macao, who has set aside for the University of Hong Kong 500 million Hong Kong dollars (US$62.5 million), 100 million each year, matching only alumni donations up to a maximum of 5 million in each donation. In the year that followed, alumni giving increased by 646 percent and number of alumni donors by 214 percent; 85 percent of the alumni donors were first-time donors. Philanthropy is, therefore, a culture where people influence people.

Many other countries are in the process of loosening restrictions for public institutions to receive private resources. Until recently, China's higher education institutions were public in the main. However, all leading institutions in China are now proud of their donation incomes. In 2002, with the "corporatization" of its public institutions, Japan allowed public institutions to receive private donations for the first time. Pakistan, as a developing country, has recognized the strength of the entrepreneur in the nation and is now actively contemplating government matching to encourage private donations.

The success of the matching grant schemes, as well as the rise of philanthropy in many countries in general, demonstrates that resources are available in the community and people are ready to make donations. The question is whether they would like to make donations to higher education. In many developing countries, the local rich people and overseas diasporas have always had the habit of making donations. They donate to temples, bridges, village schools, or sometimes foreign universities. The government matching has created an indication that higher education is also a field where money would make a useful contribution. It is an important step toward new resources strategies.

The Idea of Institutional Advancement

It is now clear that private donations to higher education are not only about more money. They often play a role that is not always achievable by other public funding. This lends itself to the notion of "institutional advancement."

Philanthropy in higher education takes on different names at different times. It is generally known as fund-raising, because the eventual tangible outcome of philanthropy is securing money from the donors. For many years, perhaps to avoid the terms "fund" and "money," philanthropy in higher education was known as "resources development." The term is still embedded in the name "development office," which often refers to the organ for fund-raising in higher education institutions. However, more recently, the term "institutional advancement" prevails in the international literature.

Institutional advancement, a term originated from the United States, vividly reflects the nature of fund-raising in higher education. In a way, institutional advancement is about fund-raising, but it is more than fund-raising. It embraces the meaning and purpose of fund-raising, which is to advance the institution to a new level of development. The following two examples, which again took place at the University of Hong Kong, may best illustrate the meaning of institutional advancement.

The first example is about laptop computers for students. In 1998, after some soul-searching and research, there was a recommendation that allowing every student to own a laptop computer would be pivotal to development on all fronts of information technology. Negotiations with dealers (IBM in this case) settled on a scheme where for each laptop machine the dealer would give a discount of about one-third the price, the students had to pay one third, and the university had to pay for the remaining third. This last bit amounted to about US$2 million, which the university, as a public institution could not come up with based on the government appropriation. At the critical moment, the then vice chancellor (i.e., the president) expressed a determination: "I will find the money!" Thus, the university became the first ThinkPad University in Asia, and thereafter owns a leading edge in learning technologies. The example demonstrates that the money was not about doing more and better than what was being doing. It was about doing things on a completely new plane. It changed the university's technology landscape. Hence it is advancement.

It is quite common, when a new idea comes through, to hear university presidents saying: "Money is not a problem!" It does not mean that they already have plenty of money in hand. What they actually mean is: "The problem is not about money!" This is antithetical to the general way of thinking in a public institution. When I was dean of education at the University of Hong Kong, before donations significantly came forth, the general mentality was to tailor our activities according to the allocated funding. When there was a budget cut, I cut my activities accordingly. Allocation, or appropriation, was the limit.

With donations in mind, sky is the limit in terms of money. The issue is whether we have a dream and whether the idea, project, or plan is convincing and strategic (i.e., an advancement). If it is, then we are confident in getting support from the community (i.e., donations). That is the general underpinning philosophy about fund-raising. It is advancement that drives fund-raising, not the other way around. In a way, donors are attracted only to advancements. According to this philosophy, the usual sigh of "but we don't have the money" could often be turned into the starting point of a good project for fund-raising.

The concept of advancement could be further illustrated in the second example. In 2006, I went to talk to one of our deans of a professional non-science faculty, which was relatively small but strong. It was a kind of needs analysis to understand the amount of resources he would need. After simple counting, he said he would need around 2 million (local currency, equivalent to US$240,000) in order to compensate for a shortfall due to a budget cut. I tested him whether an endowment of 20 million would help. It did not attract him because the interest was seen to be too small. I further cornered him with a hypothetical 200 million. He got stuck and, after some hesitation, said "No, I already have too much on my plate." Nonetheless, he raised 80 million in the following year, which is greater than his annual appropriation of 70 million. He, therefore, had established three more chair professors, started a new cutting-edge program, and created two positions for frontier academic areas. The following year, he came to me with an advancement plan, in anticipation of 800 million in five years, half of which would be for a devoted faculty building. The next year, he got the building, because he was the first dean who had a plan in hand for 400 million.

This second example shows a change in paradigm in the same dean. Typical of an administrator in a public institution, he could only tailor his activities according to the money handed down from above. There was no room for him to dream beyond the allocation. Philanthropic donations opened up a totally new window of opportunity for him, so that he could boldly dream and chart his path, because although money is a concern, it is no longer a constraint.

This is what institutional advancement is about. Compared with the situation where an institution lives only on public appropriations, I could identify a few marked differences in terms of paradigms. In the paradigm shaped by public funding: public appropriation is the ceiling; when there is no money, there is no plan; the natural consequence of any budget cut is reduction of activities; donations are meant to be small money to compensate for discrepancies in public funding; money is needed when there is a budget deficit and the department is weak; what is going to happen tomorrow is not very different from what we have been doing; and the ideal situation is a steady state. However, under the paradigm of institutional advancement: the sky is the limit in funding; it is great vision that leads to big money; money is to fulfill a big leap in development; money comes by only when we are strong; what we do tomorrow will be on a much higher plain than what we have today; and we are ever looking for new breakthroughs and starting new traditions.

The notion of institutional advancement, thus, has a liberating function. It moves academics out of the box fixed by government allocation. It puts the core values back to academic endeavors, it creates room for creative and innovative thinking, it allows dreams to be realized, and it encourages bold explorations and risk taking, which are so precious for academic inquiry and breakthroughs yet are hardly supported by public funding.

This is an essential concept for philanthropy in higher education. Donations for higher education are usually partnerships with academic excellence. Donations to higher education are indicative of community endorsement of the institutions' contributions. It is also indicative of community agreement with the missions of the institution. Hence, successful fund-raising is not only about strategies and skills. It is about articulating the nature, mission, values, and impact of the work that academics are doing.

Fund-raising in Institutions

How exactly does fund-raising work in institutions? A brief account of the salient elements for institutional advancement follows.

The Champion

Fund-raising in an institution is often led by a champion. The champion should be either the president or someone at the senior management level working closely with the president. The champion should be totally convinced about the importance of institutional advancement, taking that as a mission. Given the essential nature of fund-raising, institutional advancement should occupy a major position in the institution's policy agenda.

The champion for institutional advancement is usually the university president. This is because only he could comprehensively represent the "face" of the institution, and most donors would think they are partnering with the institution as a whole. Even if in terms of portfolio another person plays the champion of fund-raising, the president has an undeniable leadership role to play in the planning and activities of fund-raising. Institutions that start fund-raising from scratch often rely almost entirely on the president. I have seen small universities such as the University of Swaziland, a public institution, where the vice chancellor (i.e., president), proudly on his own, has solicited substantial donations for the university's advancement. Many private institutions in Indonesia are also engaged in fund-raising activities initiated by the rector (president).

Some institutions appoint a vice president with a portfolio of institutional advancement. In some cases, the champion can also be a "silver hair" professor or a few such professors who have a devoted portfolio for fund-raising. Alternatively, in some conventions, the champion can be an alumni leader who is also a prominent figure in society. In any case, the champion should be someone who commands respect both within the institution and in society, with determination to create new resources for the institution. The champion should also possess the capacity to articulate the essence of fund-raising and to inspire members of the university community to engage in institutional advancement.

Development Office

Real institutional advancement often starts with the establishment of a development office, so that fund-raising activities could be coordinated and organized. Major universities nowadays all have development offices, often modeled after the American universities. The tasks of the development office include planning, database construction and maintenance, networking, and event management. However, the majority of its tasks are interactions with donors and potential donors, which include cultivation (networking and relationship building), solicitation (asking), stewardship (maintenance of the relationship), and renewal (asking again).

The director of the development office is a crucial figure in fund-raising, whose importance in fund-raising is second only to the president. In the most successful cases, the directors have had their own social status; so that they would not be seen as merely employed fund-raisers. There is no definite career path that leads to a directorship of development. The nearest occupation to the post is marketing. Often, a person is appointed as director of development because of his/her track record of fund-raising in previous institutions, rather than because of his/her training. In institutions with a vice president in charge of institutional advancement, the vice president oversees the work of the development office. In such a case, the director could be just a professional fund-raiser.

There are different models of the organizational position of the development office. At many institutions, the development office is responsible for alumni networking, although in many cases the two positions are separate. Some institutions include fund-raising, alumni affairs, media and publicity, and universities' relations under one umbrella, often under one vice president.

No definite size exists for the development office. In the extreme case, Harvard University's central development office hosts 220 employees, with development offices of various sizes in the respective schools. Harvard typically raises around US$500 million a year. Most development offices in other American universities are much smaller. In China, the equivalent of a development office often takes the form of a secretariat to the university foundation. In Peking University, which raises funds annually to the order of US$0.5 million, some 20 people work for the foundation. In the University of Hong Kong, which has an annual yield of around US$100 million, there are 25 people in the development office, which also takes care of alumni affairs.

The size of the development office is often also governed by the investment of the institution in fund-raising. According to the Council for the Advancement and Support of Education, in the United States, the professional body for institutional fund-raisers with international membership, the investment in fund-raising could be anything between 5 to 15 percent of the annual yield. While there is no lower bound to the spending, anything about 15 percent could be seen as high.

A Campaign

Often, institutions would like to conduct fund-raising in the form of campaigns. The concept of a *campaign* distinguishes itself from the daily routines of an administrative division in an institution. A campaign typically has a starting date and a sunset date, leading to a definite target against which one could measure the degree of success of the fund-raising; it is strongly target oriented. Another feature of a campaign is that it is a project and should have a planned duration, with a schedule and a budget for investment. Theoretically, the team would be dismissed when the campaign is complete.

A campaign is also a good framework for working out the fund-raising strategies, which are often represented by a fund-raising "pyramid." The pyramid is a kind of estimation in terms of the amounts and the donors. The pyramid follows more or less a 80/20 principle, where at the top of the pyramid, a handful of donors might each give, say, 200 million "dollars"; and at the bottom, some thousands of donors may each give, say, below 500 "dollars." As one works their way down the pyramid, the amount decreases but the number of donors increases. The pyramid thus constructed can provide a starting point for adjusting fund-raising strategies to gain the optimal amount of donations. The workload and human resources requirements can also be estimated. The development office can then work out who the possible donors are and what are the "products" (items or projects to receive the donations). Fund-raising activities, events, and relational contacts are then planned, accordingly.

Donors

The described pyramid also presents the reality about donors. The majority of the donors contribute a small percentage to the sum, but a few major donors contribute to the majority of the sum. The major donations are often categorized as major gifts, because though small in number, securing them requires substantial effort such gifts and subsequently demands very careful stewardship. Stewardship here refers to maintaining close relations with the donor, involving them as a member of the university community, so that they also develop some ownership in the university's developments. Also leadership gifts exist whose amounts are often unprecedented, and hence they set the benchmark for the donations that follow.

The majority of the donors contribute small sums. For some institutions, such donations take the form of alumni annual gifts, where each person donates a fixed sum (often a small amount) every year as a token to pay back to the alma mater. Some institutions have established alumni networks, where volunteer alumni representatives pay home visits to other alumni in an effort to raise funds. Some other institutions adopt "phonathons" to encourage alumni donations through telephone contact or to solicit alumni donations electronically, through the web. In an institution mature in fund-raising, all donors are benefactors for the institution, regardless of the sum they donated.

Products

Products refer to items on which donations can be received. Classical examples of products are named buildings, often referred to as "brick and mortar." The donation money may or may not be used to cover the building costs. However, the building is named after the donor as a token of recognition and memory. There are indeed real "bricks" where the donor could leave a note of memory, which will be part of a new building, for example.

Donors donate toward professorships as a token of their appreciation and support of academic excellence. With a substantial donation, the selected discipline or academic would be named after the donor in the form of a named endowed professorship. Sometimes, the donor would like to name the particular discipline in anticipation of developments in the future.

Various kinds of scholarships would enrich students' learning experiences. These might include exchange study in another country, service learning in a developing country or in the deprived areas of the home country, or provisions to undertake internship in a local organization. All these reflect the learning activities in the institution. Of course, there are many other scholarships to provide financial assistance to students or to reward merits in their study.

The aforementioned are just a few of the most common products for higher education philanthropy. There are no limits to the design of a product for donations. In reality, much of the work of the development office is to help create or formulate donation products. Much of the task is to articulate the areas of excellence in a language understood by a layman. Often, such articulations are realized in a "case statement," which describes what the discipline is about, how it is contributing to human lives, and how a donation would make a difference. The case statement acts as a bridge between what the academic is actually working on and what could be understood by potential donors.

Conclusion

The world trend of expanding and enhancing higher education is an emerging but irreversible phenomenon. Often, it is only when governments have decided on expansion of higher education that they start looking for resources. Moving beyond public revenues and mobilizing community resources has become an urgent necessity. Among others, attracting private philanthropy should become a major task facing all institutions. While government allocation and student tuition could become the boundaries for academic endeavors in public and private institutions respectively, donations could enable institutions to scale new planes and realize new dreams. It is only with significant contribution from the community that massive higher education of high quality can become a reality.

References

Cheng, K.M. (2009) "Public-Private Partnership," in S. Bjarnason, K.M. Cheng, J. Fielden, M.J. Lemaitre, D. Levy, and N.V. Varghese, *A New Dynamic: Private Higher Education*, Paris: UNESCO.

Gates, W.H., Sr. and C. Collins (2003) *Wealth and Our Commonwealth: Why America Should Tax Accumulated Fortunes*. Boston: Beacon Press.

Levy, D.C. (2008) "Intersectoral interfaces in higher education development: Private and public in sync?" in J.Y. Lin and B. Pleskovic (eds.) *Higher Education and Development*, Washington, DC: World Bank.

Prince, R.A. and K.M. File (1994) *The Seven Faces of Philanthropy: A New Approach to Cultivating Major Donors*. San Francisco: Jossey-Bass.

10

The Challenge of University Leadership in the Developing World

D. BRUCE JOHNSTONE

If higher education leadership is thought of as combining authority and influence to make a difference—that is, to effect change—in either institutions or systems of higher education, then the challenges are formidable in the best of financial and political circumstances. Under conditions of severe financial austerity and the not uncommon political interference and instability found in many developing countries, the challenges to higher education leadership in the first decade of the twenty-first century are immense.

At the same time, the need for change, especially in the universities of the so-called developing world, is also immense. Universities in all countries must contend with the ever-changing nature of science and the ever-shifting frontiers of knowledge itself. They must change with the shifting demands of a global economy and with the changing requirements of the workplace. Especially in the developing world, universities must also increase capacity to keep up with the surging demand for higher education—fueled by increasing populations and ever-larger proportions of increasing populations seeking places in the institutions of higher education. Universities—again, especially in the developing world—must somehow accommodate (or fail to accommodate) these changes, most of which are costly, in a climate of severe and worsening austerity and frequently of political intrusion and/or instability.

This chapter is an exploration of the nature of these leadership challenges in the so-called developing world both at the level of the institution (presidents, vice chancellors, deans, and rectors) as well as the level of the state or of a multicampus system (ministers, permanent secretaries, system heads, and other high-ranking governmental officials), while seeking to achieve change mainly in public higher education systems. Under the assumption that universities and higher education systems need to change—mainly in developing countries beset with growing needs and deteriorating finances—some of the factors that impede leadership will be examined and suggestions offered to better enable leadership both at the institutional level as well as the level of governmental and systemwide policymaking.

Some individuals, because of charisma, courage, vision, interpersonal skills, and good luck will be more effective leaders than others, and most individuals in leadership positions can learn to be better leaders. To anticipate a conclusion of this chapter, it will be argued that leadership, as the capacity to effect change, is a function not just of natural gifts, or learned behaviors, or tricks of the trade but also of the policy context in which institutions and their leaders operate. Providing more and better leaders depend on careful selection and on some leadership training. Yet, more effective higher education leadership also requires better governmental policies that give people in leadership positions the freedom to make difficult decisions, the support in the face of the inevitable push back from elements in the academy against these changes, and the resources needed to implement the new policies.

The Context

The term *developing countries,* as used in this chapter, is an imprecise term, embracing all of what the World Bank classified in 2005 as low-income countries—having per capita gross national incomes below US$2,260 in purchasing power parities (corresponding to less than US$510 by exchange rates). Many of those countries, which the World Bank—on the basis of per capita incomes— would term lower-middle income countries, did have higher incomes and frequently much higher rates of economic growth; but still large proportions of their populations lived in poverty and generally exhibited other characteristics associated with underdeveloped economies.

Although these characteristics vary greatly—and again with the caveat that the term *developing* is imprecise—the higher education institutions and systems of developing countries may exhibit the following characteristics: (1) rapidly increasing demands for places due to high birthrates and rapidly expanding proportions of college-level-age young people who are completing academic secondary schools with aspirations for higher education; (2) limited higher education capacity, especially in the universities, but also relative underdevelopment of the short-cycle, nonuniversity institutions; (3) expectedly high levels of austerity, with overcrowded lecture theaters, heavy teaching loads, and inadequate resources for books and journals, equipment, computers, and telecommunications; (4) high proportions of the already inadequate governmental budgets for higher education absorbed by student maintenance expenditures and thus unavailable for the support of instruction; (5) uneven levels of academic preparedness of entering students from secondary schools combined with university curricula considered by many to be elitist and academic expectations to be unreasonable, with consequent high rates of dropouts, or wastage; and (6) great resistance to cost sharing due to the poverty of most of the students, compounded by the legacies of socialist experiments and populist democracies and the political volatility of students, especially over tuition fees and other matters of personal finance.

From these characteristics, five factors, inextricably interrelated, may be identified that frame the context of the leadership challenge in the developing world. The first is the almost ironic combination of an overemphasis on the research university form—that is, a conspicuous underdevelopment in most developing countries of the shorter cycle, more vocationally oriented, nonuniversity—together with a scholarly weakness in most institutions purporting to be research universities. This scholarly weakness is due to a combination of factors, including the inadequacy of laboratories and equipment in science and engineering (partly a function of financial austerity), the loss of scholars to universities in Europe and North America, and in many of the older universities an overemphasis on the humanities and social sciences and a commensurate underemphasis on science, engineering, agriculture, and management (in part a remnant of the old colonial universities that mainly prepared students for positions in the civil service).

Universities in many developing countries are also deeply politicized, oftentimes with regional divisions and with academic calendars punctuated by strikes and lockouts. The net effect in too many developing countries is a quality of university-based scholarship and training that falls far short of meeting the social or economic needs of the country.

A second factor, clearly contributing to the first, is the pervasive financial austerity of universities in most countries and especially those in the developing world. This austerity is a function of the high and rapidly rising unit costs of universities everywhere compounded by the surging enrollment pressures that in turn are caused by rapidly increasing youth populations and further accelerated by rapidly increasing high school completion rates. The financial austerity is further worsened in many low-income countries by a political reluctance to charge anything but the most nominal tuition fees, resulting in an excessive dependence on the restricted public treasuries and further complicated by the compelling competition for limited public revenues.

The resulting and worsening austerity in most developing countries is manifested in many ways. The shortage of operating revenues, especially for nonpersonnel needs, limits necessary expenditures on technology, library resources, scientific equipment, and maintenance. The shortage of revenue for personnel, coupled with the political difficulty of shedding faculty or staff in less-needed programs, often imposes great teaching loads, especially in programs of more recent high demand, which in turn affects the quality of teaching and the capacity to implement new programs and to update curricula. The shortage of capital revenue contributes to overcrowding and the concentration of this already limited capacity to the urban areas, in turn requiring most students to leave their homes and find accommodation in these crowded areas, adding to the expense of higher education.

The unevenness of secondary education is a third challenging factor to colleges and universities in most developing countries, contributing to high dropout rates and prolonged (and therefore costly) years in the universities. It also exacerbates disparities in access and completion between urban and rural areas and between middle and upper-middle classes (that can frequently afford private secondary schools and tutors) and low-income children.

A fourth contextual factor challenging higher education leadership in many low-income countries is the government itself. Governments may look upon the university—especially a so-called *flagship* university—as a kind of political prize and therefore a source of patronage, installing leaders who may lack both the necessary familiarity with the nature of a university and the respect of the faculty. Governments may also view the university as venue of opposition, harboring radical faculty and students who may be allied with opposition parties. Governmental controls over spending, resource allocation and reallocation, and other institutional decisions are frequently intrusive, reflecting a lack of trust in the institutional leadership. All of these problems plague colleges and universities in most countries, but they are frequently most challenging and limiting in developing countries.

Finally, the fifth factor, common to most universities in virtually all countries but especially crippling when combined with all of the other limitations in the developing country context, is the inherent conservatism of universities as institutions. Universities everywhere are hard to change. They function (or aspire to function) as seekers of truth and repositories of culture, and they are purposefully designed to resist distractions from political whims, cultural trends, or the changing needs of the economy and the workplace. In contrast to the afore-mentioned inclination of governments everywhere to intrude upon universities, this institutional conservatism is magnified by the classical university traditions of academic freedom and the supremacy of the faculty in matters of institutional governance—which traditions extend to most universities in most developing countries. Sometimes enshrined by constitutional provisions of university autonomy, these traditions are supposed to shield universities from governments as well as from influences of the market, whether stemming from students as clients or consumers or directly from the requirements of public or private employers.

Further contributing to this conservatism, faculty everywhere are resistant to direction, supervision, or requests for accountability. Faculty in the universities of many countries even assume a right to select (and perforce to remove) those in positions of some authority—rectors, dean, and department heads—which of course seriously retards the ability of those offices to effect change that carries any threat to any vested personal or institutional interests. Academic freedom and institutional autonomy get conflated with the preservation of jobs (frequently as civil servants) and with an academic lifestyle that is often accompanied by little supervision or accountability. Thus, the conservatism of the university is a kind of protection but can also constitute a barrier inhibiting change that is necessary for the social good.

In short, and as a segue to the analyses and recommendations of this chapter: (1) higher education change is imperative—and nowhere more so than in the universities and other postsecondary institutions of the developing world; and (2) the ability to effect purposeful change—that is, the essence of leadership—is difficult in all universities and especially under the conditions of austerity and political instability that mark so many developing countries.

Who Can [Might] Be Leaders in Higher Education—And How Can They Lead?

Leadership has been defined for the purpose of this chapter as the capacity to make a difference—that is, to effect change—in either individual institutions or systems of higher education. At the institutional level, then, leadership first calls to mind those at the head of the college or university: the offices of president, chancellor, vice chancellor, or rector. These offices, however, can be quite dissimilar in countries with different university governance traditions and laws. The classical continental European university head is generally referred to as a rector and is virtually always both from the faculty and elected by the faculty (or a faculty senate, which may include some individuals other than faculty members). The head of a college or university in the United States, Canada, Japan, China, and an increasing number of other countries is called either a president (most commonly) or a chancellor—the titles, at least in the United States, being interchangeable, with one frequently applied to the head of a public college or university institution and the other to the head of a multicampus public system, in order to keep the two offices distinct. Thus, the heads of the multicampus systems in California and North Carolina are called presidents and the heads of the constituent universities called chancellors, whereas the opposite nomenclature is applied in the multicampus systems of New York and Wisconsin. The heads of public colleges and universities in the United States are chosen by a governing board rather than by a faculty senate (although faculty generally have a prominent role in the search process) and thus are, at least theoretically, more independent of the faculty, more likely to come from outside of the institution, more likely to be favored by a governing board representing private and even corporate interests, and are occasionally chosen from the ranks of nonfaculty (e.g., institutional leaders other than faculty or leaders from government or even from business or the military)—none of which eventualities would be found in the European rector model. Finally, the term *vice chancellor* is employed in Britain and much of the Commonwealth (such as in East Africa) for a university head much like an American university president. The vice chancellor is usually chosen by a governing council, the head of which is frequently a prominent individual with the honorary appellation of chancellor but with little authority and is not to be confused with an American university chancellor, who could be either the head of an institution or the head of a multicampus system.

Other institutional offices can also house leaders, in the sense of individuals capable of effecting significant change in the university. Most prominent would be the heads of faculties, commonly called deans—as deans of arts and science, medicine, law, or engineering. Faculty deans are frequently the most influential university leaders in changing the composition and thus the scholarly orientations of their faculties via their importance in approving faculty appointments and promotions and in approving (and occasionally initiating) new or revised academic programs. At a higher institutional level, chief academic officers—in American universities generally called academic vice presidents or provosts— are more distant from the initial appointments and intrafaculty resource allocations than the deans but have significant influence over: (1) the appointments of faculty deans; (2) the criteria for faculty promotion (and sometimes even over individual promotion decisions); and (3) budget and faculty *line*, or *billet*, allocations among the several faculties of the university. In all cases, the ultimate authority of deans is that which the university presidents and academic vice presidents allocate (or defer) to them—which can be considerable and thus leaves the potential for such offices to exert significant leadership. The same is true, then, for chief academic officers, whose authority and influence are similarly derived from the institutional head.

Significant leadership in public higher education can also be exercised by offices external to institutions of higher education, including those directly within the government—including ministers, vice ministers, and even heads of governments and heads of state. Leadership at these highest levels of government—again, in the sense of effecting significant change—is exercised by authority or influence over the selection of the university heads themselves (i.e., the presidents or vice chancellors), the election of the members and chairs of governing boards where such exist, and authority over the institutional budgets and, therefore, over the allocation of resources and growth possibilities for individual institutions or for the different sectors of higher education.

Other offices external to the institutions themselves also provide potential for exercising higher education leadership. Such offices would include members, and especially heads, of governing boards charged with responsibilities for appointing or nominating institutional heads, setting or changing institutional missions, and approving changes in programs. These boards are sometimes referred to as *buffer bodies*, occupying a space of authority between the institution and its head and the government. Governing boards exert their influence in two directions: representing, to the institution, the needs of the government and, in a larger sense, the needs of the people while simultaneously representing the needs of the institution—mainly for resources, and also for autonomy—to the government. The principal leverage for change and thus for significant leadership possessed by a governing board, especially by its chair, lies principally in three authorities: (1) its authority to appoint (sometimes only to nominate) the college or university head; (2) its authority to approve and, in some cases, to initiate changes in programs and sometimes even in institutional mission; and (3) its ability to defend the institutional head—and by implication the president's or vice chancellor's attempts at significant change—against the inevitable opposition that such leadership invariably occasions. In this way, leadership by, say, a governing board chair is generally in collaboration with the head of either the institution or the multicampus system.

Other external boards or councils and their executive directors or chairs may look similar to governing boards and governing board chairs but lack—or may have chosen not to exercise—the authorities enumerated earlier for the true governing boards: that is, over key appointments, budgets, academic program additions and deletions, or mission determinations or alterations. Such boards, councils, or coordination bodies in the United States generally have only recommending authority, the impact of which is completely up to whatever head of government or minister or legislative body is to receive the recommendations. Thus, a head of government or minister who chooses generally to defer to the recommendations of such an official advisory body can create a context in which the chair or head of such a recommending, or advisory, body can exercise significant leadership.

In some developing countries—Kenya and Uganda come to mind—such national higher education councils have been established to advise the ministers on such potentially critical and change-eliciting matters as the division of the total higher education budgets among the several public institutions and/or sectors, campuses, and occasionally to oversee student funding and accreditation agencies. In such cases, and especially in developing countries—where the higher education issues such as sector diversification, encouragement of private institutions, and implementation of cost-sharing measures are both critical and highly contested—significant leadership can emerge in such external bodies in spite of the absence of genuine authority. The keys to this context for potential leadership are in the confluence of: (1) higher education issues that are so contested that politicians see little advantage—and considerable political peril—in taking sides and so prefer to defer difficult decisions such as the alteration of institutional missions or the implementation of fees to others, such as appointed commissioners; (2) the appointed commissioner has a known reputation for both integrity and academic respectability; and (3) this appointed commissioner or adviser has the ambition, courage, communication skills, and luck to emerge as a higher education change maker—that is, a leader.

Higher Education Leadership and the Structural/Legal Rules of the Game

At least for this chapter, leadership is defined as the making of change or the altering of institutional trajectories—that is, the way the institution would develop by its organizational inertia, apart from the purposeful application of the authority and/or the influence of a leader. Moreover, the concentration is on the leadership ability attached to the university head (i.e., president chancellor, vice chancellor, or rector). Therefore, the ability to lead a public college or university is in part a function of the structural/legal limits that a particular government places upon that office. For example, a university president in the United States—an office generally considered the most authoritative of all public college and university heads—serves either for a prescribed term or more commonly at the pleasure of the governing board, which means that he or she can be removed, generally by a majority of the board. At the same time, the American president, unlike the European rector, is somewhat insulated from the judgment of the faculty (thus able to continue in office even after formal votes of no confidence from the faculty). A university president in China must both manage and lead alongside a more-or-less parallel university head of the Chinese Communist Party, who has certain authorities over, for example, personnel and curriculum. A university rector in Germany (as in Austria and Switzerland) both manages and leads alongside a governmentally appointed chancellor, who is not an academic and initiates little or nothing but who must approve that the budgets, financial transactions, and other executive actions by the rector are in accordance with applicable laws and regulations. A university president in Japan, after the significant 2004 change that corporatized the national universities and greatly augmented the authority of the presidents, is nominated by the university's management council but is still approved by the minister. In many developing countries, a university president is formally appointed and presumably may be removed by the head of state. In short, the ability to lead a public university—in the sense of making a difference and almost inevitably eliciting the opposition of at least some powerful vested interests—is in part a function of these structural/legal constraints, including who in the government has the power to appoint and/or remove the university head. And by extension, if higher education in any country—and especially in a developing country—is deemed to be in need of change and therefore in need of more effective leadership, then governments can generally enhance the likelihood of effective leadership from the top by altering the structural/legal mode of the appointment and removal of the head of the institution or, if there be one, the multicampus system or the national advisory council or coordinating body.

At the same time, the structural/legal constraints on leadership of public institutions of higher education are more likely to emanate not from the manner in which the president (or vice chancellor or rector) is appointed but from authority that is granted to these offices—or placed elsewhere in the government—over decisions most critical to any university. The most important of these are probably the following five: (1) the ability to appoint and reward (and perforce to remove) other top members of the university's management team—as opposed to having the vice presidents, deans, directors, and even department chairs appointed by an external authority; (2) the ability to substantially influence the appointment, promotion, and compensation of faculty—as opposed to being constrained by civil-service provisions applicable to all governmental employees; (3) the ability to reallocate resources to and from programs and thus to add and shed faculty and staff from them—as opposed to having to seek governmental permission to reallocate or to carry forward revenues; (4) the ability (within certain governmentally imposed limits) to supplement governmental revenues with entrepreneurial revenue from grants gifts, contracts, and fees—as opposed to having fees (or the freezing of fees or the lack thereof) imposed by the government; and (5) the ability to execute contracts, borrow, and otherwise act in the capacity of the chief executive officer of a true public corporation. Thus, a president (vice chancellor or rector) can be granted great institutional authority and effectively shielded from faculty and other sources of opposition, but if the decisions that matter—such as the selection of the management team, the terms and conditions of faculty and staff employment, the ability to shift revenues among programs or to add and drop programs, and the ability to supplement scarce (and quite possibly declining) governmental revenue—are denied, then no university head, regardless of intelligence, charisma, or executive skills, is likely to be able to accomplish significant change or to earn the mantle of a strong leader.

Academic Leadership and the Enigma of Authority versus Influence

Effecting change in most organizations, both public and private, is a relatively simple matter of exercising the authority attached to the office. As the office of a university president (or rector or vice chancellor) is undisputedly the highest in the university, with nearly unlimited authority, the capacity to effect change, and thus to effectively lead, should be a relatively simple matter. Alas, most universities are not the classic bureaucracies described by Max Weber. The authority of the office of university president, vice chancellor, or rector is limited not merely by the external constraints of structure and law, as described in the preceding section, but also by the nature of the university as an organization and the nature of higher education production—that is, teaching and scholarship. Faculty are not merely resistant to supervision over both their teaching and their research. Rather, the technology of these activities—what the economist would call the higher education production function—is simply not sufficiently defined, nor is the output of teaching and research sufficiently measurable to admit to the supervision and control found in most other producing organizations. Individuals and units within the university operate according to patterns established and maintained less by authority and supervision than by norms of the academic profession.

Thus, the ability to effect change in a university (and similarly but less so in other forms of higher education institutions) is as much a matter of influence as it is of authority and most effective when authority and influence are

combined in one individual. Authority is a function of office and the powers
that are ascribed to that office—in the case of public colleges and universities by
law or delegated by the government. Influence in a university setting, however,
is more a function of individual attributes—including among other aspects,
academic credibility and prestige, a reputation for integrity, the ability to communicate effectively, and charisma (as long as one is not viewed as too charis-
matic). Influence in a college or university is also a function of one's perceived
ability to attract revenue (ever in short supply). In a public college or university, influence is greatly heightened by political connections and the ability to
maximize public revenues. Political connections in many developing countries
tend to follow personal, ideological, ethnic, or even tribal allegiances. Thus,
there may be a disconnect in some developing countries between the ability to
influence the faculty that matter for effecting academic change and the ability to influence the politicians or members of the government that matter for
negotiating favorable budgets. In addition, the most-effective higher education
leadership would feature the ability to influence faculty as well as the ability to
influence significant politicians—in combination with the authority to effect
the desired changes.

Enhancing Leadership

As set forth at the start of this chapter, the challenges confronting higher education in all countries, and especially higher education in developing countries, are formidable and call for effective leadership. This leadership must be
able to bring about change in individual institutions and/or national systems.
Leadership is needed—again, more than ever in the developing world—in the
setting and changing of institutional and systemwide missions. Leadership is
needed in developing the academic programs that conform to these missions
and in the kinds of faculty recruited, developed, promoted, and retained in
pursuit if the programs. It is needed in the quest both for addition resources,
such as the always politically contested implementation of fees, as well as in
the difficult decisions that must be taken to maximize the efficiency and productivity of the (inevitably inadequate) resources that are ultimately available.
Leadership in higher education is needed to overcome the resistance at times
from the faculty and at other times from the politicians.

Effective higher education leaders in all countries will have certain capacities.
They must be able to inspire the faculty with academic credibility, integrity, a
willingness to listen, as well as an ability—after an appropriate period of listening—to make difficult decisions. They must be able to pick a strong administrative team, give direction and then delegate to this team, and make changes in
the team when necessary. The leaders must be able to inspire this team with a
sense of strength and composure, especially in times of great institutional stress
and austerity. They must be able to elicit advice from the best givers of advice,

while never being captured or daunted by so-called experts. They must be able to synthesize and make order out of what will frequently seem to be a cacophony of conflicting advice and interests so that the institution can move on in some purposeful direction. Effective academic leaders must be able on some occasions to maintain fundamental academic principles and stay on course in the face of pressures to do otherwise—on other occasions to take the institution off of its established trajectory and bring about change—and to make wise decisions about which of these courses to pursue. Finally, academic leaders must be able to communicate effectively—to faculty, students, civic leaders, and politicians alike.

Much of these various capacities are attributes that leaders are born with. Some can be learned or perfected with training and mentoring. At the same time, a theme of this chapter has been that effective leadership of public institutions of higher education, and especially in the challenging context of developing countries, needs more than individuals with the attributes of leadership. Effective leadership needs governments to empower the offices of potential leaders, both of the universities and other institutions of higher education, and to empower also the councils, commissions, and governing boards that have significant roles in appointing, guiding, and defending the heads of the institutions.

If effective leadership is conceived as the capacity to effect change and if the most needed change in higher education will be contested by some parties, then more effective leadership in higher education in developing countries must be developed. Governments should create the structural/legal context in which presidents, vice chancellors, deans, and other potential leaders have the authority to make the difficult decisions like mission differentiation, resource allocation and reallocation, and the critical hiring, promoting, compensating—and, indeed the shedding—of faculty and staff to realize the necessary changes. *Great* leaders may be born—albeit infrequently. But *effective* leaders can be discovered, encouraged, appointed, empowered, and protected—mainly by wise governments and enlightened statesmen and stateswomen. Developing countries desperately need all the effective higher education leadership they can get.

11

Access and Equity

LIZ REISBERG AND DAVID WATSON

In the academic and policy arenas, access has come to be understood as enrolling larger percentages of the population who desire higher education. Equity requires that these opportunities are equally available to all citizens. Most nations have succeeded in expanding the enrollment of the traditional age cohort, but it has become increasingly apparent that this trend does not necessarily include all segments of the population. Moreover, equity does not result naturally from greater access; new kinds of interventions are required to address the underlying factors that determine who enrolls and who persists until graduation. Governments and higher education institutions are beginning to address the challenges of recruiting, selecting, and supporting students across a broader spectrum of the age cohort, focusing on students from underrepresented groups. This growing diversity obliges universities to confront new challenges to ensure that most (if not all) of these new students complete their program of study. The public concern with equity reflects the growing expectation that universities must assume a larger role in civil society that reaches beyond the institution itself.

Nearly every society confronts inequities, but the inequalities that play out in education are based on different historical, social, and economic factors—for example, in Botswana and Switzerland, the United States and India, Malaysia and Australia. To appreciate the constraints and opportunities for widening access and securing equity in each environment one has to understand the culture and demography of the society and the education system. Concerning access and equity, countries cannot implement universal solutions.

The policy of equity raises larger questions about the institution's interface with the society around it. What is a university's responsibility for solving complex issues embedded in conditions that often have deep roots in history and culture? To what extent should university communities reflect the makeup of the society that hosts them? How does an institution balance social obligations against other commitments? Who defines the university's obligations and decides when these obligations have been met?

However, difficult choices are not only the burden of individual institutions but likewise must be exerted by all stakeholders—students, parents, sponsors, and policymakers. Consensus about the problem or its solutions is not easily reached. Furthermore, every choice has consequences and often requires that to extend benefits in new directions, there are necessary costs that may affect others.

Greater and more inclusive participation in higher education goes far beyond the issue of social justice. In a globalized world where economic success depends on the ability to manage vast amounts of knowledge and technology, the development of human capital is key. The economic prosperity of most countries depends on an increasingly well-educated workforce, and thus access to higher education must be a national priority.

Nonfinancial benefits to education also need to be taken into account. The Wider Benefits of Learning Group at the Institute of Education in the United Kingdom has demonstrated (for cohorts born in 1958, 1970, and now 2000) that participants in higher education in the United Kingdom are likely to be happier, healthier, and more democratically tolerant (Schuller et al. 2004).

A recent report published by the state of Washington in the United States shows the same findings. Compared to families with parents who hold a first university degree, families whose parents have only a high school diploma are three times more likely to live below the poverty line and require publically subsidized services. Not only does more education promote financial independence and thus less dependence on tax-supported programs, but higher levels of education correlate directly with individuals reporting excellent health, less likelihood of criminal activity, higher levels of participation in elections and a greater inclination to do volunteer work (HECB 2010).

Data from many other countries support these findings. No society can benefit in the long run from overlooking the education of the population as a whole. Higher education has an important role to play here and is gaining greater attention from policymakers and international donors.

The Scope of the Problem

Access Does Not Ensure Equity

Participation in higher education has most certainly expanded in recent decades. Most countries have experienced success in enrolling larger percentages of their population in primary and secondary schools. The urgency of raising the median level of education even higher has contributed to the momentum of higher education "massification." Progress has been made in encouraging secondary school leavers to pursue additional study—confirmed by data from UNESCO (United Nations Educational, Scientific, and Cultural Organization). Worldwide, the gross-enrollment ratio has increased from 19 percent to 26 percent (2000 to 2007, respectively). In high-income countries, participation during this period has increased from 57 percent of the age cohort to 67 percent. In several countries enrollment growth has been particularly impressive. Brazil has increased enrollment from 16 to 30 percent, China from 8 to 23 percent, and the Czech Republic from 29 to 55 percent (Altbach, Reisberg, and Rumbley 2009). But gross enrollment ratios reflect national averages and do not convey critical data about the domestic profile of enrollment.

Increased enrollment has not included all sectors of the population equally. As a result, many countries have introduced programs to encourage underrepresented groups to enroll, sometimes giving these students priority through affirmative-action programs, reservation or quota programs, and special financing programs. But the problem is not easily solved, drawing policymakers and scholars to look more deeply at the factors that influence participation. More thorough examination has brought to light the complexity of the equity issue. The underlying factors are as diverse as they are pernicious and involve circumstances that universities are not in a position to resolve—such as, poorquality preparation in primary and secondary school, family income, or parental levels of education.

As mentioned earlier, global progress in increasing the gross-enrollment ratio tells only part of the story. Higher education systems have been expanding and diversifying in response to the growing demand for wider access. It is important to examine *where* the enrollment expansion is taking place. A university degree benefits all graduates but alumni of elite institutions enjoy additional benefits and advantages that enhance the value of their degrees. While elite institutions have done much to diversify their enrollment, most of the expansion has taken place at less-prestigious universities, polytechnic and vocationally oriented institutions, new private universities, community colleges, and online providers.

A debate has been highlighted over the social significance of persons from the disadvantaged strata enrolling at "second-tier" and less-selective institutions, and questions have been raised as to whether this pattern continues to privilege select sectors of the population.

> Some scholars suggest that higher education expansion, especially when it occurs through hierarchical differentiation, is a process of *diversion*, whereby members of the working class are diverted from elite opportunities and are channeled to positions of lower status. . . . Others have noted, however, that even lower-tier postsecondary schooling represents enhanced opportunity, so that the important effect of expansion may be one of *inclusion*.
>
> (Arum, Gamoran, and Shavit 2007, 2)

Investments focused on key institutions have contributed to China's increasingly stratified higher education system and demonstrates the way differentiation can influence future opportunities and channel privilege. Students, parents, and employers have taken careful note of the emerging hierarchy. National research revealed that more than 67 percent of surveyed employing units indicated that they advocated or promoted the prestige of the degree when considering whom to hire. Fewer than 5 percent of the respondents indicated that they were not influenced by the institution where a job applicant had studied. Chinese elite institutions generally remain beyond the reach of the rural poor (Hong 2004).

The dispute over whether the growing diversity of students and institutions opens opportunity or protects privilege pervades the literature (Morley, Leach, and Lugg 2009; David 2007). Undisputed is the limited space at elite research universities and the need for high-quality alternatives for those individuals unable to qualify for top-tier institutions. The extent to which the differentiation of institutions leads to various subsequent opportunities over the life-course merits more research.

What Does Equity Mean?

Inequality tends to sustain itself unless a kind of intervention is underway. More perverse forms of affirmative action have been practiced at elite colleges for a long time, such as priority given to the children of alumni and children of wealthy potential donors (Golden 2006). That said, many societies now use affirmative action, quotas, or reservation programs to remedy the inequitable distribution of opportunities in the past.

Recent studies have called attention to the limited attainment of the beneficiaries of expanded access and targeted admissions programs (Bowen, Chingos, and McPherson 2009; Rose 2005). This research underscores that equity means more than opening the door wider.

> The definition of equity is broad and emphasizes both equity in opportunities and equity in educational outcome. Equity in education is thus not only a question of opportunities provided in the educational system, but it is also concerning the actual results of the various educational choices and performances of different groups of pupils and students through the educational system.
>
> (OECD 2007)

Among the many problems, unequal opportunity often begins long before tertiary education. Students who are disadvantaged for any reasons (economic background, racial prejudice, geographic location, or physical disability) are often inadequately prepared for postsecondary study. The preparation gap is exacerbated by the fact that students from middle- and upper-middle-class backgrounds often have the advantage not only of better schools but of additional tutoring and preparation before beginning tertiary study. Subsequently, institutions face the challenge of not only widening access but also addressing deficiencies and disadvantages that have accumulated over years of schooling if these targeted populations are to be integrated successfully at the university level.

In sum, equity signifies making access available with the resources and support necessary for individuals to succeed and benefit from new opportunities. New services are required to provide academic monitoring, support and tutoring, counseling to assist with social and academic culture at the university level, and financial support to ameliorate economic hardship. Students from disadvantaged groups are likely to lack university-educated parents who offer support that is influential in insuring persistence and success. Universities must fill in many gaps if progress is to be made.

Who Is Underrepresented?

The issue of equity moves the discussion of access beyond numbers and percentages. Equity implies fair access to all, but patterns of underrepresentation appear in nearly all countries. *Who* qualifies as a member of a disadvantaged group is defined by a broad range of characteristics, as alluded to earlier.

> Inequalities in higher education participation are evident throughout the life course and include differences in terms of time (and age), place, gender, ethnicity, first language, parental (and sibling) social class, parental education, type of school attended, housing tenure, health/disability, criminal activity, learning difficulties, family structure and religious background. Multiple social disadvantages can result in initial education and, subsequently, participation in other forms of learning. Parental income and education are particularly influential. Occupational status and family size are also relevant. . . . Quality of life factors (such as infant health) are important for understanding disengagement from education rather than participation within it. . . . The question is raised as to whether policymakers should seek to reduce inequality in education directly, or seek to reduce the wider inequalities that are reflected in education.
>
> (Gorard et al. 2006)

The underlying causes that favor some groups and discriminate against others vary widely, sometimes a reflection of policy and sometimes of circumstance. Parental education and family wealth seem to be particularly influential.

Some individuals confront multiple obstacles that disadvantage them from an early age. An example in the United Kingdom is the group now called "cared-for" children, children born without the prospect of a healthy or stable family and for whom the state has taken responsibility. These children tend to grow up in either foster or residential homes and reflect a "perfect storm" in the sense that they have limited support for academic development, an unpredictable home environment, limited financial means, and other conditions that place them at the margin of society. Although this group may not belong to a targeted subsector it is regularly at the bottom of almost every test of educational progression and subsequently disadvantaged at the point of entry into higher education (Jackson, Ajayi, and Quigley 2005).

Around the world, different factors create unequal opportunities and produce unequal outcomes. The Chinese minority in Malaysia has been denied access to higher education in the past by the preferential and legal entitlement of the Malayan majority—even though those citizens' education and income levels are high; Arab-Israelis have been prejudiced by entrance tests; aspirant ethnic communities in eastern and central Europe have suffered from policies in support of ethnic cleansing; and non-Afrikaans speakers in South Africa have been excluded, perpetuating patterns of participation based on race (Watson 2005). The United States has, likewise, overtly or indirectly limited access to different minority groups at various points in history. Despite intervention on behalf of minorities by the courts, black and Hispanic enrollment still represents a small percentage of the enrollment at US degree-granting institutions as well as taking much longer to complete their degree than their white counterparts (Bowen, Chingos, and McPherson 2009).

The social dynamic can be fluid; the people who become disadvantaged in a society can change over time. Women were once barely present in higher education. Today, women outnumber men in many countries. A special focus issue of *University World News* noted that with the exception of a few fields (engineering, science, and information technology) women outnumber men in Europe, North America, Latin America, and the Caribbean with the Arab states not far behind (*University World News* 2009b). Within the Organization for Economic Cooperation and Development (OECD) at present only a few countries still have a male majority of enrollments—Japan, Turkey, and Korea. Sweden actually had affirmative action for men to boost their enrollment numbers at university until challenged recently by a group of women in the courts. Women represent 60 percent of university enrollment in Sweden (*Chronicle of Higher Education* 2010). Worldwide, women are more likely than men to complete their studies based on data collected from OECD countries, an interesting departure from the past (OECD 2009).

Here again the quantitative data need further examination. Although gender parity of students enrolled in higher education might seem to be within sight in most countries, inequities persist. Globally, women are concentrated in disciplinary areas associated with lower-waged postgraduation—such as education, welfare, and health—giving rise to questions about factors that influence the selection of course of study (Morley, Leach, and Lugg 2009).

Ironically, in the past, quotas have been used to exclude as well as to include people in higher education. In the United States, the enrollment of Jews was once limited by quotas, particularly at elite institutions, to avoid representation disproportionate to their presence in the larger society (Golden 2006).

Today, without quotas, Jews represent 25 percent of Harvard's undergraduate enrollment (Harvard Hillel 2010), although they account for less than 2 percent of the US population. A similar issue involves Asian-American students, who represent upwards of 40 percent of the undergraduates at the University of California at Los Angeles, Berkeley, San Diego, and Irvine, while they represent 12 percent of California's population (Chea 2009). Here again, the issue is more complicated than it may initially appear as neither Jewish Americans or Asian Americans are a homogenous group. Still, high enrollment from these two groups raises another issue—whether the objective of equity policies is to have enrollment reflect the percentage of a minority group in the larger population and whether universities should hold to those percentages and limit the participation of some minority groups.

In many countries, the factors that determine who has access to higher education and who will be successful have changed. Today, economic status is as likely as race, gender, or ethnicity to determine who has access to the best opportunities for postsecondary education and who is most likely to complete a degree. In fact students are often disadvantaged by "multiple markers of identity" (Morley, Leach, and Lugg 2009) rather than by a single characteristic (Schwartzman 2006). Distributing equitable opportunity, determining if a particular group should gain special consideration in admission, and whether the participation of another group should be constrained, all contribute to the dilemmas of social responsibility that higher education is being asked to address. While the goal of greater equality is generally shared, determining *who* and *how* is less easily resolved, and separate countries have pursued different strategies in the pursuit of a more equal society.

A Comparative Look at Challenges and Solutions

Affirmative action—based on quota and reservation programs—is being used in many countries to address the unequal participation of minority or disadvantaged groups within each society. While they may appear to allow underrepresented groups to "catch up," these programs are usually controversial. Moreover, research as to the impact of these policies is limited.

Brazil

In Brazil, there are four times more white citizens with 15 years of education, or more, than black citizens or citizens of mixed race (Schwartzman 2006). Much progress has been made in improving access to secondary school, where less diversity in participation by race exists. Progress at the tertiary level has continued to be skewed toward white students. Competitive entrance examinations to the more prestigious public universities have given advantage to a predominantly white population with the resources to attend better-quality secondary schools.

There are sufficient university seats to accommodate all secondary school graduates, but low-income and racial minorities (when they do enroll) are not well distributed throughout the higher education system (Schwartzman 2006). The irony of lower-income families finding greater access in tuition-driven institutions while wealthier students enroll in free public universities has in fact been perceived by policymakers. In response, the government has introduced quotas to reserve space in the public sector for more nonwhite students. Several public universities now add points to the admissions-exam score of students from public secondary schools that enroll students from disadvantaged groups. On the surface this action forms a mechanism for "leveling the playing field," but as pointed out by Simon Schwartzman this disadvantages students from low-income families who have been able to enroll in private schools. He also notes that students given the benefit of additional points enter at an academic disadvantage, raising the liability that they might drop out or (at the least) remain isolated in remedial courses.

In Brazil, as elsewhere, inequities are easier to identify than to resolve. The quota system has stirred considerable controversy. One notable response was more than 300 lawsuits filed against the Federal University of Rio de Janeiro by applicants who felt they were harmed by the quota system. There are concerns about whether the quota system will actually aggravate racial tension in Brazil, and it remains hard to determine how (in a largely mixed-race society) race will be defined (Tavolaro 2008).

India

Access to higher education in India has expanded rapidly with the inauguration of many new public and private institutions. Still, not only is the overall gross enrollment relatively low, at less than 15 percent but participation rates dip below 6 percent in the most rural states where access to higher education institutions is scarce (Jayaram 2008; Altbach, Reisberg, and Rumbley 2009).

India is home to an extremely diverse population, where a rigid hierarchy has governed the allocation of educational and economic opportunities in the past. The government of India, like Brazil, introduced affirmative action in the form of quotas or reservations with the objective of distributing social benefits more equally to "backward classes and scheduled tribes." Since 1961, the constitution has mandated that 22.5 percent of the space in higher education be reserved for scheduled classes and tribes. In some states 50 percent of the space is reserved. The program has resulted in much more diversity in higher education, but like Brazil, India has had trouble defining clearly exactly who belongs to the targeted groups. As a perverse affect of the program, while the classification might seem degrading, some groups claimed these identities to take advantage of the places in the civil service and universities reserved for members of these groups (De Zwart 2000).

The reservation program has also provoked protests from students and professionals who warned that this strategy would only serve to replace qualified candidates with unqualified and unprepared individuals (Neelakantan 2006). Yet, the question is how and whether inequities would be addressed without some type of forced intervention, leading one observer to state, "Reservations are needed because of the innate inability of Indian society to be just and fair by itself to all its constituents" (Punwani 2006).

Africa

Despite their complications quota systems continue to provide great appeal internationally where large inequities exist and no better alternatives are apparent. A lecturer at the University of Malawi observed:

> I was part of the team that administered Unima entrance exams in Mzuzu. If you had the spirit of the living God in you, you could not control a tear of sympathy from your eyes when you saw the gulf between candidates from rich versus poor families, rural versus urban areas and private versus public schools. These and other concerns about the poor in rural areas are the reason why we need a quota system as an equalization policy that benefits the rural poor and not a region or tribe.
>
> (*University World News* 2009a)

Throughout Africa, participation in higher education remains low for all population groups. Progress toward improved gross-enrollment ratios continues, but in this region, women are not keeping pace with men. In Tanzania and Ghana, for example, despite affirmative action and quota programs the social group most likely to enroll in higher education is men from the top socioeconomic groups. In Ghana where women are making slow progress, they are also most likely to be from the wealthier class (Morley, Leach, and Lugg 2009). It has been stated that gender has cultural associations not dissipated by quotas and that women in many African societies are expected to conform to traditional female roles not compatible with higher levels of education. "Parental message systems" (Morley, Leach, and Lugg 2009, 61) more than affirmative action seem to help women break through the constraints of traditional culture; encouragement from fathers is particularly influential.

* * *

Quota programs, reservation programs, and affirmative-action programs have undoubtedly opened doors wider but are limited in the social conditions they can change. They also tend to base eligibility on a single characteristic not always easy to assign and where individuals in the target groups are generally disadvantaged by multiple factors. Without focusing on these deeper challenges, initiatives that attempt to extend admissions opportunity based on a single characteristic will most likely have limited impact.

Toward the Fair Distribution of Opportunity

The unfair distribution of wealth and poverty and the subsequent circumstances that can be ascribed to each is a problem across the globe. Most individuals are born to advantages or disadvantages due to no act or choice of their own. The challenge is finding a solution that apportions social benefits where they have been scarce, without depriving those who are poised to enjoy them.

Addressing Past Deficits

One of the dilemmas of programs to improve equitable access to the full spectrum of higher education institutions is bridging the gaps in preparation. Raising aspirations of fair access to prestigious institutions on the part of well-qualified nonstandard students is hindered by the challenge of getting more prepared students to matriculation. In March 2008, during a public debate over the achievement gap in the United Kingdom it was disclosed that:

> Only 176, or just over half a percent, of the nearly 30,000 pupils who got three A's at A-level last year were eligible for free meals, according to figures which show that household income is the biggest single predictor of a child's academic success. . . . They [new statistics] were released by ministers in response to questions from the shadow children's secretary, Michael Gove, who said they illustrated the struggle top universities face in trying to recruit top candidates from the poorest backgrounds.
>
> (Curtis 2008)

It is important to understand the effect of decisions made by and for students during primary and secondary education that derail their preparation for higher education. In addition, the gap widens as students from wealthier families are more likely to supplement their required classroom attendance with tutoring to improve their performance on universities' entrance examinations, a practice evident in countries from Brazil to Japan.

When elite universities pursue diversity in their student body the results reveal a perplexing pattern of advantage and disadvantage. A study of admission to elite US colleges, found that whites received more offers than students of Asian heritage; Hispanics received offers disproportionately to whites; African Americans were at least five times as likely to be accepted as whites; and athletes were twice as likely to be admitted as nonathletes (Espenshade and Radford 2009). Students from private schools were twice as likely to be admitted as students from public high schools (Clark 2009). Thus, in the pursuit of diversity, elite schools are giving preferences based on a dizzying number of variables. Although minority students tend to be more successful at more-selective than less-selective institutions, it has been warned that selecting students who are underprepared for the academic expectations of elite institutions ("over matched") put these students at higher risk of not completing their degree than their more privileged peers (Bowen, Chingos, and McPherson 2009).

Students who are not sufficiently competitive to be attractive to elite schools—hard to reach groups—tend to remain concentrated in less-demanding institutions (typically, polytechnics, community colleges, and large colleges under local authority). Additionally, these students tend to stay closer to home for economic, familial, and cultural reasons. This is often especially true with children in indigenous communities that are often isolated. Subsequently, the quality of the education that students from underrepresented groups pursue may be linked to the geography (Gibbons and Vignoles 2009; Piquet 2006).

The Impact of Fees

The massification of higher education, coupled with the growing tendency to count education as a "private good," have encouraged governments toward cost-sharing and cost-recovery schemes for financing higher education.

Even before the trend to introduce fees, an inequitable cost burden existed for university attendance. Students from lower-socioeconomic backgrounds are more likely to struggle to fund living expenses and the ancillary costs of study (books, materials, etc.) and less likely to be in a position to forgo immediate income than their middle- and upper-class peers who receive family support. Only a few countries provide subsidies to adequately cover the full cost of tertiary study, and in these states massification has put a strain on these subsidies.

Where at least full-time initial higher education has been free in the past, the imposition of student fees in jurisdictions is a phenomenon that has been spreading across Europe and Australasia over the past decade. To insure that fees will not become a barricade to participation, complex arrangements for student support (financial aid, loans, and subsidies) and postgraduate fee recovery through the tax system have been springing up, even in the most traditionally "statist" systems, such as Germany. For institutional leaders and policymakers, cost-recovery schemes present a wicked dilemma. The commitment to free higher education (like access to national health services) has strong populist appeal, not the least to students and their parents. Still, subsidies to higher education have not distributed benefits equally to all sectors of the population in the past. At the same time institutions need additional revenue in a context of declining public subsidy. The dilemma requires unattractive compromises that have unequal impact on different segments of the population.

Data measuring the impact of new cost-sharing schemes are still limited and confusing. In China, for example, rapidly rising fees do not take into account the income disparities between urban and rural populations. Furthermore, the most prestigious and best institutions tend to be concentrated in large urban areas, placing attendance out of reach for rural students whose family income can afford neither fees nor the cost of living in China's expensive cities (Hong 2004).

Willingness to assume debt seems to vary by culture, but in most cases, students from low-income families are more risk averse and less likely to take advantage of low-interest study loans. Loans are often less available to lower-income students where they require cosigners or collateral. Making credit available to lower-income student has demonstrated a positive effect on attendance (Johnstone and Marucci 2003; Canton and Blom 2004). Some countries reward merit with scholarship, producing the perverse (but not surprising) effect of offering additional subsidies to wealthier students (Usher 2009). D. Bruce Johnstone's chapter on "the funding of universities" in this book provides further analysis of these issues.

A standard issue concerns whether policy accomplishes stated objectives or something else. In England, in 2006, a system of intended variable fees to students was introduced with the provision that the government would cover the gap to institutions and recover them from the graduates later in life through the income tax system. Meanwhile, under the supervision of a newly formed Office for Fair Access institutions are required to dedicate part of the income resulting from fees to student bursaries and related "out-reach" work. Claire Callender reflects:

> [R]ather than eliminate price as a factor in university choice, which was central both to the rationale underpinning the introduction of bursaries and to the political rhetoric surrounding their establishment, HEIs are turning net price to their advantage in the competitive struggle for students.
>
> (Callender forthcoming)

It is generally agreed that free tuition or even quite low-cost higher education is not sustainable in the era of massification and the growing tendency to classify higher education as a "private good." The challenge now is to ensure that access and equity are protected in an increasingly difficult fiscal environment for higher education.

Retention and Persistence to Graduation

As the issue of access gets more attention from researchers and policymakers it becomes increasingly apparent that increased access has less social impact if study programs are not completed. The challenges of retaining students to graduation are many and even greater when a student is the first in his or her family to enroll in tertiary study, less prepared for his or her peers, or combating the disadvantages often associated with race, ethnicity, or disability. Evidence indicates that students from disadvantaged backgrounds are more likely to drop out even if they are equally qualified when they enter higher education (Chowdry et al. 2008). Although there is evidence that each additional year of postsecondary study boosts income potential, a significantly larger-wage premium is earned by individuals who complete their degree (Bowen, Chingos, and McPherson 2009).

In the United States data from the National Center for Educational Statistics show that the six-year graduation rate for black students is less than 50 percent, 20 percentage points lower than white students (Carey 2008). Innovative programs demonstrate that despite preuniversity academic deficits and social challenges, new participants in higher education can be successful with appropriate intervention. The Center for Academic Retention and Enhancement at Florida State University offers a broad, multifaceted approach to enrolling and graduating "hard to reach" students. CARE works with secondary schools to identify talented students as early as sixth grade and offers summer and after-school programs to encourage and guide them. A bridge program provides academic and social orientation during the summer between high school graduation and university matriculation. Ongoing tutoring and counseling are available after enrolling. The result has been that these students graduate at nearly the same rate as their non-CARE peers (Carey 2008).

The previous assumption that any higher education is better than none has become doubtful, for persistence to graduation is becoming as decisive for future opportunities as access to university study. It appears that individuals who commence postsecondary study yet drop out fall behind economically, comparable to their peers who never pursued tertiary study at all. With the expansion of access to higher education, retention and completion have become as relevant to success (measured as social and economic participation after graduation) as widening participation.

The ability to persist is directly related to prior educational success and represents another way in which institutions of higher education should have a strong motivation to contribute to the improvement of the performance of primary and secondary education. Institutions also have a greater leverage (through research and their role in forming relevant professionals) than they often acknowledge. They also have the option of forming innovative partnerships with previous levels of education, as demonstrated in the example of Florida State University.

Challenges for Leadership

Does Greater Equity Compromise Quality?

Whether or not widening participation can be achieved without compromising the quality of what is offered, is another dilemma. This issue concerns politicians and policymakers. Here is a UK House of Commons select committee's reflection on access and equity: "Our values and democratic commitments press us to answer the old question 'Can we be equal and excellent too?' with a resounding 'yes'" (UK House of Commons 2001).

Excellence is a word often used in political rhetoric but without much utility in practice. When higher percentages of the age cohort enroll, new and more practical definitions of excellence will be needed.

> By definition, as one passes 50 percent, to continue to increase participation means to involve people who are below the median in terms of academic achievement and these people tend to come from society's more disadvantaged groups who have always been less likely to attend postsecondary education.
>
> (Usher 2009, 6)

Elite institutions will be able to increase diversity with little effect; these institutions will always be in a position to select students with high potential for success and (often) provide the environment and services needed to sustain high completion rates. For other institutions, diversity will introduce students with broadly varied levels of preuniversity preparation and talent, and that will require more accommodation and flexibility in the classroom.

The report of the Task Force on Higher Education and Society suggests that higher education must "combine tolerance at points of entrance with rigor at the point of exit" (2000, 41). The challenge will be to put this goal into practice, given the realities of local circumstance and resources.

New pressures on higher education are likely to compete with continued progress toward greater equity. The definition of excellence has become tied to the notion of "world class." In this context, emphasis is placed on research productivity, media interest, graduate destinations, infrastructure, and international recruitment. These are unlikely characteristics of most "demand-absorbing" institutions. Many of the common-sense elements of performance—like teaching quality, widening participation and social mobility, services to business and the community, support of rural in addition to metropolitan communities, as well as contributions to other public services—are conspicuously absent from this new take on excellence (Watson 2007, 34–46). World class and improved access and equity may sit together well in theory and rhetoric but require different kinds of policy and support. As more governments become preoccupied with developing "world-class" universities, it is possible that the endeavor could divert resources necessary to accommodate the participation of new populations in higher education. The following example from the United Kingdom underscores the disproportionate allocation of funding from the perspective of social justice. The Funding Council in England in 2007 reported expenditures as follows: £40 million on access for full-time undergraduates (based on educational disadvantage in different census wards); £54 million on access for part-time undergraduates; £187 million on retention of full-time undergraduates; £56 million on retention of part-time undergraduates; and £13 million on support and facilities for disabled students. A total of £354 million was allocated to support broader access and retention. This is in contrast to the £1.4 billion for research funding. Investment in broader access represents about 2.5 percent of the research-related funding (HEFCE 2007).

Pedagogy and Student Engagement

New entrants to higher education from historically underrepresented groups will not only reflect diverse preuniversity experience but are also likely to demonstrate other inclinations and needs. As already mentioned, a great need will be under way for tutoring and other academic support, as students from poor secondary schools are likely to be unprepared for the demands of university study. There is also likely to be a growing "disconnect" between traditional teaching and the culture and expectations of first-generation college students and other students from historically underrepresented groups. This is most likely to be seen by faculty as a student problem rather than an incentive to develop new pedagogy (Gorard et al. 2006). Going forward, diversity will oblige institutions to rethink the way higher education is delivered.

> As universalization progresses, most new students are simply less interested in the kind of education provided by existing higher education institutes or are simply less academically gifted. In order to attract these students, new tactics need to be introduced.
>
> (Usher 2009, 9)

There may be courses on offer that are perceived to be more attractive (especially those related to health, service, and cultural professions), and the teaching styles may be felt to be more appropriate in the so-called "new" universities. The Higher Education Policy Institute has pointed to the greater frequency of contact with mainstream academic staff in these institutions (as opposed to research and teaching assistants), and there is some evidence of greater attention to pedagogical practice (Bekhradnia, Whitnall, and Sastry 2007).

Some countries are experimenting with new approaches to pedagogy at institutions that serve indigenous populations. New Mexican "intercultural universities" are developing approaches to teaching and learning that are congruent with cultural values, language, and history (Brunner et al. 2006). Pedagogy and the organization of degree programs will have to be reconsidered along with measures of performance and criteria for achievement and excellence as higher education becomes increasingly diverse.

Conclusion

It is generally agreed that there is a worldwide need for the reallocation of privilege. The concentration of social benefits to a small segment of society is no longer acceptable. To continue past patterns of inequality will stunt the expansion of economic prosperity and democracy. Access to higher education has become a serious component of building stable and prosperous modern societies.

Access to postsecondary education was long the privilege of small segments of society until the last half of the twentieth century. The massification of most higher education systems expanded opportunities worldwide but not equally within all sectors of society. Nations today are trying to address those inequities through a range of strategies.

Perfect solutions are not in evidence. Public resources are limited and need to address a broad spectrum of social problems, and all needs will not be met. Some individuals will likely lose opportunities, even though they are not directly responsible for past patterns of discrimination. Their possibly required sacrifices might contribute to further divisiveness as will continuing to exclude sectors of the population from access to opportunities. The situation cannot remain static, and universities have an important role to play.

Despite a lot of rhetoric, widening participation is not solely dependent on higher education admissions offices. University admissions have improved distributional fairness (Gorard et al. 2006).

Widening participation is about improving the quality of school-based experience for all students, especially those from underrepresented groups. Improving success in compulsory education is vital. The gap in higher education participation between richer and poorer students is largely explained by the weak academic achievement of disadvantaged children in secondary school (Chowdry et al. 2008). Ultimately, eliminating obstacles to successful participation requires intervention well before the point of entry into higher education and increasing the attainment of children from poorer backgrounds at earlier ages.

Inside the university the obligation is to understand the current pattern of recruitment, orientation, and integration of diverse populations. New initiatives to ensure retention (or persistence) and the eventual success of all groups (in employment as well as graduation) are needed. This involves sustaining a professional dialogue about a range of issues, including any cultural, curriculum, or pedagogical adjustments that might be necessary within institutions as well as in the policy arena. Across the sector an obligation is needed to collaborate and cooperate to improve progression. New and relevant research is badly needed.

At the level of public policy and debate, university leadership must work in partnership with schools at the compulsory phase of education, with other types of social institutions, and with public and private employers.

Above all, universities should strive to get the balance right between self-reflection (via institutional research) and constructive criticism of the other social and political enterprises that figure into this equation. Positive engagement with access and equity represents a long haul; it is, however, immensely worthwhile in the light of the commitment of universities to social justice.

References

Altbach, Philip G., Liz Reisberg, and Laura E. Rumbley (2009) *Trends in Global Higher Education: Tracking an Academic Revolution*, Chestnut Hill, MA: Center for International Higher Education, Boston College.
Arum, Richard, Adam Gamoran, and Yossi Shavit (2007) "More inclusion than diversion: Expansion, differentiation, and market structure in higher education," in Yossi Shavit, Richard Arum, Adam Gamoran, and Gila Menachem (eds.), *Stratification in Higher Education: A Comparative Study*, Stanford, CA: Stanford University Press.
Bekhradnia, Bahram, Carolyn Whitnall, and Tom Sastry (2007) *The Academic Experience of Students in English Universities: 2007 Report*, Oxford: Higher Education Policy Institute.
Bowen, William G., Matthew M. Chingos, and Michael S. McPherson (2009) *Crossing the Finish Line: Completing College at America's Public Universities*, Princeton, NJ: Princeton University Press.
Brunner, José Joaquin, Paulo Santiago Carmen García Gaudilla, Johann Gerlach, and Léa Velho (2006) *Thematic Review of Tertiary Education*, Paris: Organization for Economic Cooperation and Development.
Callender, Claire (forthcoming) "Institutional aid in England: Promoting widening participation or perpetuating inequalities?" in Jane Knight (ed.) *Financing Higher Education: Access and Equity*, Rotterdam: Sense.
Canton, Erik and Andreas Blom (2004) *Can Student Loans Improve Accessibility to Higher Education and Student Performance: An Impact Study of the Case of SOFES, Mexico*, Washington, DC: World Bank.
Carey, Kevin. 2008. Graduation rate watch: Making minority student success a priority. Education Sector Reports. Available: http://www.educationsector.org/usr_doc/Graduation_Rate_Watch.pdf.
Chea, Terence (2009) University of Calif. admissions rule angers Asian-Americans, *USA Today*, April 24. Available: http://www.usatoday .com/news/education/2009-04-24-university-cali-fornia-asian_N.htm.
Chowdry, Haroon, Claire Crawford, Lorraine Dearden, Alissa Goodman, and Anna Vignoles (2008) Understanding the determinants of participation in higher education and the quality of institute attended: Analysis using administrative data, Institute of Fiscal Studies. Available: http://www.ifs.org.uk/publications.php?publication_id = 4234.
Chronicle of Higher Education (2010) Swedish universities to end gender-based affirmative action, 13 January. Available: http://chronicle.com/blogPost/Swedish-Universities-to-End/20444/.
Clark, Kim (2009) Do elite private colleges discriminate? *US News*, October 7. Available: http://www.usnews.com/articles/education/2009/10/07/do-elite-private-colleges-discriminate-against-asian-students.html?PageNr = 2.
Curtis, Polly (2008) Free school meal pupils lose out in race for top A-levels. *Guardian*, February 23. Available: http://www.guardian.co.uk/education/2008/feb/23/schools.alevels.
David, Miriam (2007) "Equity and diversity: Towards a sociology of higher education for the 21st century?" *British Journal of Sociology of Education* 28(5): 675–90.
De Zwart, Frank (2000) "The logic of affirmative action: Caste, class and quotas in India," *Acta Sociologica*, 43: 235–49.
Espenshade, Thomas J. and Alexandra Walton Radford (2009) *No Longer Separate, Not Yet Equal: Race and Class in Elite College Admission and Campus Life*, Princeton, NJ: Princeton University Press.
Gibbons, Steven and Anna Vignoles (2009) Access, choice and participation in higher education, London: Teaching and Learning Research Programs. Available: http://www.tlrp.org/dspace/handle/123456789/1599.
Golden, Daniel (2006) *The Price of Admission: How America's Ruling Class Buys Its Way Into Elite Colleges and Who Gets Left Outside the Gates*, New York: Crown.
Gorard, Stephen, Emma Smith, Helen May, and Liz Thomas (2006) Review of widening participation research: Addressing the barriers to participation in higher education, Higher Education

Funding Council for England. Available: http://www.hefce.ac.uk/pubs/rdreports/2006/rd13_06/

Harvard Hillel (2010) Available: http://www.hillel.org/HillelApps/JLOC/Campus.aspx?AgencyId=17431 on January 28, 2010.

HECB (Higher Education Coordinating Board) (2010) Key facts about higher education in Washington (2009–10). Available: http://www.hecb.wa.gov/keyfacts.

HEFCE (Higher Education Funding Council for England) (2007) *Funding Higher Education in England: How HEFCE Allocates its Funds*, July 20, Bristol, UK: HEFCE Guide.

Hong, Shen (2004) Access to higher education for disadvantaged groups in China. *Chinese Education and Society*, 37(4): 439–57.

Jackson, Sonia, Sarah Ajayi, and Margaret Quigley (2005) *Going to University from Care*, London: Institute of Education.

Jayaram, Narayna (2008) "Disparities in access to higher education in India: Persistent issues and the changing context," paper presented at Hurst Seminar, "Higher Education and Equality of Opportunity," Beer Sheva, Israel, June.

Johnstone, D. Bruce and Pamela Marucci (2003) "Cost Sharing and higher education access in Southern and Eastern Africa," *International Higher Education*, no. 30 (Winter): 9–11.

Morley, Louise, Fiona Leach, and Rosemary Lugg (2009) Democratising higher education in Ghana and Tanzania: Opportunity structures and social inequalities. *International Journal of Educational Development* 29: 56–64.

Neelakantan, Shailaja (2006) "Quota protests increase across India," *Chronicle of Higher Education*, May 26, A49.

OECD (Organization for Economic Cooperation and Development) (2007) Equity in Education Thematic Review: Norway. Available: http://www.oecd.org/LongAbstract/0,3425,en_2649_39263231_38692819_1_1_1_1,00.html.

—— (2009) Education at a glance 2009: OECD indicators. Available: http://www.oecd.org/document/24/0,3343,en_2649_39263238_43586328_1_1_1_1,00.html.

Piquet, Martine (2006) "Australian multicultural equity and fair go," in Elaine Kennedy-Dubourdie (ed.) *Race and Inequality: World Perspectives on Affirmative Action*, Surrey, UK: Ashgate.

Punwani, Jyoti (2006) "Caste system has become subtle and sophisticated," *Times of India*, April 25. Quoted in Gupta, Asha (2006) *Affirmative Action in Higher Education in India and the US: A Study in Contrasts*. Berkeley: Center for Studies in Higher Education, University of California, Berkeley.

Rose, Heather (2005) "The effects of affirmative action programs: Evidence from the University of California at San Diego," *Educational Evaluation and Policy Analysis*, 27 (3): 263–89.

Schuller, T., Preston, J., Hammond, C., Brassett-Grundy, A., and Bynner, J. (2004) *The Benefits of Learning: The Impact of Education on Health, Family Life and Social Capital*, London: RoutledgeFalmer.

Schwartzman, Simon (2006) A Questão da inclusão social na universidade Brasileira. Simpósio Universidade e Inclusão Social, Universidade Federal de Minas Gerais, 24 novembro.

Task Force on Higher Education and Society (2000) *Higher Education in Developing Countries: Peril and Promise*, Washington, DC: World Bank.

Tavolaro, Lília G. M. (2008) "Affirmative action in contemporary Brazil: Two institutional discourses on race," *International Journal of Politics, Culture, and Society*, 19: 145.

UK House of Commons (2001) "Higher Education: Access, Education and Employment Committee 4th Report," February, para. 116.

University World News (2009a) Politician arrested over quotas, December 13. Available: http://www.universityworldnews.com/article.php? story=2009 1212124142253.

—— (2009b) SPECIAL REPORT: Women in higher education, October 25. Available: http://www.universityworldnews.com/publication/archives.php?mode=archive&p_id=UWorld&issueno=98&format = html.

Usher, Alex (2009) "Ten years back and ten years forward: Developments and trends in higher education in the Europe region," paper presented at the UNESCO Forum on higher education in the Europe region, "Access, values, quality and competitiveness," Bucharest, Romania, May 21–24.

Watson, David (2005) "What I think I know and don't know about widening participation in HE," in Chris Duke and Geoff Layer (eds.) *Widening Participation: Which Way Forward for English Higher Education?* Leicester, UK: National Institute of Adult Continuing Education.

—— (2007) *Managing Civic and Community Engagement*. Maidenhead, UK: Open University.

12

The Academic Profession
The Realities of Developing Countries

PHILIP G. ALTBACH

The academic profession worldwide is united by its commitment to teaching and the creation and transmission of knowledge. Yet, as pointed out by Burton R. Clark, it is also composed of "small worlds" and "different worlds" divided by discipline, role, and other factors (Clark 1987). This chapter examines the conditions of the academic profession and workplace in developing countries. A growing proportion of the world's postsecondary students are found in developing countries, and the rate of expansion of higher education is greatest in this part of the world. In 2010, there are more than 150 million postsecondary students worldwide, with at least half studying in developing or middle-income countries (Altbach, Reisberg, and Rumbley 2009). China and India are now the largest and third largest academic systems in the world, respectively, and most of the enrollment expansion in the coming 30 years will be in developing countries. Further, many developing countries are building up large and complex academic systems, including research universities. There are an estimated 3,500,000 full-time academics in developing and middle-income countries, with perhaps an equal number of part-time teachers. Yet little is known about the professionals responsible for teaching and research in these universities.

What is recognized about the conditions of the academic profession and of academic work in the developing world is not positive. The conditions of work and levels of remuneration are inadequate, involvement in institutional governance often limited, and the autonomy to build both an academic career and academic programs in the university is often constrained.

While some of these circumstances exist in middle-income nations such as the countries of the former Soviet Union, this chapter is mainly concerned with developing countries—nations with low-level per capita income. There are major variations among the developing countries and, indeed, within the academic systems of these countries. Larger countries, such as India and China, have some universities and specialized postsecondary institutions with excellent facilities that operate at international levels, although they have not yet achieved the status of top world-class institutions. However, these higher education systems are overall of fairly low quality. As with most comparative analyses, the generalizations presented here do not fully apply to all of the countries or higher education systems discussed in the chapter.

The academic profession is at the heart of any university; without committed and well-educated professors, no university can achieve its potential. Professors perform the central tasks of the university—teaching, research, and service. They must be taken into account in every decision made by the university. Their working conditions and remuneration must enable them to perform well. Universities have traditionally involved the professoriate in governance and, thus, in decisions concerning the central functions of the university—who is admitted for study, what is taught, who is hired to the profession, who is promoted up the ranks, what are the requirements for academic degrees, and who is awarded a degree. The academic freedom and job security of the professoriate must be protected.

Yet, as will be discussed in this chapter, the conditions of the academic profession in the twenty-first century are far from ideal and in some ways are deteriorating. This is true worldwide. The impact of massification, the privatization of higher education, and the impact of the financial crisis have all contributed to the challenges faced by the academic profession.

Worldwide Trends

Many of the conditions affecting the academic profession in developing countries are central realities worldwide. For example, G.R. Evans (2002) points out that the British academic profession has been drawn away from its traditional values and that in many ways this has weakened the country's universities. As she points out, these trends are observable worldwide. The central realities of higher education in the twenty-first century—massification, accountability, privatization, and marketization—affect universities everywhere and academics, to differing degrees. Massification has led, among other things, to an expanded academic profession and an academic community that is increasingly fragmented. Accountability has limited the traditional autonomy of the profession, more tightly regulating academic work and eroding one of the major attractions of the academic profession. Privatization has, in some contexts, placed pressure on academics to generate income for themselves and for the university through consulting and other nonteaching activities. Marketization has forced academics to become more aware of students' curricular interests. Professors have also been encouraged to engage in entrepreneurial activities. The sad fact in the era of mass higher education is that the conditions of academic work have, for most academics, deteriorated everywhere.

There has been a major shift in the nature of academic institutions and academic work in many countries and for a substantial part of the academic profession. These changes have implications for the career structure of the professoriate, choices for research and teaching, the relationship of academic staff to administration, and the participation of academics in the governance of institutions—to mention a few factors. In industrialized nations, the top segments of increasingly differentiated academic systems have thus far managed to retain the ability to engage in high-level teaching and research and to protect the central values of the university. While the problematic trends described earlier affect academics everywhere, the impact may be especially severe in developing countries, where the traditional roles of the professoriate are often less well established, financial and other resources less adequate, and the pressures greater.

Centers, Peripheries, and Dependency

The professoriate in the developing countries is a profession on the periphery (Altbach 1998). With few exceptions, research is undertaken at the major universities in the industrialized countries, and the norms of academic work at these institutions set the standard everywhere. The academic world is itself hierarchical, and research universities in the industrialized countries are at the center of an international knowledge system (Shils 1972). These institutions produce most of the research and control the key international journals and other means of communication. They train researchers and top scholars and in most countries educate the elites (Geiger 2004). Peripheries are not, of course, limited to developing countries. Academics in teaching-oriented universities generally are peripheral to those at the major research universities. The academic profession in developing countries is also peripheral to the international centers.

The academic systems of developing countries are, without exception, imported from the North. Indeed, all contemporary universities are based on the medieval University of Paris model, with the exception of the al-Azhar University in Cairo. In part, the European model was imposed by the colonial powers, but even in Ethiopia, Thailand, and Japan, where foreign academic patterns were not imposed, European models prevailed over existing indigenous academic traditions. Following independence, when developing countries had the chance to change the nature of the university, none of them chose to do so. Indeed, in many cases, even the language of the colonial power was retained for instruction and research. The European and increasingly the American academic models—based on departments, competition among academic staff, institutional hierarchy, and specific definitions of science and scholarship—continue to prevail throughout the developing world and are increasingly influential elsewhere.

Language is one element of the peripherality of the academic profession in developing countries. In the twenty-first century, English is the main language for academic communication—in journals and Internet networks, as well as at international meetings (Crystal 1997). Major Western languages—such as French and to a lesser extent German and Spanish—are also widely used. Other languages may be used for teaching and perhaps local publications but have little international relevance for scientific research. This is as true for Danish or Hungarian as it is for Chinese or Swahili. A significant number of developing countries use English or French for instruction—permitting the use of textbooks and curricular materials in those languages but also weakening the connection to local cultures and realities.

Larger and wealthier than their counterparts in the South, the long-established academic communities of the North possess resources that permit them to maintain leadership in all areas of academic work. Universities in the North also have close relationships with multinational corporations and other consumers of research. These links provide further funding sources and outlets for research and other academic work. This combination of wealth, resources, and position ensures the centrality of the universities of the North.

Global realities are in the process of change. Not only has globalization created an international knowledge system in which academics and universities worldwide can participate, but some of the larger developing countries are rapidly building research universities and may be shedding their peripheral status (Altbach and Balán 2007; Salmi 2009). China, for example, has provided significant support to a small number of its top universities, and these institutions produce research and train doctorates. Countries that have in the past half century moved ahead economically—such as South Korea, Singapore, and Taiwan—have also built research universities that can compete with the best in the world. These institutions offer working conditions and remuneration to the academic profession necessary to sustain a research university.

Related to peripherality is dependency. Third World academics often perceive themselves to be dependent on the main centers of knowledge and the world scientific networks. The vast inequality in wealth, size, and access to resources and institutional infrastructure contributes to dependency. The policies and practices of academic systems in the North also play a role in the power imbalance. For example, scholarly journals select articles based on the interests as well as the methodological and scientific norms that prevail in the North, which often places Third World researchers at a disadvantage in getting their work published and recognized internationally. In many developing countries, funding for research, participation in international conferences and programs, and access to academic collaboration is often dependent on external support from the North. The decision-making structures are based in the North and reflect the interests and concerns of the dominant academic communities. The situation is most extreme for Africa, where almost all research and funding for international linkages come from external sources—foreign governments, multilateral agencies such as the World Bank, philanthropic foundations, and so on. African scholars and scientists are dependent on foreign funds and must comply with the particular priorities and programs of the funders for their research (Teferra and Altbach 2002).

The fact is that most academics work in the "small worlds" of their departments and universities, spend most of their time teaching, and are thus unaffected in their daily lives by the trends in international scholarship. While research and knowledge communication at the top of the system are directly involved in the peripherality and dependency discussed here, the daily lives of most academics operate at a different level—less directly affected by academic globalization. Academics in developing countries function in a world of peripherality and, depending on the country and region, dependency, but at the same time are deeply embedded in national realities.

The Domination of External Values

The universities of the developing world are in many ways dependent on the world academic system. Not only is the institutional model and, often, language of instruction adopted from the North but many of the norms and values of the academic profession as well. The Third World also looks to the North for validation of academic quality and respectability. For example, academics are expected to publish in Northern academic journals, and promotion sometimes depends on such publication. Even where local scholarly publications exist, many academic decision makers do not consider them of sufficient quality. While it is understandable that in small and relatively new academic systems there may be the desire to implement external validation of the work of scholars and scientists, relying on foreign journals has implications for the professoriate. Internationally circulated journals are often highly competitive, but they may not place much value on research topics relevant in developing countries. Moreover, it is always more difficult for authors to write in a language that is not their own. Journal editors, for their part, must be guided by the methodological and topical predilections of their colleagues and are as a result less interested in work done by Third World authors, who are disadvantaged by the lack of access to the library and laboratory facilities available at the major universities of the North.

Third World academic systems, however, rely on the major Western academic institutions to give legitimacy to their academic work. China and other developing countries measure the research productivity of academics in part by relying on the Science Citation Index (SCI) and, to a lesser extent, the Social Science Citation Index (SSCI). This measurement of the impact of scholarly work counts the citations in a group of internationally circulated journals. The number of journals covered is only a small proportion of those published, and almost all of them are edited and published in the North. Thus, the scientific work produced in the developing countries is largely overlooked. The SCI and SSCI are the only major scholarly citation indexes available. Their prominence augments the power of international scientific networks, further undervaluing scientific work carried out in developing countries. While Third World academics strive to keep abreast of world science, they are at a distinct competitive disadvantage. The way in which the world of scientific publishing is organized discourages national and regional scientific communities from emerging in the Third World. While understandable and probably necessary for universities seeking to engage in research and teaching at the highest international levels, an overreliance on these external norms distorts academic development and introduces unrealistic expectations for institutions and for the academic profession.

The Impact of Globalization

The globalization of higher education has had a broad structural impact on systems everywhere (Scott 1998), and certain elements are specifically affecting the academic profession. The most visible aspect of globalization is the emergence of a worldwide market for academic talent, stimulated in part by the large numbers of students who study abroad. It must be emphasized that the international labor market for scholars and scientists and most of the flows of foreign students are South-to-North phenomena. In 2009, more than 2.5 million students were studying outside the borders of their own countries; the vast majority of these students were from developing countries, and their destinations were in the industrialized nations. The United States is the host country for close to 660,000 students, with western Europe, Australia, and Canada absorbing most of the rest. The flow of students from North to South is tiny, although there is some South-South flow. A large majority of international students from developing countries study for advanced degrees—in contrast to patterns from the industrialized nations, where students tend to study for their first degree or spend just a semester or year abroad. A significant number of students who obtain their degrees abroad do not return home, and those who do return and join the academic profession and bring the values and orientations of the country in which they studied back with them.

While foreign study has received considerable attention, its impact on the academic profession has not been analyzed. In many developing countries, academics with foreign degrees constitute a significant part of the professoriate. Furthermore, these returnees are clustered at the top of the profession and dominate research-oriented universities. They are the "power elite" of the academic community. These trends are linked to a number of factors. Foreign academic degrees are valued not only because of the perceived quality of the training and the exposure to the best facilities and professors available but also because foreign study is deemed to be more prestigious than receiving training at home. Scholars returning from abroad often wish to employ the values they absorbed during their studies to upgrade local standards, whether or not such replication is practical or desirable in local conditions. These academics follow the latest international academic developments and seek to maintain links with the countries in which they studied, often importing scientific equipment as well as ideas. Conflicts between foreign-returned academics and their locally educated colleagues are common.

There is also an increasingly important flow of academic talent around the world. Again, the flow is almost exclusively from South to North. It takes many forms, including migration from one country to another on a permanent basis, stints as visiting scholars or postdoctoral fellows, or temporary work assignments abroad. Statistics are difficult to obtain, but some 106,000 visiting scholars were at American universities in 2008—up from 80,000 just eight years earlier. It is a well-known fact that there is a large flow of academics and professionals from a number of African countries to North America and Europe. For example, more Ghanaian medical doctors are practicing outside of Ghana than at home. There is now a flow from sub-Saharan African nations to South Africa, while at the same time South African academics are taking jobs in the North.

What used to be called the "brain drain" has evolved into a much more complex phenomenon. For academic and scientific personnel, settling in another country no longer means permanent emigration. In some cases, people from developing countries employed in the North return home when attractive opportunities open up after domestic circumstances have improved in terms of living conditions, academic infrastructures, and the intellectual and political climate. As Taiwan and Korea developed in the 1960s and became stable democracies, academics and scientists who had settled abroad began returning home to take jobs in universities. More common is the phenomenon of scientists and scholars from developing countries, who have emigrated, maintaining active relationships with their countries of origin (Choi 1995). They serve as consultants, visiting professors, lecturers, or advisers to universities, governments, and sometimes companies in their countries of origin. In this way, they act as important links between centers and peripheries. Migrants understand conditions in their countries of origin and regularly participate in academic life there as well as at their new homes. A growing number of foreign-educated Chinese are returning home as the universities and working conditions for academics improve.

In the twenty-first century, the diaspora of professors, scientists, and intellectuals from developing countries who study or live in the North represents a significant factor in the academic culture of the developing world. Globalization makes this human flow possible. An international academic culture, the willingness of universities worldwide to accept students and in many cases faculty members from abroad, and immigration policies that permit migration all contribute to this diaspora. While the bulk of the flow is from South to North, there is also significant movement among the industrialized countries. Academics move from countries with relatively low salaries and poor working conditions to those with greater resources. For example, large numbers of academics from the former Soviet Union have moved to western Europe and North America in recent years. Smaller numbers have gone from the United Kingdom to the United States and Canada because of deteriorating salaries and working conditions in the United Kingdom. There has also been a modest South-South flow—Indians can be found teaching in a number of English-speaking African countries and South Africa has attracted academics from other African countries. Egyptians and Palestinians staff universities in the Gulf and Saudi Arabia. The costs and benefits of this massive international migration are considerable—with most of the benefits accruing to the wealthier academic systems.

Information technology (IT) is also closely related to globalization and is beginning to affect universities and the academic profession in many ways. Two basic elements are of concern here: the use of IT for scientific communication worldwide and for pedagogical purposes, both through distance education and for improving instruction and learning in traditional universities. The IT revolution has yet to fully unfold and will increase its impact on higher education everywhere. It is likely to be especially influential in developing countries, where the demand for access is greatest.

IT is a new phenomenon in much of the developing world—Africa, for example, has been connected to the Internet for a relatively short time, and even now many African academics have only sporadic access to it (Teferra 2003). The issue of access is central. In the academic context of developing countries, many academic staff do not have their own computers and must rely on spotty access and service. Personal e-mail accounts are by no means universal. Connectivity is unreliable and often slow, due to inadequate and poorly maintained telephone systems—meaning that many sophisticated databases will not run well. Prices are often high, and this means that individuals cannot afford their own accounts, and universities may ration access. Despite these serious problems, IT has provided many academics in developing countries with unprecedented access to current scientific information, which to some extent makes up for the inadequate libraries that exist in virtually all developing countries. Just as important, the Internet has permitted academics to communicate with colleagues worldwide, dramatically decreasing traditional isolation.

While IT has given access to knowledge on a scale hitherto unknown, it has in some ways increased the peripherality of developing-country academics (Castells 2000). Studies show that developing countries use information from the North but contribute relatively little to the total flow of knowledge. Developing countries are, in sum, users of knowledge produced by others.

Developing countries are making use of IT-based distance education—indeed, 7 out of the 10 largest distance-education providers are located in developing countries—in countries such as Turkey, India, and China. With the exception of the few academics who have been involved with developing and delivering curriculum in these distance-based universities, few individuals in developing countries have had their teaching affected by IT.

The impact of the Internet and IT on the academic profession is in many ways similar to the patterns of inequality described earlier in the chapter. Academics in developing countries are largely dependent on outsiders for the technology, basic equipment, and content. These assets have helped developing-country academics to keep abreast of scientific research, communicate with international colleagues, and participate in scientific debates on a more equal basis. However, academics in developing countries are still peripheral in many ways in the Internet-based knowledge system.

The Shape of the Profession

The professoriate is changing in many parts of the world, and developing countries are not free from these changes. In developing countries, a higher proportion of academics work on part-time contracts or are subject to irregular hiring practices. In many developing countries, a large part of the profession is composed of part-time staff who teach a few courses and do not have regular academic appointments or real links to the university. This is the norm at most Latin American universities, except for Brazil, where full-time permanent staff are a small proportion of the total academic labor force. In many countries, tenure is not guaranteed, and even full-time academics have little formal job protection, although, in fact, relatively few are actually fired. Clear guarantees of academic freedom or the assurance of a stable career are often missing.

There are curious contradictions in the nature of academic appointments. On the one hand, those hired in regular full-time positions are generally given de facto security of appointment, without much evaluation as to job performance, competence in teaching or research, or other attributes of a successful academic career. At the same time, while few appointees are in fact removed from their academic posts, many academic systems do not offer a formal tenure system that protects academic freedom or inhibits interference by university authorities in the intellectual life of academic staff.

In many Latin American countries, the pattern of academic appointments includes periodic "contests" for academic posts, which require each professor to defend his or her position publicly and permit others to apply for the post. Often, contests do not occur due to the inability of university authorities to organize open competitions on a regular basis. In reality, few faculty are removed from posts they already hold, but the possibility of removal remains a fact. In many developing countries, the terms and conditions of academic appointments are not clearly spelled out, leaving considerable latitude for administrative or governmental interference in an academic career.

The requirements for academic appointments vary greatly in developing countries and are in general less rigorous than is the case in most industrialized nations. In the North, the standard requirement for an academic appointment includes holding a doctoral degree or the equivalent—the highest degree possible in the country. In Germany, Russia, and other countries following the German academic model, a second doctorate—the habilitation or its equivalent—is required for appointment to a full professorship.

It is probably the case that a significant minority—in some cases a majority—of academics in most developing countries hold just a bachelor's degree. Those in senior academic positions almost always have higher academic qualifications, but much of the academic labor force has modest qualifications for their jobs. A number of countries, including India and Brazil, have engaged in successful efforts to increase the qualifications of their academic staff by providing opportunities for study to those already in academic positions and increasing the minimum qualifications for appointments. The lack of qualifications has meant that academic upward mobility is limited for many junior staff. It also means, of course, that the level of expertise possessed by many teachers is quite modest, affecting the quality and depth of the instruction provided to many students.

It is unlikely that, on balance, the qualifications of academic staff will improve dramatically in the coming period. Continued expansion throughout the developing world means that large numbers of new teachers will be required, and selectivity will be minimal. The bulk of enrollment growth worldwide will be in developing countries. In India, for example, enrollments will almost double in the next two decades. The challenge of providing teachers to instruct these students will place severe strains on the limited capacities in most developing countries for advanced training in the universities.

The mixed qualifications of academic staff have resulted in a highly differentiated academic profession. The small minority of well-qualified professors, many of whom hold foreign doctoral degrees, are located at the top of the system. The large majority of poorly qualified teachers at the bottom possess few possibilities for mobility. Missing is a successful middle rank of scholars. A wide gulf exists between the thin wedge of highly qualified personnel and the large, poor, and marginally qualified group of teachers.

In spite of the limited data on the socioeconomic backgrounds of the academic profession in developing countries, some generalizations can be made. The involvement of women in the profession varies and is surprisingly high in some countries. In many Latin American nations and in South Asia, the proportion of women holding academic positions is high—often higher than in industrialized countries. As of 1993, more than one-third of academics in three large Latin American countries (Brazil, Mexico, and Chile) were women (Boyer, Altbach, and Whitelaw 1994). Only a few industrialized nations have reached that level. In developing countries, academics tend to come from well-educated, urban families, although the majority of the population remains largely uneducated and rural. Academics do not, however, come mainly from elite families, due in part to the fact that salaries are not high and chances for mobility are limited.

The academic profession in developing countries differs significantly from the professoriate in the North. In developing countries, there are more part-time staff. Full-time professors have less job security and are sometimes subject to insecure terms of appointment; they are not as well qualified; and they come from more modest backgrounds. While there have been efforts to upgrade academic skills in some developing countries, massification has meant that qualifications have not kept up with the need for more teachers in the classrooms of the Third World.

Developing-Country Realities

While the basic roles of academics everywhere are similar—teaching, research, and service—in all countries most academics are mainly teachers, with research and service a minor or negligible part of their work. Academics worldwide have recently suffered from a deterioration in income, working conditions, and, in some cases, prestige (Altbach 2002). Working conditions for academics in developing countries are, in general, significantly less favorable than for their colleagues in the North, and there is less emphasis on the research and service roles of the profession.

Institutional Environment

The working environment for most Third World academics is far different than what is the norm in the industrialized nations. While this chapter is not intended as an analysis of the infrastructures of academic institutions, it is necessary to point out that conditions vary considerably across and within countries. For example, India has a few academic institutions—such as the Indian Institutes of Technology, several management schools, and the Bhabha Atomic Research Centre—with facilities comparable to average institutions in the industrialized countries, although not the very best. But the vast majority of Indian universities, colleges, and other academic institutions fall far below the level of the average postsecondary institutions in the North. While precise figures do not exist, it is probably the case that 95 percent of Indian academics work in an environment that is well below international levels (Jayaram 2003). The situation is significantly better in China, which has a growing number of academic institutions that seek to compete on a global level in terms of research and teaching. However, in China, the large majority of academics work in substandard conditions, and most staff teaching in postsecondary education do not hold an advanced degree. In many developing countries, especially smaller nations, no academic institutions exist that even approach international standards in terms of facilities or quality. Even large countries, such as Ethiopia or Nigeria, have few if any academic institutions that can offer working conditions permitting scholars and scientists to function competitively on an international basis. Even in fairly well-developed academic systems in relatively affluent countries such as Argentina, the physical facilities available to most academics are quite limited. What is surprising in the developing world is the ability of many academics to work effectively under such difficult circumstances.

The academic environment is characterized by inadequacies at all levels. The cost of maintaining up-to-date facilities and resources has increased with the escalating prices of journals and books and the complexity and sophistication of scientific equipment. In the twenty-first century, it is increasingly costly to stay competitive in world science. Further, all of these scientific products would have to be imported at unfavorable exchange rates and in an environment of financial scarcity.

In fact, many academics lack even a desk on which to place a computer, even if one were available. Office space is in short supply, limiting the possibility for academic work and consultation with students and colleagues. Many academics have nothing but the books they use as texts or perhaps a few related publications. The physical infrastructure available to most academics is inadequate for scientific research and scholarship and barely adequate for teaching. Indeed, in much of the developing world, facilities are actually deteriorating due to financial shortages and the pressures of ever-increasing numbers of students.

Bureaucracy and Politics

Universities everywhere are bureaucratic institutions. In the North, the concept of shared governance is the norm, with the professoriate sharing or controlling (decreasingly) the key governing structure of universities. Professorial power has weakened everywhere as academic institutions expand and demands for accountability mount. However, academics' control over key aspects of the curriculum, the hiring of new faculty members, issues of instruction and evaluation, and related issues remains largely intact.

The same cannot be said for many universities in developing countries. First of all, the tradition of professorial power and shared governance is weak. In countries formerly under colonial rule, universities were founded with strong bureaucratic structures and firm controls to ensure loyalty and adherence to the norms of the colonial authorities. In other countries, academic institutions, which were often directly established by government, also lacked the traditions of faculty power. Governments have been concerned about institutional stability, student political activism and unrest, and the risk that universities could become sources of dissent in society. These factors led to the buildup of strong bureaucratic controls and prevented the growth of professorial autonomy and strong faculty governance. Even in Latin America, with its long tradition of formal autonomy for the universities, the academic profession has attained less control over working conditions and over institutional structures.

Many universities in developing countries have become politicized, which has directly affected the academic profession. In developing countries, universities are important political institutions—not only do they train elites but they also play a direct political role as a forum for student political activism, dissident perspectives, and even mobilization of opposition activities. Especially in societies with unstable governments, universities often serve an oppositional political function.

In many developing countries, two kinds of politics affect higher education: academic politics within the university and societal politics. Academic politics can be found everywhere—in departments, among colleagues, and in the university at large. In the North, while factions may be present in departments, institutions and units within them are generally not disrupted by politics or governed by political considerations. Seldom does the partisan politics in broader society intrude into the on-campus operation of the institution. In developing countries, politics is more prevalent at universities and is not infrequently a motivating force in academic policy decisions, the hiring or promotion of academic staff, and other areas.

A number of factors explain the intrusion of politics into academe. In the developing-country context, the university is an institution with considerable resources. In such a resource-scarce environment, the decisions made on campus—including the hiring of staff (faculty and administrators), student admissions, the creation of new programs, and so on—have broader implications. Universities in developing countries have a tradition of being politicized, the result of a long history of involvement in independence movements or other struggles. Politics has continued to be an element of campus life in the absence of the norms in the North that keep partisan politics away from the university.

In Latin America, parts of South Asia, some African countries, and elsewhere, party politics sometimes determines the election of academics to administrative posts. Candidates for rector or dean may stand for election backed by a political party or a campus faction. Political partisanship is often felt in the appointment of professors and other staff. Occasionally, even student admissions or examination results may be influenced by political considerations.

Universities are complex bureaucratic institutions. In developing countries, bureaucratic control, government involvement in academic decisions, and the politicization of all elements of higher education have been detrimental to the academic profession and the strength of academic norms and values in higher education.

Academic Freedom

Not surprisingly, given the realities discussed here, academic freedom is often not well protected in developing countries. The institutional protections common in the North are often missing—such as tenure or civil service status, as well as academic freedom. A number of factors have combined to put professors in developing countries in a more vulnerable position than their counterparts in the North. The history of higher education in developing countries, as noted, is one of governmental oversight and bureaucratic control. Colonial regimes as well as postindependence governments worried about the political loyalty of the professoriate and of the university. To a certain extent, a tradition of subservience exists in the academic profession of developing countries (Gilbert 1972). Academic freedom is often more highly contested in developing countries because the work of professors can have direct political relevance—that is, their writings can have an immediate impact on society. The campus environment is often highly volatile, and professors may contribute to dissent on campus and in society. Protecting professorial freedom of expression and academic work does not receive a high priority from governments.

These limitations on academic freedom damage the professoriate, creating problems for expression and research. When professors step over an often undefined line, they can suffer serious consequences—ranging from mild sanctions to loss of their positions or imprisonment. In some countries, research, especially in the social sciences, is restricted. Publications are closely monitored, and professors who express views in opposition to government policy face problems. Most academics, however, do not perceive the situation regarding academic freedom as problematic. In the sciences few restrictions are imposed. Most academics are in any case involved exclusively in teaching, and classroom expression is seldom monitored. However, the lack of a respected culture of academic freedom has an impact on the intellectual atmosphere of the university.

Working Conditions

In general, the professoriate in developing countries works under much-less-favorable conditions than what is standard in the North. Again, there are significant variations—with a small proportion of academics at the top universities enjoying conditions similar to the North. Few classrooms have anything more than the most rudimentary teaching aids. Class size tends to be large, and in any case the almost universally accepted method of instruction consists of the lecture, with little opportunity for discussion or questions. In some countries, the lack of laboratories and equipment deprives students of an essential component of scientific training. Rote learning constitutes the norm in many places.

Teaching loads, even for senior professors, are high by international standards, and academic staff typically spend more time in the classroom than do their peers in the North. There are some exceptions, such as China, where teaching loads are less onerous. The trend, with enrollment pressures and financial shortfalls, is toward ever-higher teaching loads. The practice of assigning advanced graduate students to assist professors is virtually unknown. Academic staff may spend

20 or more hours per week in direct teaching. Little time remains for research, course preparation, advisement, or other academic activities. Academic staff often possess little control over what courses are taught. Differences do exist by country, rank, and institution, with academics at the most prestigious universities teaching less than their colleagues further down on the academic hierarchy. Junior staff often teach more than senior academics.

In a growing number of countries, academics are expected to engage in remunerative activities unrelated to their basic teaching. Consulting; extra instruction in the form of revenue-producing, noncredit courses, or other programs; extramural service; and other activities increasingly constitute part of the academic workload. These forms of work produce additional income for universities as well as for individual faculty members. The traditional job of the professor is expanding to include entirely new kinds of responsibilities.

Remuneration

Without adequate salaries, professionals would be hard pressed to perform their best-quality work. The gulf between the industrialized nations and the developing countries, with regard to salaries, is immense. Of course, academics everywhere earn less than people with similar qualifications in the rest of the labor force, but people do not become professors to get rich. Nonetheless, in most industrialized countries, it is possible for academics to achieve a modest middle-class standard of living based on their salaries. With variations by country, discipline, and rank, academic salaries are usually sufficient to live on in the industrialized countries. In developing countries, however, with some exceptions, this is not the case (Rumbley, Pacheco, and Altbach 2008).

In many developing countries, a full-time academic salary cannot support what is considered to be a middle-class standard of living. This is almost universally the case for junior academics but is also true of senior professors in many countries. Thus, in many countries, academics must hold more than one job. Their main appointments provide a portion of their income, but they must earn additional income from teaching at other universities, consulting, or even holding jobs in business or in service occupations unrelated to their academic work. In many countries, academics provide tutoring or other ancillary teaching to boost their income, even when such activities are proscribed by the university. In the industrialized world, professors also take on outside consulting in order to earn extra income. The difference in developing countries is that, without this additional income, academics could not survive, and many cannot be the sole breadwinners in their families.

Salaries do, of course, vary significantly across and within institutions. Private universities often pay higher salaries than public institutions. The majority of academics in developing countries work at public universities. Income is linked to rank, but in some countries professors engaged in research and graduate teaching can earn higher salaries. In a few countries, professors receive additional payment for publications and other evidence of academic productivity. In Mexico there is an elite cadre of research-active professors who receive additional remuneration in recognition for their work. Salaries tend to be higher at the most prestigious institutions, in business schools, and other specialized schools. In some countries, academic salaries are not paid regularly, placing great strains on the affected academics, civil servants, and other public officials. The many part-time professors earn much less than full-time professors, in some cases just a token payment.

As a general rule, the low academic salaries in developing countries are unlikely to improve. Salary structure produces a significant impact, as the poor salary levels have led to brain drain. The best scholars and scientists in developing countries can earn many times their local salaries by relocating to the North, and many take this option. Few academics in developing countries are able to devote their full attention to their academic work because of the need to supplement their incomes. Thus, an academic career in the Third World is less than a full-time occupation, even for academics who hold regular full-time positions. This has negative consequences for research and academic productivity, generally. When combined with the structural impediments discussed earlier, it is hardly surprising that the research productivity of academics in developing countries is so low. Salary structure also negatively affects morale.

Corruption

While not much analyzed, corruption in higher education is an issue of concern in some developing countries. Corrupt practices take many forms that affect the professoriate. Student admission may be dependent on the payment of bribes that can take many forms, including expensive tutoring courses by professors in charge of admissions. Professors may engage in plagiarism of different kinds or may purchase research papers that they publish as their own. Professorial appointments may be based on nonacademic criteria such as personal relationships, religious, political, or ethnic affiliations, or others. Promotions or salary increments may be given for nonacademic reasons. In a few countries, corruption is widespread in academic life—and in the society as well—and the academic profession is significantly affected. In a larger number of cases, corruption is an occasional matter, but it is deeply damaging to core academic values and to the profession. Without a transparent and meritocratic environment, the academic profession cannot flourish and the university cannot achieve its goals.

Future Prospects

This overview of the academic profession in developing countries has provided a generally gloomy perspective. Although the outlook for improvement is not promising, some specific changes may enhance morale, productivity, and, perhaps most importantly, the quality of universities and other academic institutions. These suggestions are not complex—in some instances stating the obvious—but implementation will be a challenge in many countries.

- Adequate salaries and a stable career path should be provided to at least a key segment of the professoriate that holds full-time positions at the main universities.
- At the top academic institutions, university facilities need to be upgraded sufficiently so that the most-well-qualified professors are able to pursue research and offer excellence in teaching.
- Procedures for involving the professoriate, along with administrators (and in some cases students), in academic decision making are essential to ensure that the academic staff have a significant role in the governance of the institution.
- In some countries, the academic profession must be depoliticized— this would involve links between political parties and academics, close ties between the professoriate and student activists, and the partisan nature of academic decision making and elections.
- Academic freedom must finally become a recognized part of university life, with guarantees protecting freedoms regarding research and publications, teaching, and reasonable expression in the public sphere.
- The academic profession itself must develop a sense of responsibility with regard to expression and publication, especially on controversial topics.
- The academic profession must receive adequate training—the doctorate, for those involved in research as well as teaching; the master's degree, for those who are exclusively teachers; and for all, some exposure to training in pedagogical methods.
- Academics must be provided with the means to keep up with current trends in their fields.
- Great care needs to be taken to ensure that part-time and temporary academic staff are well qualified and provided with appropriate benefits.

Conclusion

This chapter has presented an almost unremittingly pessimistic picture of the current state of the academic profession in developing countries. Yet, what is surprising is that so many people who are working in higher education institutions freely chose the academic life and persevere under difficult circumstances. Fortunately, academic work in developing countries does have many rewarding aspects. Scholars are generally held in high regard, and a professorship, even if poorly paid, is an occupation with high status. Learning is respected, and those who possess knowledge are held in high esteem. Despite the circumstances described here, university life holds considerable attraction. It is, after all, the life of the mind, and those who are inspired to heed the call for intellectual pursuits will put up with many hardships to pursue an academic career.

Yet, as is clear from this analysis, the profession is truly in crisis. The continued deterioration in the conditions of the professoriate has not only had a negative impact on one of the most highly educated and potentially productive segments of the population but has weakened higher education as well, since academic institutions cannot perform well without a committed, well-trained, and stable academic profession. In the context of globalization, developing countries require access to the wider world of science and technology, and the academic profession represents a central link to the international knowledge network. As the primary educator of future generations, the academic profession is in many ways the linchpin of development.

Note: An earlier version of this chapter appeared in Philip G. Altbach, ed., *The Decline of the Guru: The Academic Profession in Developing and Middle-Income Countries* (Chestnut Hill, MA: Boston College Center for International Higher Education, 2002).

References

Altbach, Philip G. (1998) "Gigantic peripheries: India and China in the world knowledge system," in *Comparative Higher Education: Knowledge, the University and Development*, Greenwich, CT: Ablex.

—— (2002) "How are faculty faring in other countries?" in Richard P. Chait (ed.) *The Questions of Tenure*, Cambridge, MA: Harvard Univ. Press.

Altbach, Philip G. and Jorge Balán (2007) *World Class Worldwide: Transforming Research Universities in Asia and Latin America*, Baltimore, MD: Johns Hopkins Univ. Press.

Altbach, Philip G., Liz Reisberg, and Laura E. Rumbley (2009) *Trends in Higher Education: Tracking an Academic Revolution*, Chestnut Hill, MA: Boston College Center for International Higher Education.

Boyer, Ernest L., Philip G. Altbach, and Mary Jean Whitelaw (1994) *The Academic Profession: An International Perspective*, Princeton, NJ: Carnegie Foundation for the Advancement of Teaching.

Castells, Manuel (2000) *The Rise of the Network Society*, Oxford: Blackwell.

Choi, Hyaeweol (1995) *An International Scientific Community: Asian Scholars in the United States*, Westport, CT: Praeger.

Clark, Burton R. (1987) *The Academic Life: Small Worlds, Different Worlds*, Princeton, NJ: Carnegie Foundation for the Advancement of Teaching.

Crystal, David (1997) *English as a Global Language*, Cambridge: Cambridge Univ. Press.

Evans, G.R. (2002) *Academics and the Real World*, Buckingham, UK: Open Univ. Press.

Geiger, Roger (2004) *Knowledge and Money: Research Universities and the Paradox of the Marketplace*, Stanford, CA: Stanford Univ. Press.

Gilbert, Irene (1972) "The Indian academic profession: The origins of a tradition of subordination," *Minerva* 10:384–411.

Jayaram, N. (2003) "The fall of the guru: The decline of the academic profession in India," in Philip G. Altbach (ed.) *The Decline of the Guru: The Academic Profession in Developing and Middle-Income Countries*, New York: Palgrave.

Rumbley, Laura E., Iván Pacheco, and Philip G. Altbach (2008) *International Comparison of*

Academic Salaries: An Exploratory Study. Chestnut Hill, MA: Boston College Center for International Higher Education.

Salmi, Jamil (2009) *The Challenge of Establishing World-Class Universities,* Washington, DC: World Bank.

Scott, Peter (ed.) (1998) *The Globalization of Higher Education,* Buckingham, UK: Open Univ. Press.

Shils, Edward (1972) "Metropolis and province in the intellectual community," in *The Intellectuals and the Powers and Other Essays,* Chicago: Univ. of Chicago Press.

Teferra, Damtew (2003) *Scientific Communication in African universities: External Assistance and National Needs,* New York: RoutledgeFalmer.

Teferra, Damtew and Philip G. Altbach (2002) "Trends and perspectives in African higher education," in D. Teferra and P.G. Altbach (ed.) *African Higher Education: An International Reference Handbook,* Bloomington: Indiana Univ. Press.

13

The Challenge of Establishing World-Class Research Universities in Developing Countries*

JAMIL SALMI

The ranking of world universities published by the *Times Higher Education Supplement* in September 2005 created a major controversy in Malaysia when it showed the country's top two universities falling by almost 100 places from the previous year. Notwithstanding the fact that the big drop was mostly the result of a change in the ranking methodology—which was a little known fact and of limited comfort—the news was so traumatic that widespread calls followed for the establishment of a royal commission of inquiry to investigate the matter. A few weeks later, the vice chancellor of the University of Malaya stepped down. This strong reaction was not out of character for a nation whose current Ninth Development Plan aims at shaping the transformation of the country into a knowledge-based economy, with emphasis on the important contribution of the university sector. And though apparently extreme, this reaction is not uncommon in developing countries around the world.

Preoccupations about university rankings reflect the general recognition that economic growth and global competitiveness are increasingly driven by knowledge and that research universities play a key role in that context. Indeed, rapid advances in science and technology across a wide range of areas—from information and communications technologies to biotechnology to new materials—provide great potential for developing countries to accelerate and strengthen their economic development. The application of knowledge results in more efficient ways of producing goods and services and delivering them more effectively and at lower costs to a greater number of people.

Tertiary education plays a critical role in that context. It helps countries build globally competitive economies by developing a skilled, productive, and flexible

* The findings, interpretations, and conclusions expressed in this chapter are entirely those of the author and should not be attributed in any manner to the World Bank, the members of its Board of Executive Directors, or the countries they represent. This chapter is derived from a book published in February 2009, *The Challenge of Establishing World-Class Universities*, Washington DC: World Bank.

labor force and by creating, applying, and spreading new ideas and technologies. A recent global study of patent generation has shown, for example, that universities and research institutes, rather than firms, drive scientific advances in biotechnology (Cookson 2007). Tertiary education institutions can also play a vital role in their local and regional economies (Yusuf and Nabeshima 2007).

According to *Constructing Knowledge Societies*, the World Bank's policy report on the contribution of tertiary education to sustainable economic development (World Bank 2002), high-performing tertiary education systems encompass a wide range of institutional models—not only research universities but also polytechnics, liberal arts colleges, short-duration technical institutes, community colleges, open universities, and so forth—that together produce the variety of skilled workers and employees sought by the labor market. Each type of institution has an important role to play, and achieving a balanced development among the various components of the system is often a major preoccupation of many governments.

Within a tertiary education system, research universities play a critical role in training the professionals, high-level specialists, scientists, and researchers needed by the economy and in generating new knowledge in support of the national innovation system (World Bank 2002). An increasingly pressing priority of many developing countries is, therefore, to ensure that their top universities are actually operating at the cutting edge of intellectual and scientific development despite the financial constraints that most of them face.

The main objective of this chapter is to explore the challenges involved in setting up globally competitive research universities in developing countries that will be expected to compete effectively with the best of the best. Is there a pattern or template that might be followed to allow more rapid advancement to world-class status? What kind of leadership is needed to inspire and drive research institutions? To answer these questions, the chapter starts by constructing an operational definition of a world-class research university and reviews the role of university leaders in that context. It then outlines and analyzes possible strategies and pathways for establishing such universities and identifies the multiple challenges, costs, and risks associated with these approaches. It concludes by examining some lessons from recent and ongoing experiences to set up new research universities in developing countries.

What Is the Meaning of World-Class University?

In the past decade, the term "world-class university" has become a catch phrase, not simply for improving the quality of learning and research in tertiary education but also, more importantly, for developing the capacity to compete in the global tertiary education marketplace through the acquisition, adaptation, and creation of advanced knowledge. With governments keen on maximizing the returns on their investments in research universities, global standing is becoming an increasingly important concern for institutions around the world (Williams and Van Dyke 2007). The paradox of the world-class university, however, as Philip G. Altbach has succinctly and accurately observed, is that "everyone wants one, no one knows what it is, and no one knows how to get one" (Altbach 2004).

Becoming a member of the exclusive group of world-class universities is not achieved by self-declaration; rather, elite status is conferred by the outside world on the basis of international recognition. Until recently, the process involved a subjective qualification, mostly that of reputation. For example, Ivy League universities in the United States, such as Harvard, Yale, or Columbia; the Universities of Oxford and Cambridge in the United Kingdom; and the University of Tokyo have traditionally been counted among the exclusive group of elite universities, but no direct and rigorous measure was available to substantiate their superior status in terms of outstanding results such as training of graduates, research output, and technology transfer. Even the higher salaries captured by their graduates could be interpreted as a signaling proxy as much as the true value of their education.

With the proliferation of league tables in the past few years, however, more systematic ways of identifying and classifying world-class universities have appeared (IHEP 2007). Although most of the 45 best-known rankings purport to categorize universities within a given country, there have also been attempts to establish international rankings. The two most comprehensive international rankings, allowing for broad benchmark comparisons of institutions across national borders, are those prepared by the renamed *Times Higher Education* (*THE*) and Shanghai Jiao Tong University, which prepares the Academic Ranking of World Universities (ARWU).

To compare the international stature of institutions, these league tables are constructed by using objective or subjective data (or both) obtained from the universities themselves or from the public domain. The *THE* ranking selects the top 200 universities in the world. First presented in 2004, the methodology for this ranking focuses most heavily on international reputation, combining subjective inputs (such as peer reviews and employer recruiting surveys), quantitative data (including the numbers of international students and faculty), and the influence of the faculty (as represented by research citations). Operating since 2003, ARWU uses a methodology that focuses on objective indicators exclusively, such as the academic and research performance of faculty, alumni, and staff, to identify the top 500 universities in the world. The measures evaluated include publications, citations, and exclusive international awards (such as Nobel Prizes and Fields Medals). Table 13.1 shows the results of the latest *THE* and ARWU world rankings.

Notwithstanding the serious methodological limitations of any ranking exercise (Salmi and Saroyan 2007), world-class universities are recognized in part for their superior outputs. They produce well-qualified graduates who are

Table 13.1 Top 20 Universities in *Times Higher Education* and *Academic Ranking of World Universities* World Rankings, 2009

Rank	THE(2009)	Rank	ARWU(2009)
1	Harvard University	1	Harvard University
2	Yale University	2	Stanford University
3	University of Cambridge	3	University of California, Berkeley
4	University of Oxford	4	University of Cambridge
5	California Institute of Technology	5	Massachusetts Institute of Technology
6	Imperial College London	6	California Institute of Technology
7	University College London	7	Columbia University
8	University of Chicago	8	Princeton University
9	Massachusetts Institute of Technology	9	University of Chicago
10	Columbia University	10	University of Oxford
11	University of Pennsylvania	11	Yale University
12	Princeton University	12	Cornell University
13	Duke University	13	University of California, Los Angeles
14	Johns Hopkins University	14	University of California, San Diego
15	Cornell University	15	University of Pennsylvania
16	Australian National University	16	University of Washington, Seattle
17	Stanford University	17	University of Wisconsin, Madison
18	University of Michigan	18	University of California, San Francisco
19	University of Tokyo	19	Johns Hopkins University
20	McGill University	20	University of Tokyo

Sources: THE 2009; ARWU 2009

in high demand on the labor market; they conduct leading-edge research published in top scientific journals; and in the case of science-and-technology–oriented institutions, they contribute to technical innovations through patents and licenses.

As illustrated by table 13.1, most universities recognized as world class originate from a small number of countries, mostly Western. In fact, the University of Tokyo is the only non-US, non-UK university among the top 20 in the ARWU ranking. If one considers that there are only between 30 and 50 world-class universities in total, according to the ARWU ranking they all come from a small group of 8 North American and Western European countries, Japan being again the only exception. The *THE* ranking has a slightly wider range of countries of origin among the top 50 universities (11 countries), including Hong Kong, China; New Zealand; and Singapore besides the usual North American and Western European nations (figure 13.1).

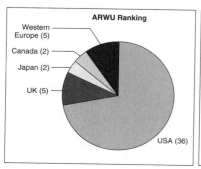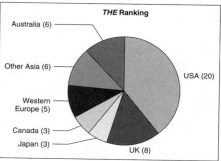

Figure 13.1 Geographical Distribution of World-Class Universities (Top 50 in 2009)
Source: ARWU 2009 and *THE* 2009

Having defined what world-class universities possess that regular universities do not, a few scholars have identified a number of basic features, such as highly qualified faculty; excellence in research; quality teaching; high levels of government and nongovernment sources of funding; international and highly talented students; academic freedom; well-defined autonomous governance structures; and well-equipped facilities for teaching, research, administration, and (often) student life (Altbach 2004; Khoon et al. 2005; Niland 2000, 2007). Recent collaborative research on this theme between UK and Chinese universities (Alden and Lin 2004) has resulted in an even longer list of key attributes, ranging from the international reputation of the university to more abstract concepts such as the university's contribution to society, both very difficult to measure in an objective manner.

In an attempt to propose a more manageable definition of world-class universities, this chapter makes the case that the superior results of these institutions—highly sought after graduates, leading-edge research, and dynamic technology transfer—can essentially be attributed to three complementary sets of factors (a) a high concentration of talent (faculty and students); (b) abundant resources to offer a rich learning environment and to conduct advanced research; and (c) favorable governance features that encourage strategic vision, innovation, and flexibility and that enable institutions to make decisions and to manage resources without being encumbered by bureaucracy.

Concentration of Talent

The first and perhaps foremost determinant of excellence is the presence of a critical mass of top students and outstanding faculty. World-class universities are able to select the best students and attract the most qualified professors and researchers.

In the sciences, being at the right university—the one where the most state-of-the-art research is being done in the best-equipped labs by the most visible scientists—is extremely important. George Stigler describes this as a snowballing process, where an outstanding scientist gets funded to do exciting research, attracts other faculty, then the best students—until a critical mass is formed that has an irresistible appeal to any young person entering the field.

(Csikszentmihalyi 1997)

This has always been the hallmark of the Ivy League universities in the United States or the Universities of Oxford and Cambridge in the United Kingdom. And it is also a feature of the newer world-class universities, such as the National University of Singapore or Tsinghua University in China.

Beijing's Tsinghua University said last month it would increase the number of awards this year. Students with high scores, such as champions of each province and winners of international student academic competitions, will be entitled to scholarships of up to 40,000 yuan ($5,700), more than double that of last year.

(*University World News* 2008)

Important factors are the ability and the privilege of these universities to select the most academically qualified students. For example, Peking University, China's top institution of higher learning, admits the 50 best students of each province every year.

One corollary of this observation is that tertiary education institutions in countries where there is little internal mobility of students and faculty are at risk of academic inbreeding. Indeed, universities that rely principally on their own undergraduates to continue into graduate programs or that hire principally their own graduates to join the teaching staff are not likely to be at the leading edge of intellectual development. A 2007 survey of European universities found an inverse correlation between endogamy in faculty hiring and research performance: the universities with the highest degree of endogamy had the lowest research results (Aghion et al. 2008).

It is also difficult to maintain high selectivity in institutions with rapidly growing student enrollment and fairly open admission policies. The huge size of the leading universities of Latin American countries such as Mexico or Argentina—the Universidad Nacional Autónoma de México (Autonomous University of Mexico) has 190,418 students, and the University of Buenos Aires (UBA) has 279,306—is certainly a major factor in explaining why these universities have failed to enter the top league, despite having a few excellent departments and research centers that are undoubtedly world class. At the other extreme, Peking

University maintained its overall enrollment at less than 20,000 until the early 2000s and even today has no more than 30,000 students.

World-class universities also tend to have a high proportion of carefully selected graduate students, reflecting their strength in research and the fact that graduate students are closely involved in the research activities of these institutions.

The international dimension is becoming increasingly important in determining the configuration of these elite institutions. This enables them to attract the most talented people, no matter where they come from, and open themselves to new ideas and approaches. At the University of Cambridge, 18 percent of the students are from outside the United Kingdom or European Union countries. The US universities ranked at the top of the global surveys also show sizable proportions of foreign academic staff. For instance, the proportion of international faculty at Harvard University, including medical academic staff, is approximately 30 percent. By contrast, only 7 percent of all researchers in France are foreign academics. Unquestionably, the world's best universities enroll and employ large numbers of foreign students and faculty in their search for the most talented.

Abundant Resources

Abundance of resources is the second element that characterizes most world-class universities, in response to the huge costs involved in running a complex, research-intensive university. These universities have four main sources of financing: government budget funding for operational expenditures and research, contract research from public organizations and private firms, the financial returns generated by endowments and gifts, and tuition fees.

In western Europe, public funding is by far the principal source of finance for teaching and research, although the top UK universities have some endowment funds, and "top-up fees" have been introduced in recent years. In Asia, the National University of Singapore, which became a private corporation in 2006, has been the most successful institution in terms of substantial endowment funding. It has managed to build up a sizable portfolio of US$774 million through effective fund-raising, making it richer than any British university after Cambridge and Oxford. The United States and, to a lesser extent, Japan have thriving private research universities.

A comparative analysis of the ARWU rankings of US and western European universities confirms that level of expenditures is one of the key determinants of performance. Globally, total spending on tertiary education (public and private) represents 3.3 percent of gross domestic product in the United States versus only 1.3 percent in the 25 European Union countries. Per student spending is about US$54,000 in the United States, compared with US$13,500 in the European Union (Aghion et al. 2008). Similarly, there are large spending variations among European universities that are correlated with the rankings results of the respective countries. The United Kingdom and Switzerland have relatively well-funded universities and achieve the highest country scores in terms of rankings, while universities from the southern European countries—as well as France and Germany—have lower ranking scores associated with low levels of funding (Aghion et al. 2007). The availability of abundant resources creates a virtuous circle that allows the concerned institutions to attract even more top professors and researchers.

Favorable Governance

The third dimension concerns the overall regulatory framework, the competitive environment, and the degree of academic and managerial autonomy that universities enjoy. The *Economist* (2005) referred to the tertiary education system in the United States as "the best in the world" and attributed this success not only to its wealth but also to its relative independence from the state, the competitive spirit that encompasses every aspect of it, and its ability to make academic work and production relevant and useful to society. The report observed that the environment in which universities operate fosters competitiveness, unrestrained scientific inquiry, critical thinking, innovation, and creativity. Moreover, institutions that have complete autonomy are also more flexible because they are not bound by cumbersome bureaucracies and externally imposed standards, even in light of the legitimate accountability mechanisms that do bind them.

The comparative study of European and US universities mentioned earlier also found that governance was, along with funding, the other main determinant of rankings. "European universities suffer from poor governance, insufficient autonomy and often perverse incentives" (Aghion et al. 2007). A subsequent paper reporting on a survey of European universities found that research performance was positively linked to the degree of autonomy of the universities in the sample, especially with regard to budget management, the ability to hire faculty and staff, and the freedom to set salaries (Aghion et al. 2008). With respect to the composition of university boards, the report concludes that "having significant outside representation on the board may be a necessary condition to ensure that dynamic reforms taking into account long-term institutional interests can be decided upon without undue delay" (Aghion et al. 2008, 39).

The autonomy elements outlined earlier are necessary, though not sufficient, to establish and maintain world-class universities. Other crucial governance features are needed, such as inspiring and persistent leaders; a strong strategic vision of where the institution is going; a philosophy of success and excellence; and a culture of constant reflection, organizational learning, and change.

Alignment of Factors

Finally, the combination of these three sets of features—concentration of talent, abundant funding, and appropriate governance—implements differentiation. The dynamic interaction among these three groups of factors is the distinguishing characteristic of high-ranking universities.

The results of the recent survey of European universities mentioned earlier confirm that funding and governance influence performance together. They indicate clearly that the higher-ranked universities tend to enjoy increased management autonomy, which, in turn, increases the efficiency of spending and results in higher research productivity (Aghion et al. 2008). A study of the influence of governance arrangements on the research output of public universities in the United States arrives to the same conclusion. When competitive research funding is available, the more autonomous universities tend to be more successful in producing patents (Aghion et al. 2009).

Having an appropriate governance framework without sufficient resources or the ability to attract top talent does not work either. Similarly, just investing money in an institution or making it selective in terms of student admissions is not sufficient to build a world-class university, as illustrated by the case of Brazil's top university, the University of São Paulo (USP). Brazil is the 5th-most-populated nation and the 10th-largest economy on the planet, it is among the 6 largest producers of cars in the world, it has world-class companies such as Embraer and Aracruz Celulose, but there is no Brazilian university among the 100 top-ranked universities in the world.

How is it that USP, the country's foremost research university, does not make it into the top group in the international rankings, despite having some of the features of world-class universities? When it was created in 1934, the founders and first leaders of USP made it a point to hire only prominent professors from all over Europe (Schwartzman 2005). Today, it is the most-selective institution in Brazil, it has the highest number of top-rated graduate programs, and every year it produces more PhD graduates than any US university. At the same time, its ability to manage its resources is constrained by rigid civil service regulations, even though it is the richest university in the country. It has few linkages with the international research community, and only 3 percent of its graduate students are from outside Brazil. The university is quite inward looking: most students come from the state of São Paulo, and the majority of professors are USP graduates (this latter feature of endogamy being a typical feature of European universities, as discussed earlier). Foreign professors cannot be recruited, by law, and it is forbidden to write a doctoral dissertation in a language other than Portuguese. According to Schwartzman (2005), the key missing element is the absence of a vision of excellence to challenge the status quo and transform the university. The lack of ambitious strategic vision can be observed as much at the national and state government levels as among the university leadership.

Paths to Transformation

Two complementary perspectives need to be considered in examining how to establish world-class research universities. The first dimension, of an external nature, concerns the role of government and the resources that can be made available to enhance the stature of institutions. The second dimension is internal. It has to do with the individual institutions themselves and the necessary evolution and steps that they need to take to transform themselves into world-class research universities.

The Role of Government

In the past, the role of government in nurturing the growth of world-class universities was not a critical factor. The history of the Ivy League universities in the United States reveals that, by and large, they grew to prominence as a result of incremental progress, rather than by deliberate government intervention. Similarly, the UK Universities of Oxford and Cambridge evolved over the centuries of their own volition, with variable levels of public funding, but with considerable autonomy in terms of governance, definition of mission, and direction. Today, however, it is unlikely that a world-class university can be rapidly created without a favorable policy environment and direct public initiative and support, if only because of the high costs involved in setting up advanced research facilities and capacities.

International experience shows that three basic strategies can be followed to establish world-class research universities: (a) upgrading a small number of existing universities that have the potential of excelling (picking winners); (b) merging existing institutions to form a new university that would achieve the type of synergies corresponding to a world-class research institution (hybrid formula); and (c) creating new world-class universities from scratch (clean-slate approach).

Upgrading Existing Institutions

One of the main benefits of this first approach is that the costs can be significantly less than those of building new institutions from scratch. This is the strategy followed by China since the early 1980s, with a sequence of carefully targeted reforms and investment programs. Indeed, Peking University and Tsinghua University, China's top two universities, have been granted special privileges by the national authorities, allowing them to select the best students from every province before any other university, much to the consternation of the other leading universities around the country.

But this approach is unlikely to succeed in countries where the governance structure and arrangements that have historically prevented the emergence of

234 · Jamil Salmi

world-class universities are not drastically revised. A comparison of the experiences of Malaysia and Singapore can serve to illustrate this point. Because
Singapore was initially one of the provinces of the Malaysian Kingdom during the first few years following independence from the British, the contrasting
stories of the University of Malaya and of the National University of Singapore
(NUS) can be quite instructive, given their common cultural and colonial origins.

At independence, the University of Malaya operated as a two-campus university, one in Kuala Lumpur and the other in Singapore. The former evolved
into the flagship University of Malaya from the beginning, and the other
became the University of Singapore, which merged with Nanyang University
in 1980 to create NUS. By all global ranking measures, NUS today functions
as a true world-class university (ranked 19th by the 2006 *THE* ranking), while
the University of Malaya struggles as a second-tier research university (ranked
192nd). In examining the different evolutionary paths of these two institutions,
several factors appear to be constraining the University of Malaya's capacity
to improve and innovate as effectively as NUS: affirmative action and restrictive admissions policies, lower levels of financial support, and tightly controlled
immigration regulations regarding foreign faculty.

The affirmative action policy implemented by the Malaysian government in
favor of the children of the Malay majority population (*Bumiputras*) has significantly opened up opportunities for that segment of the population. The
proportion of Malay students—the Malay population represents 52 percent of
the total Malaysian population—went from about 30 percent to two-thirds of
the total student population between the early 1970s and the late 1980s. The
proportion of Chinese students decreased from 56 to 29 percent over the same
period (Tierney and Sirat 2008).

The downside of these equity policies was that they prevented the university
from being very selective in its student admissions to target the best and brightest in the country. Large numbers of academically qualified Chinese and Indian
students, in particular, were unable to attend Malaysia's best universities and
had to seek tertiary education abroad, thereby removing important talent from
Malaysia. In addition to restrictions among its own population, the Malaysian
Ministry of Higher Education places a 5 percent cap on the number of foreign
undergraduate students that public universities can enroll.

By contrast, the proportion of foreign students at NUS is 20 percent at the
undergraduate level and 43 percent at the graduate level. The cost of their
studies is highly subsidized by NUS. The primary consideration for attracting
these foreign students is not to generate income, as often happens in UK and
Australian universities, but to bring in highly qualified individuals who will
enrich the pool of students.

NUS is also able to mobilize nearly twice as many financial resources as the
University of Malaya (US$205 million annual budget versus US$118 million,

respectively) through a combination of cost sharing, investment revenue, fund-raising, and government resources. The success of NUS's fund-raising efforts is largely the result of the generous matching-grant program set up by the government in the late 1990s as part of the Thinking Schools, Learning Nation Initiative, which provided a three-to-one matching at the beginning and is now down to one-to-one. As a result, the annual per student expenditures at NUS and the University of Malaya were US$6,300 and US$4,053, respectively, in 2006.

Finally, in Malaysia, on one hand, civil service regulations and a rigid financial framework make it difficult, if not impossible, to provide competitive compensation packages to attract the most-competent professors and researchers, particularly foreign faculty. NUS, on the other hand, is not bound by similar legal constraints. The PS21 public service reform project in the early 2000s aimed at promoting a culture of excellence and innovation in all public institutions, including the two universities. NUS is therefore able to bring in top researchers and professors from all over the world, pay a global market rate for them, and provide performance incentives to stimulate competition and to retain the best and the brightest. Indeed, a good number of Malaysia's top researchers have been recruited by NUS.

Merging Existing Institutions

The second possible approach to building up a world-class research university consists of promoting mergers among existing institutions. In China, for example, a number of mergers have taken place to consolidate existing institutions. Beijing Medical University merged with Peking University in 2000; similarly, in Shanghai, Fudan University merged with a medical university, and Zhejiang University was created out of the merger of five universities. In 2004, in the United Kingdom, the Victoria University of Manchester (VUM) and the University of Manchester Institute of Science and Technology (UMIST) merged, creating the largest university in the United Kingdom, with the purposefully stated goal of being "top 25 by 2015" (http://www.manchester.ac.uk/research/about/strategy/). The government of the Russian Federation is also relying on amalgamation as a key policy within its overall strategy of developing elite research universities. In 2007, two pilot federal universities were set up by merging existing institutions in Rostov-on-Don in southern Russia and in the Siberian city of Krasnoyarsk. The two new institutions will also receive additional funding to support efforts to allow them to recruit highly qualified researchers and equip state-of-the-art laboratories (Holdsworth 2008).

The great advantage of mergers is that they can result in stronger institutions able to capitalize on the new synergies that their combined human and financial resources may generate. But mergers can also be risky, potentially aggravating problems instead of resolving them. In the case of France, for example, recently proposed mergers would augment the critical mass of researchers and bring about a higher place in the Academic Ranking of World Universities, which favors research output, but they would not address the fundamental limitations of French universities—including inflexible admissions policies, a weak financial basis, rigid governance arrangements, and outdated management practices.

Another danger associated with mergers is that the newly consolidated institution could suffer because of clashing institutional cultures. It has become clear, for example, that the previously mentioned merger between VUM and UMIST has not been as successful as expected or originally perceived. Currently acknowledging a £30 million budget deficit and the likelihood of up to 400 jobs lost on the campus, the University of Manchester has had immediate experience with the complexities of merging (Qureshi 2007). Among the main problems encountered are duplication of staff and curricular offerings, the political challenges of engendering support for the merger by making promises that have proven detrimental to keep, and the short-term absorption of labor contracts and institutional debt. In addition, the newly formed institution, with its commitment to achieving world-class status, invested heavily in hiring "superstar" academic staff and supplying them with correspondingly superstar facilities. This exacerbated further the staffing debt that the institution inherited with the merging of the distinct and separate institutional staff members into the one university. Still, five years later, the University of Manchester is emerging from the pains of the merger in relatively strong shape.

Creating New Universities

In countries where institutional habits, cumbersome governance structures, and bureaucratic management practices prevent traditional universities from being innovative, creating new universities may be the best approach, provided that it is possible to staff them with people not influenced by the culture of traditional universities and that financial resources are not a constraint. New institutions can emerge from the private sector, or governments can allow new public institutions to operate under a more favorable regulatory framework. One of the earlier success stories in that respect was the establishment of the Indian Institutes of Technology, which, in the past decades, have gradually risen to world-class status.

Kazakhstan is a country intent on following this path as it seeks to make its economy less dependent on oil and more competitive overall. The government has decided to set up a new international university in Astana. The plan is that this university will follow a highly innovative multidisciplinary curriculum designed in cooperation with leading foreign universities. In the same vein, the government of Saudi Arabia announced in late 2007 its plans for a US$3 billion graduate research university, King Abdullah University of Science and Technology, which would operate outside the purview of the Ministry of Higher Education, to allow for greater management autonomy and academic freedom than the regular universities of the kingdom enjoy.

Time is an important dimension that also needs to be factored into the strategic plan of any aspiring world-class university. Governments are often under pressure to show immediate results, running the risk of taking precipitous decisions, and overlooking the fact that the establishment of a strong research university is a long-term process. Building ultramodern facilities before adequately defining programs, curricula, and pedagogical practices that are fully aligned, or hiring star researchers from overseas without matching them with a critical mass of national faculty are common mistakes. Developing a culture of excellence in research and teaching does not happen from one day to the next; it requires proper sequencing of interventions, careful balance among the various quantitative and qualitative objectives of the project, and a long-term view.

* * *

The creation of new institutions may have the side benefit of stimulating existing ones into becoming more responsive to the global competitive environment. In several countries, the emergence of high-quality private institutions has provoked the existing public universities into becoming more strategically focused. In Uruguay, for example, the venerable University of the Republic—which had exercised a monopoly over tertiary education in the country for 150 years—started a strategic planning process and considered establishing postgraduate programs for the first time only after being confronted in the mid-1990s with competition from newly established private universities. Similarly, in Russia, the creation of the Higher School of Economics and of the Moscow School of Social and Economic Sciences in the 1990s pressured the Department of Economics at the State University of Moscow to revamp its curriculum and get more actively involved in international exchanges.

Strategies at the Institutional Level

The establishment of a world-class research university requires, above all, strong leadership, a bold vision of the institution's mission and goals, and a clearly articulated strategic plan to translate the vision into concrete targets and programs. Universities that aspire to better results engage in an objective assessment of their strengths and areas for improvement, set new stretch goals, and design and implement a renewal plan that can lead to improved performance. By contrast, many institutions are complacent in their outlook, lack an ambitious vision of a better future, and continue to operate as they have in the past, ending up with a growing performance gap compared with that of their national or international competitors.

Recent research on university leadership suggests that in the case of top research universities, the best-performing institutions have leaders who combine good managerial skills and a successful research career (Goodall 2006). To be able to develop an appropriate vision for the future of the university and to implement this vision in an effective manner, the university leader needs to fully understand the core agenda of the institution and be able to apply the vision with the necessary operational skills.

A case study of the University of Leeds in the United Kingdom illustrates how the arrival of a new leader in 2003 marked the beginning of a conscious effort to reverse a downward trend through carefully planned and implemented strategic change. Rapid growth in student numbers (the second-largest university in the United Kingdom) had led to tensions between the teaching and research missions of the university, resulting in diminishing research income and results. Among the main challenges faced by the new vice chancellor was the need to create a sense of urgency among the entire university community and to convince everyone of the importance of achieving a better alignment between corporate goals and the contribution of individual faculties and departments with a long tradition of autonomy.

> For the University of Leeds, our reputation and profile made this challenge harder. As a great institution we had to demonstrate the vulnerability of our current position, alongside the importance and achievability of our vision. Staff were not going to engage in a strategy unless its credibility and relevance could be clearly established. To achieve this we used a variety of internal and external measures of performance reputation and ranking to clearly articulate the current position and the vision. . . . Considerable time and effort was dedicated to developing the vision of "by 2015 our distinctive ability to integrate world-class research, scholarship and education will have secured us a place among the top 50 universities in the world."
> (Donoghue and Kennerley forthcoming)

A crucial element of the vision is the selection of niche domains of research toward which the institution will seek to build and maximize its comparative advantage. In that respect, it is important to underline that a research university—even a world-class university—most likely cannot excel in all areas. Harvard University, widely recognized as the number one institution of higher learning in the world, is not the best-ranked university in all disciplines. Its strengths are especially noted in economics, medical sciences, education, political science, law, business studies, English, and history.

Conclusion

The highest-ranked universities are the ones that make significant contributions to the advancement of knowledge through research, teach with the most-innovative curricula and pedagogical methods under the most conducive circumstances, make research an integral component of undergraduate teaching, and produce graduates who stand out because of their success in intensely competitive arenas during their education and (more important) after graduation.

There is no universal recipe or magic formula for "making" a world-class research university. National contexts and institutional models vary widely. Therefore, each country must choose, from among the various possible pathways, a strategy that plays to its strengths and resources. International experience provides a few lessons regarding the key features of such universities—high concentrations of talent, abundance of resources, and flexible governance arrangements—and successful approaches to move in that direction, from upgrading or merging existing institutions to creating new universities altogether.

Furthermore, the transformation of the university system cannot take place in isolation. A long-term vision for creating world-class universities—and its implementation—should be closely articulated with (a) the country's overall economic and social development strategy; (b) ongoing changes and planned reforms at the lower levels of the education system; and (c) plans for the development of other types of tertiary-education institutions to build an integrated system of teaching, research, and technology-oriented institutions.

Finally, the building pressures and momentum behind the push for world-class research universities must be examined within the proper context to avoid overdramatization of the value and importance of world-class institutions and distortions in resource allocation patterns within national tertiary education systems. Even in a global knowledge economy, where every nation—both industrial and developing—is seeking to increase its share of the economic pie, the hype surrounding world-class institutions far exceeds the need and capacity for many systems to benefit from such advanced education and research opportunities, at least in the short term.

References

ARWU (Academic Ranking of World Universities) (2009) Academic Ranking of World Universities 2009. Available: http://www.arwu.org/ARWU2009.jsp (accessed March 14, 2010).

Aghion, P., M. Dewatripont, C. Hoxby, A. Mas-Colell, and A. Sapir (2007) "Why reform Europe's universities?" *Bruegel Policy Brief*, issue 2007/04, September.

—— (2008) "Higher aspirations: An agenda for reforming European universities," Bruegel Blueprint Series, no. 5.

—— (2009) "The Governance and performance of research universities: Evidence from Europe and the U.S.," National Bureau of Economic Research, Working Paper no. 14851, April.

Alden, J. and G. Lin (2004) *Benchmarking the Characteristics of a World-Class University: Developing an International Strategy at University Level.* London: UK Higher Education Leadership Foundation, May.

Altbach, P.G. (2004) "The costs and benefits of world-class universities," *Academe.* January–February. Available: www.aaup.org (accessed April 10, 2006).

Cookson, C. (2007) "Universities drive biotech advancement," *Financial Times*, May 6.

Csikszentmihalyi, M. (1997) *Creativity: Flow and the Psychology of Discovery and Invention*, New York: Harper Collins.

Donoghue, S. and M. Kennerley (forthcoming) "Our journey towards world class: Leading transformational strategic change," *Higher Education Management and Policy*, Paris: OECD.

Economist (2005) "Secrets of success," September 10, vol. 376, 6.

Goodall, A. (2006) "The leaders of the world's top 100 universities," *International Higher Education*. no. 42, Winter, 3–4.

Holdsworth, N. (2008) "Russia: Super league of 'Federal' universities," *University World News*. 26 October.

IHEP (Institute for Higher Education Policy) (2007) *College and University Ranking Systems: Global Perspectives and American Challenges*. Washington DC: IHEP.

Khoon, K.A., R. Shukor, O. Hassan, Z. Saleh, A. Hamzah, and R. Ismail (2005) "Hallmark of a world-class university," *College Student Journal*, December. Available: http://findarticles. com/p/articles/mi_mOFCR/is_4_39/ai_n16123684 (accessed April 10, 2007).

Niland, J. (2000) "The challenge of building world class universities in the Asian region," *On Line Opinion*, February 3. Available: http://www.onlineopinion.com.au/view.asp?article = 997 (accessed April 10, 2006).

—— (2007) "The challenge of Building world-class universities," in Sadlak, J. and Liu, N.C. (eds.), *The World Class University and Ranking: Aiming Beyond Status*, Bucharest, Romania: UNESCO-CEPES

Qureshi, Yakub (2007) "400 university jobs could go," *Manchester Evening News*, March 9. Available: http://www.manchestereveningnews.co.uk/news/education/s/1001/1001469_400_ university_jobs_could_go.html (accessed May 20, 2007).

Salmi, J. (2009) *The Challenge of Establishing World-Class Universities*, Washington, DC: World Bank.

Salmi, J. and A. Saroyan (2007) "League tables as policy instruments: Uses and misuses," *Higher Education Management and Policy*, 19 (2).

Schwartzman, S. (2005) *Brazil's Leading University: Between Intelligentsia, World Standards and Social Inclusion*. Instituto de Estudos do Trabalho e Sociedade.

Tierney, W. and M. Sirat (2008) "Challenges facing Malaysian higher education," *International Higher Education*, no. 53, Fall, 23–24.

THE *(Times Higher Education)* (2007) See Times Higher World University Rankings 2007. Available: http://www.thes.co.uk/worldrankings/ (accessed March 30, 2008).

—— (2009) *Times Higher Education*-QS World University Rankings 2009: TOP 200 WORLD UNIVERSITIES. Available: http://www.timeshighereducation.co.uk/hybrid.asp?typeCode = 438 (accessed March 14, 2010).

University World News (2008) "China: Growing competition for top students." Available: http:// www.universityworldnews.com (accessed June 14, 2008).

Williams, R. and Van Dyke, N. (2007) "Measuring the international standing of universities with an application to Australian Universities," *Higher Education*, 53, 819–41.

World Bank (2002) *Constructing Knowledge Societies: New Challenges for Tertiary Education*, Washington, DC: World Bank.

Yusuf, S. and K. Nabeshima (2007) *How Universities Promote Economic Growth*, Washington, DC: World Bank.

Index

academic freedom xii, 12, 35, 46–48,
72, 77, 80–81, 84, 88, 98–99, 179,
206, 213, 221, 228; and academic
profession 213, 217–18; and
autonomy 14–16; and private
donations 165, 167; and world-
class research universities 228,
237
academic governance *see* governance
academic leadership *see* leadership
academic profession 47, 49, 85, 184;
academic freedom 47, 48,
80, 84, 179, 206, 213, 218;
appointments 47–48; in
developed countries 47; in
developing countries 205–22;
expansion 206; governance 206;
international labor market 210;
foreign degrees 210; information
technology 212–13; job
security 47, 206; politics 217;
privatization 206; problems
with 205, 206, 214, 220;
research 208; salaries 49;
traditional norms 47–48, 184,
206, 218
academic quality 5, 132, 136, 139, 209
Academic Ranking of World Universities
(ARWU) 80, 147–49, 151,
155–56, 226–28, 230, 236
academic salaries 4, 220–21
access xiii, 2, 17, 33, 52, 62, 64, 67, 187,
208; disadvantaged students xiv;
at elite universities 196;
and equity 2, 187–202; and
technologically-assisted
instruction xiv, 61–62, 65, 68,
108, 112, 114, 125–26, 162, 197
accountability xii, 84, 128–30, 133,
163, 179, 206; vs. autonomy 1,
12, 34–35, 46–47, 131–33, 137,
206, 231; demand and support
for 18, 83–84, 128, 129, 161,

216; growth of 5, 12, 33–34, 35,
49–50, 206; impact of 33, 47, 132,
137; limitation or lack of support
of 12, 179
accreditation 34, 122–23, 130–33,
135–37, 141–42; agencies 34,
38, 118, 121, 122, 141, 148;
international accreditation 114,
117, 118, 122, 123, 141; mills 123;
and standards 133–35
Addis Ababa University 79
affirmative action xiii, 78, 189–90, 192,
193, 195–96, 234, 252
Africa (higher education) xii, 15,
112, 117–18, 195; African
foreign students 91; benefits
of change 72–73; culture 14;
dependency 208; anglophone
countries 212; East Africa 63,
180; flow of academics 211;
francophone countries xiii;
funding 14, 64; government
authority 12, 14; information
technology 212; Internet xvi;
North Africa 73; politics xvii,
217; quality and ratings
xvi–xvii; South to South student
and faculty flows 109, 212;
student-loan trends 63–64, 66;
women xiv; world class xvi
sub-Saharan Africa: enrollments 54,
62, 72–73; flow of academics 211;
gender inequity xiii, xiv;
government revenues 55–56;
qualified faculty xv; tuition fees
and "user charges" 63; *see also*
specific countries
African Leadership Forum 118
African Virtual University 62
Aga Khan University 118
Al-Ahram Canadian University 120
Al-Ahram Organization 120
Al-Azhar University 116, 207